In the Break

In the Break

The Aesthetics of the Black Radical Tradition

Fred Moten

University of Minnesota Press
Minneapolis • London

Portions of chapter 1 were originally published as "Voices/Forces: Migration, Surplus, and the Black Avant-Garde," in *Writing Aloud: The Sonics of Language,* edited by Brandon LaBelle and Christof Migone (Los Angeles: Errant Bodies Press, 2001); reprinted by permission of Errant Bodies Press. Portions of chapter 1 also appeared as "Sound in Florescence: Cecil Taylor Floating Garden," in *Sound States: Innovative Poetics and Acoustical Technologies,* edited by Adalaide Morris (Chapel Hill: University of North Carolina Press, 1998); copyright 1998 by the University of North Carolina Press; reprinted by permission of the University of North Carolina Press. An earlier version of chapter 2 appeared as "From Ensemble to Improvisation," in *Hambone* 16 (Fall 2002); reprinted by permission of *Hambone.* An earlier version of chapter 3 appeared as "Black Mo'nin' in the Sound of the Photograph," in *Loss,* edited by David Kazanjian and David Eng (Berkeley: University of California Press, 2002); copyright 2002 by the Regents of the University of California; reprinted by permission of the University of California Press.

Translated poetry by Antonin Artaud in chapter 1 originally appeared in *Watchfiends and Rack Screams: Works from the Final Period,* edited and translated by Clayton Eshleman and Bernard Bador (Boston: Exact Change, 1995); reprinted courtesy of Exact Change. *Lush Life,* by Billy Strayhorn, copyright 1949 (renewed) by Music Sales Corporation (ASCAP) and Tempo Music Corporation (BMI); all rights administered by Music Sales Corporation (ASCAP); international copyright secured; all rights reserved; reprinted by permission. Lines from "The Dead Lecturer," by Amiri Baraka, in chapter 2 are reprinted by permission of Sterling Lord Literistic, Inc.; copyright 1964 by Amiri Baraka.

Published by the University of Minnesota Press
111 Third Avenue South, Suite 290
Minneapolis, MN 55401-2520
http://www.upress.umn.edu

Library of Congress Cataloging-in-Publication Data

Moten, Fred.
   In the break : the aesthetics of the Black radical tradition / Fred Moten.
      p. cm.
Includes bibliographical references (p.) and index.
   ISBN 0-8166-4099-8 (HC : alk. paper)—ISBN 0-8166-4100-5 (PB : alk. paper)
   1. African Americans—Intellectual life. 2. African Americans—Politics and government. 3. Radicalism—United States. 4. African American aesthetics. 5. African American arts. 6. Arts—Political aspects—United States. I. Title.

E185 .M895 2003
700'.89'96073—dc21

                                        2002151661

Printed in the United States of America on acid-free paper

The University of Minnesota is an equal-opportunity educator and employer.

25 24 23 22 21   13 12 11 10 9

for B

black radicalism cannot be understood within the particular
context of its genesis ...

—Cedric Robinson, *Black Marxism*

... an insistent previousness evading each and every natal occasion ...

—Nathaniel Mackey, *Bedouin Hornbook*

Contents

Acknowledgments

All love and thanks to my comrade and companion, Laura Harris.

I hope my work is animated by the material spirit of my beautiful grandparents, Marie and Charlie Jenkins.

Thanks to my sister and brother, Glynda White and Mike Davis, for everything; my aunt, Bertha Marks, my cousin, Rev. L. T. Marks, and all of my family in Kingsland, New Edinburgh, and all parts north and west; and Q. B., Eloise, Valorie, Dalorie, and Tony Bush for letting me be part of their family.

Mark and Susan Harris have sustained Laura and me through difficult times with great generosity and love.

I want to thank my mentors Martin Kilson and Julian Boyd for their knowledge, support, and *time*. In both of them, the richest style moves in perfect harmony with the deepest substance.

William Corbett, Masao Miyoshi, Avital Ronell, Ann Banfield, Stephen Booth, Herman Rapaport, Kathryne Lindberg, Cedric Robinson, Hortense Spillers, Angela Davis, Amiri Baraka, Samuel R. Delany, Cecil Taylor, and above all Nathaniel Mackey have been invaluable examples.

The sense of working together on a collective project with Alan Jackson, Errol Louis, Steve Harney, Eric Chandler, Akira Lippit, Seth Moglen, Avery Gordon, Chris Newfield, Josie Saldaña, David Kazanjian,

May Joseph, David Eng, Barbara Browning, Nahum Chandler, Paul Kottman, Karen Hadley, Sandra Gunning, Kate McCullough, Mary Pat Brady, Stephanie Smith, José Muñoz, and Tom Sheehan (my spiritual coauthor) has meant everything to me.

Laurie Chandler, Joe Torra, Alice Key, Kate Butler, Gwen Rahner, Maya Miller, Alycee Lane, Kevin Kopelson, Doris Witt, Max Thomas, Margaret Bass, Helene Moglen, Anna McCarthy, Herman Bennett, André Lepecki, Angela Dillard, Phil Harper, Bob Stam, Robin Kelley, Saidiya Hartman, Farah Griffin, Jason King, Anita Cherian, Lara Nielsen, Heather Schuster, Tracie Morris, Abdul-Karim Mustapha, Eric Neel, Kevin Floyd, Hakan Dibel, Cynthia Oliver, Phil Round, Linda Bolton, Dee Morris, Brooks Landon, Ed Folsom, Fred Woodard, David Depew, Mary Depew, Mary Ann Rasmussen, Stephen Vlastos, John Nelson, Alan Weiss, Christof Migone, Richard Schechner, Jennifer Fink, Lisa Duggan, Lauren Berlant, Laurence Rickels, Julie Carlson, Peggy Phelan, Barbara Kirshenblatt-Gimblett, L. O. Aranye Fradenburg, Randy Martin, Charles Rowell, Ange Mlinko, Jim Behrle, and Murray Jackson have been supportive friends, editors, and colleagues.

I thank José Muñoz and Laura Harris for reading all of the manuscript and Sarah Cervenak for her help with the index.

Robert O'Meally accepted me with grace and friendship into the Jazz Study Group he convenes at Columbia University. The chance to join the scholars he brings together has been a highlight of my intellectual life and very important to the work I have tried to do in this book.

Over the past three or four years, in the course of finishing this book, I have often returned to Stanley Cavell's words at the end of *A Pitch of Philosophy*: "Am I ready to vow ... that I have the ear, that I know my mother's mother tongue of music to be also mine?" My mother, B Jenkins, taught me the value of trying to reach for something and in her "absence" that value, the essence of her tradition, dawns on me every morning in a different way as old and new desire. I want to go as far out from where she was as she wanted me to go, all the way back to her ground and line. All my work is dedicated to her with all my love.

Resistance of the Object:
Aunt Hester's Scream

The history of blackness is testament to the fact that objects can and do resist.[1] Blackness—the extended movement of a specific upheaval, an ongoing irruption that anarranges every line—is a strain that pressures the assumption of the equivalence of personhood and subjectivity. While subjectivity is defined by the subject's possession of itself and its objects, it is troubled by a dispossessive force objects exert such that the subject seems to be possessed—infused, deformed—by the object it possesses. I'm interested in what happens when we consider the phonic materiality of such propriative exertion. Or, to invoke and diverge from Saidiya Hartman's fundamental work and phrasing, I'm interested in the convergence of blackness and the irreducible sound of necessarily visual performance at the scene of objection.

Between looking and being looked at, spectacle and spectatorship, enjoyment and being enjoyed, lies and moves the economy of what Hartman calls hypervisibility. She allows and demands an investigation of this hypervisibility in its relation to a certain musical obscurity and opens us to the problematics of everyday ritual, the stagedness of the violently (and sometimes amelioratively) quotidian, the essential drama of black life, as Zora Neale Hurston might say. Hartman shows how narrative always echoes and redoubles the dramatic interenactment of "contentment and abjection," and she explores the massive discourse of the cut, of rememberment and redress, that we always hear in narratives where blackness marks simultaneously both the performance of the object and the performance of humanity. She allows us to ask: what have objectification and humanization, both of which we can think in relation to a certain notion of subjection, to do with the essential historicity, the quintessential modernity, of black performance? Whatever runs off us, a certain offense runs through us. This is a double ambivalence that requires analyses of looking and being looked at; such game requires, above all, some thinking about the opposition of spectacle and routine, violence and pleasure. This thinking is Hartman's domain.

A critique of the subject animates Hartman's work. It bears the trace, therefore, of a movement exemplified by an aspect of Judith Butler's massive theoretical contribution wherein the call to subjectivity is understood also as a call to subjection and subjugation and appeals for redress or protection to the state or to the structure or idea of citizenship—as well as modes of radical performativity or subversive impersonation—are always already embedded in the structure they would escape.[2] But if Hartman moves in this field she also moves in another tradition that forces another kind of questioning. Consulting Frederick Douglass on all of this is mandatory and the best place to consult him is in the moments when he describes and reproduces black performance. But this is to move in the tradition of a mode of reading Douglass that conflates his story (and its graphic and emblematic primal scene) with the story of slavery and freedom; this is to risk an uncritical covering of the assertion of Douglass's originarity; this is to approach the natal occasion that our musico-political tradition must evade. In order to sidestep this problematic, Hartman has both to avoid and to arrive at Douglass, must both repress and return to him.

Everything moves, for Hartman, after an opening decision regarding these questions of comportment:

> The "terrible spectacle" that introduced Frederick Douglass to slavery was the beating of his Aunt Hester.... By locating this "horrible exhibition" in the first chapter of his 1845 *Narrative of the Life of Frederick Douglass*, Douglass establishes the centrality of violence to the making of

the slave and identifies it as an original generative act equivalent to the statement "I was born." The passage through the blood-stained gate is an inaugural moment in the formation of the enslaved. In this regard, it is a primal scene. By this I mean that the terrible spectacle dramatizes the origin of the subject and demonstrates that to be a slave is to be under the brutal power and authority of another; this is confirmed by the event's placement in the opening chapter on genealogy.

I have chosen not to reproduce Douglass's account of the beating of Aunt Hester in order to call attention to the ease with which such scenes are usually reiterated, the casualness with which they are circulated, and the consequences of this routine display of the slave's ravaged body. Rather than inciting indignation, too often they immure us to pain by virtue of their familiarity—the oft-repeated or restored character of these accounts and our distance from them are signaled by the theatrical language usually resorted to in describing these instances—and especially because they reinforce the spectacular character of black suffering. What interests me are the ways we are called upon to participate in such scenes. . . . At issue here is the precariousness of empathy and the uncertain line between witness and spectator. Only more obscene than the brutality unleashed at the whipping post is the demand that this suffering be materialized and evidenced by the display of the tortured body or endless recitations of the ghastly and terrible. In light of this, how does one give expression to these outrages without exacerbating the indifference to suffering that is the consequence of the benumbing spectacle or contend with the narcissistic identification that obliterates the other or the prurience that too often is the response to such displays? This was the challenge faced by Douglass and the other foes of slavery, and this is the task I take up here.

Therefore, rather than try to convey the routinized violence of slavery and its aftermath through invocations of the shocking and the terrible, I have chosen to look elsewhere and consider those scenes in which terror can hardly be discerned. . . . By defamiliarizing the familiar, I hope to illuminate the terror of the mundane and quotidian rather than exploit the shocking spectacle. What concerns me here is the diffusion of terror and the violence perpetrated under the rubric of pleasure, paternalism and property.[3]

The decision not to reproduce the account of Aunt Hester's beating is, in some sense, illusory. First, it is reproduced in her reference to and refusal of it; second, the beating is reproduced in every scene of subjection the book goes on to read—in both the ritual performances combining terror and enjoyment in slavery and the fashionings and assertions of citizenship and "free" subjectivity after emancipation. The question here concerns the inevitability of such reproduction even in the denial of it. This is the question of whether the performance of subjectivity—and the subjectivity that Hartman is interested in here is definitely performed—always and everywhere reproduces what lies before it; it is also the question of whether performance in general is ever outside the economy of reproduction.[4] This is not to say that Hartman tries but cannot make disappear the originary performance of the violent subjection of the slave's body. Indeed, Hartman's considerable, formidable, and rare brilliance is present in the space she leaves for the ongoing (re)production of that performance in all its guises and for a critical awareness of how each of those guises is always already present in and disruptive of the supposed originarity of that primal scene. What are the politics of this unavoidably reproducible and reproductive performance? What is held in the ongoing disruption of its primality? What shape must a culture take when it is so (un)grounded? What does this disturbance of capture and genesis give to black performance?

Douglass's *is* a primal scene for complex reasons that have to do with the connectedness of desire, identification, and castration that Hartman displaces onto the field of the mundane and the quotidian, where pain is alloyed with pleasure. However, this displacement somehow both acknowledges and avoids the vexed question of the possibility of pain and pleasure mixing in the scene and in its originary and subsequent recountings. For Hartman the very specter of enjoyment is reason enough to repress the encounter. So lingering in the psychoanalytic break is crucial in the interest of a certain set of complexities that cannot be overlooked but must be traced back to this origin precisely in the interest of destabilizing its originarity and originarity in general, a destabilization Douglass founds in his original recitation, which is also an originary repression. It's the ongoing repression of the primal scene of subjection that one wants to guard against and linger in. Douglass passes on a repression that Hartman's critical suppression extends. Such transfer demands that one ask if every recitation is a repression and if every reproduction of a performance is its disappearance. Douglass and Hartman confront us with the fact that the *conjunction* of reproduction and disappearance is performance's condition of possibility, its ontology and its mode of production. The recitation of Douglass's repression, the repression embedded in his recitation, is there in Hartman as well. Like Douglass, she transposes all that is unspeakable in the scene to later, ritualized, "soulfully" mundane and quotidian performances. All that's missing is the originary recitation of the beating, which she reproduces in her reference to it. This is to say that there is an intense dialogue with Douglass that structures *Scenes of Subjection*. The dialogue is opened by a refusal of recitation that reproduces what it refuses. Hartman swerves away from Douglass and thereby runs right back to him. She also runs through him into territory he could not have recognized, territory no one has charted as thoroughly and as convincingly as she has done. Still, this turn away from Douglass that is also a turn to and through Douglass is a disturbance that is neither unfamiliar nor unfamilial. *In the Break* addresses such resemblance by way of the following questions: Is there a way to disrupt the totalizing force of the primality Douglass represents? Is there a way to subject this unavoidable model of subjection to a radical breakdown?

My attempt to address these questions will, I hope, justify another engagement with the terribly beautiful music of Douglass's recitations of the beating of his Aunt Hester. The engagement moves initially through and against Karl Marx, by way of Abbey Lincoln and Max Roach. I want to show the interarticulation of the resistance of the object with Marx's subjunctive figure of the commodity who speaks. According to Marx, the speaking commodity is an impossibility invoked only to militate against mystifying notions of the commodity's essential value. My argument starts with the historical reality of commodities who spoke—of laborers who were commodities before, as it were, the abstraction of labor power from their bodies and who continue to pass on this material heritage across the divide that separates slavery and "freedom." But I am interested, finally, in the implications of the breaking of such speech, the elevating disruptions of the verbal that take the rich content of the object's/commodity's aurality outside the confines of meaning precisely by way of this material trace. More specifically with regard to Douglass's prefatory scene and its subsequent restagings, I'm interested in establishing some procedures for discovering the relationship between the "heart-rending shrieks" of Aunt Hester in the face of the master's violent assault, the discourse on music that Douglass initiates a few pages after the recitation of that vicious encounter, and the incorporation or recording of a sound figured as external both to music and to speech in black music and speech.

In his critical deployment of such music and speech, Douglass discovers a hermeneutic that is simultaneously broken and expanded by an operation akin to what Jacques Derrida refers to as "invagination."[5] This cut and augmented hermeneutic circle is structured by a double movement. The first element is the transference of a radically exterior aurality that disrupts and resists certain formations of identity and interpretation by challenging the reducibility of phonic matter to verbal meaning or conventional musical form. The second is the assertion of what Nathaniel Mackey calls "'broken' claim(s) to connection"[6] between Africa and African America that seek to suture corollary, asymptotically divergent ruptures—maternal estrangement and the thwarted romance of the sexes—that he refers to as "wounded kinship" and the "the sexual 'cut.'"[7] This assertion marks an engagement with a more attenuated, more internally determined, exteriority and a courtship with an always already unavailable and substitutive origin. It would work by way of an imaginative restoration of the figure of the mother to a realm determined not only by verbal meaning and conventional musical form but by a nostalgic specularity and a necessarily endogamous, simultaneously virginal and reproductive sexuality. These twin impulses animate a forceful operation in Douglass's work, something like a revaluation of that revaluation of value that was set in motion by four of Douglass's "contemporaries"—Marx, Nietzsche, Freud, and Saussure. Above all, they open the possibility of a critique of the valuation of meaning over content and the reduction of phonic matter and syntactic "degeneracy" in the early modern search for a universal language and the late modern search for a universal science of language. This disruption of the Enlightenment linguistic project is of fundamental importance since it allows a rearrangement of the relationship between notions of human freedom and notions of human essence. More specifically, the emergence from political, economic, and sexual objection of the radical materiality and syntax that animates black performances indicates a freedom drive that is expressed always and everywhere throughout their graphic (re)production.

In *Caribbean Discourse* Edouard Glissant writes:

> From the outset (that is from the moment Creole is forged as a medium of communication between slave and master), the spoken imposes on the slave its particular syntax. For Caribbean man, the word is first and foremost sound. Noise is essential to speech. Din is discourse.... Since speech was forbidden, slaves camouflaged the word under the provocative intensity of the scream. It was taken to be nothing but the call of a wild animal. This is how the dispossessed man organized his speech by weaving it into the apparently meaningless texture of extreme noise.[8]

Lingering with Glissant's formulations produces certain insights. The first is that the temporal condensation and acceleration of the trajectory of black performances, which is to say black history, is a real problem and a real chance for the philosophy of history. The second is that the animative materiality—the aesthetic, political, sexual, and racial force—of the ensemble of objects that we might call black performances, black history, blackness, is a real problem and a real chance for the philosophy of human being (which would necessarily bear and be irreducible to what is called, or what somebody might hope someday to call, subjectivity). One of the implications of blackness, if it is set to work in and on such philosophy, is that those manifestations of the future in the degraded present that C. L. R. James described can never be understood simply as illusory. The knowledge of the future in the present is bound up with what is given in something Marx could only subjunctively imagine: the commodity who speaks. Here is the relevant passage from volume 1 of *Capital*, at the end of the chapter on "The Commodity," at the end of the section called "The Fetishism of the Commodity and Its Secret."

> But, to avoid anticipating, we will content ourselves here with one more example relating to the commodity-form itself. If commodities could speak they would say this: our use-value may interest men, but it does not belong to us as objects. What does belong to us as objects, however, is our value. Our own intercourse as commodities proves it. We relate to each other merely as exchange-values. Now listen how those commodities speak through the mouth of the economist:
>
> "Value (i.e., exchange-value) is a property of things, riches (i.e., use-value) of man. Value in this sense necessarily implies exchanges, riches do not."
>
> "Riches (use-value) are the attribute of man, value is the attribute of commodities. A man or a community is rich, a pearl or a diamond is valuable. . . . A pearl or a diamond is valuable as a pearl or diamond."
>
> So far no chemist has ever discovered exchange-value either in a pearl or a diamond. The economists who have discovered this chemical substance, and who lay special claim to critical acumen, nevertheless find that the use-value of material objects belongs to them independently of their material properties, while their value, on the other hand, forms a part of them as objects. What confirms them in this view is the peculiar circumstance that the use-value of a thing is realized without exchange, i.e. in a social process. Who would not call to mind at this point the advice given by the good Dogberry to the night-watchman Seacoal?

"To be a well-favoured man is the gift of fortune; but reading and writing comes by nature."[9]

The difficulty of this passage is partly due to its dual ventriloquizations. Marx produces a discourse of his own to put into the mouth of dumb commodities before he reproduces what he figures as the impossible speech of commodities magically given through the mouths of classical economists. The difficulty of the passage is intensified when Marx goes on to critique both instances of imagined speech. These instances contradict one another but Marx comes down neither on the side of speech he produces nor on that of the speech of classical economists that he reproduces. Instead he traverses what he conceives of as the empty space between these formulations, that space being the impossible material substance of the commodity's impossible speech. In this regard, what is at stake is not *what* the commodity says but *that* the commodity says or, more properly, that the commodity, in its inability to say, must be made to say. It is, more precisely, the idea of the commodity's speech that Marx critiques, and this is because he believes neither in the fact nor in the possibility of such speech. Nevertheless, this critique of the idea of the commodity's speech only becomes operative by way of a deconstruction of the specific meaning of those impossible or unreal propositions imposed upon the commodity from outside.

The words Marx puts into the commodity's mouth are these: "our use value ... does not belong to us as objects. What does belong to us as objects, however, is our value," where value equals exchange value. Marx has the commodity go on to assert that commodities only relate to one another as exchange-values, that this is proven by the necessarily social intercourse in which commodities might be said to discover themselves. Therefore, the commodity discovers herself, comes to know herself, only as a function of having been exchanged, having been embedded in a mode of sociality that is shaped by exchange.

The words of the commodity that are spoken through the mouths of the classical economists are roughly these: riches (i.e., use-value) are independent of the materiality of objects, but value, which is to say exchange-value, is a material part of the object. "A man or a commodity is rich, a pearl or a diamond is valuable." This is because a pearl or a diamond is exchangeable. Though he agrees with the classical economists when they assert that value necessarily implies exchange, Marx chafes at the notion that value is an inherent part of the object. "No chemist," he argues, "has discovered exchange-value either in a pearl or a diamond." For Marx, this chemical substance called exchange-value has not been found because it does not exist. More precisely, Marx facetiously places this discovery in an unachievable future without having considered the conditions under which such a discovery might be made. Those conditions are precisely the fact of the commodity's speech, which Marx dismisses in his critique of the very idea. "So far no chemist has ever discovered exchange-value either in a pearl or a diamond" because pearls or diamonds have not been heard to speak. The impossible chemical substance of the object's (exchange-)value is the fact—the material, graphic, phonic substance—of the object's speech. Speech will have been the cutting augmentation of the already existing chemistry of objects, but the object's speech, the commodity's speech, is impossible, that impossibility being the final refutation of whatever the commodity will have said.

Marx argues that the classical economists believe "that the use-value of material objects belongs to them independently of their material properties." He further asserts that they are confined in this view by the nonsocial realization of use-value—the fact that its realization does not come by way of exchange. When he makes these assertions, Marx moves in an already well-established choreography of approach and withdrawal from a possibility of discovery that Douglass already recited: the (exchange-)value of the speaking commodity exists also, as it were, *before* exchange. Moreover, it exists precisely as the capacity for exchange and the capacity for a literary, performative, phonographic disruption of the protocols of exchange. This dual possibility comes by a nature that *is* and at the same time is social and historical, a nature that is given as a kind of anticipatory sociality and historicity.

To think the possibility of an (exchange-)value that is prior to exchange, and to think the reproductive and incantatory assertion of that possibility as the objection to exchange that is exchange's condition of possibility, is to put oneself in the way of an ongoing line of discovery, of coming upon, of invention. The discovery of the chemical substance that is produced in and by Marx's counterfactual is the achievement of Douglass's line given in and as the theory and practice of everyday life where the spectacular and the mundane encounter one another all the time. It is an achievement we'll see given in the primal scene of Aunt Hester's objection to exchange, an achievement given in speech, literary phonography, and their disruption. What is sounded through Douglass is a theory of value—an objective and objectional, productive and repro-ductive ontology—whose primitive axiom is that commodities speak.

The impossible example is given in order to avoid anticipation, but it works to establish the impossibility of such avoidance. Indeed, the example, in her reality, in the materiality of her speech as breath and sound, anticipates Marx. This sound was already a recording, just as our access to it is made possible only by way of recordings. We move within a series of phonographic anticipations, encrypted messages, sent and sending on frequencies Marx tunes to accidentally, for effect, without the necessary preparation. However, this absence of preparation or foresight in Marx—an anticipatory refusal to anticipate, an obversive or anti- and anteimprovisation—is condition of possibility of a richly aug-mented encounter with the chain of messages the (re)sounding speech of the commodity cuts and carries. The intensity and density of what could be thought here as his alternative modes of preparation make pos-sible a whole other experience of the music of the event of the object's speech. Moving, then, in the critical remixing of nonconvergent tracks, modes of preparation, traditions, we can think how the commodity who speaks, in speaking, in the sound—the inspirited materiality—of that speech, constitutes a kind of temporal warp that disrupts and augments not only Marx but the mode of subjectivity that the ultimate object of his critique, capital, both allows and disallows. All of this moves toward the secret Marx revealed by way of the music he subjunctively mutes. Such aurality is, in fact, what Marx called the "sensuous outburst of [our] essential activity."[10] It is a passion wherein "the senses have . . .

become theoreticians in their immediate practice."[11] The commodity whose speech sounds embodies the critique of value, of private property, of the sign. Such embodiment is also bound to the (critique of) reading and writing, oft conceived by clowns and intellectuals as the natural attributes of whoever would hope to be known as human.

In the meantime, every approach to Marx's example must move through the ongoing event that anticipates it, the real event of the commodity's speech, itself broken by the irreducible materiality—the broken and irreducible maternity—of the commodity's scream. Imagine a recording of the (real) example that anticipates the (impossible) example; imagine that recording as the graphic reproduction of a scene of instruction, one always already cut by its own repression; imagine what cuts and anticipates Marx, remembering that the object resists, the commodity shrieks, the audience participates. Then you can say that Marx is prodigal; that in his very formulations regarding Man's arrival at his essence, he has yet to come to himself, to come upon himself, to invent himself anew. This nonarrival is at least in part an ongoing concealment internal to a project structured by an attunement to the revealed secret. What remains secret in Marx could be thought as or in terms of race or sex or gender, of the differences these terms mark, form, and reify. But we can also say that the unrevealed secret is a recrudescence of an already existing notion of the private (or, more properly, of the proper) that operates within the constellation of self-possession, capacity, subjectivity, and speech. He can point to but not be communist. What does the dispropriative event have to do with communism? What's the revolutionary force of the sensuality that emerges from the sonic event Marx subjunctively produces without sensually discovering? To ask this is to think what's at stake in the music: the universalization or socialization of the surplus, the generative force of a venerable phonic propulsion, the ontological and historical priority of resistance to power and objection to subjection, the old-new thing, the freedom drive that animates black performances. This is all meant to begin some thinking of the possibility that the Marxian formulation of sociality-in-exchange is grounded in a notion of the proper that is disrupted by the essential impropriety of the (exchange-)value that precedes exchange.

Part of the project this drive animates is the improvisation through the opposition of spirit and matter that is instantiated when the object, the commodity, sounds. Marx's counterfactual ("If the commodity could speak, it would say . . .") is broken by a commodity and by the trace of a subjectivity structure born in objection that he neither realizes nor anticipates. There is something more here than alienation and fetishization that works, with regard to Marx, as a prefigurative critique. However, according to Ferdinand de Saussure, and in extension of Marx's analytic, the value of the sign is arbitrary, conventional, differential, neither intrinsic nor iconic, not reducible to but rather only discernible in the reduction of phonic substance.

> In any case, it is impossible that sound, as a material element, should in itself be part of the language. Sound is merely something ancillary, a material the language uses. All conventional values have the characteristic of being distinct from the tangible element which serves as their vehicle. It is not the metal in a coin which determines its value. A crown piece nominally worth five francs contains only half that sum in silver. Its value varies somewhat according to the effigy it bears. It is worth rather more or rather less on different sides of a political frontier. Considerations of the same order are even more pertinent to linguistic signals. Linguistic signals are not in essence phonetic. They are not physical in any way. They are constituted solely by differences which distinguish one such sound pattern from another.[12]

The value of the sign, its necessary relation to the possibility of (a universal science of and a universal) language, is only given in the absence or supercession of, or the abstraction from, sounded speech—its essential materiality is rendered ancillary by the crossing of an immaterial border or by a differentializing inscription. Similarly, the truth about the value of the commodity is tied precisely to the impossibility of its speaking, for if the commodity could speak it would have intrinsic value, it would be infused with a certain spirit, a certain value given not from the outside, and would, therefore, contradict the thesis on value—that it is not intrinsic—that Marx assigns it. The speaking commodity thus cuts Marx; but the shrieking commodity cuts Saussure, thereby cutting Marx doubly: this by way of an irruption of phonic substance that cuts and augments meaning with a phonographic, rematerializing inscription. That irruption breaks down the distinction between what is intrinsic and what is given by or of the outside; here what is given inside is that which is out-from-the-outside, a spirit manifest in its material expense or aspiration. For Saussure such speech is degraded, say, by accent, a deuniversalizing, material difference; for Chomsky it is degraded by a deuniversalizing agrammaticality, but Glissant knows that "the [scarred] spoken imposes on the slave its particular syntax." These material degradations—fissures or invaginations of a foreclosed universality, a heroic but bounded eroticism—are black performances. There occurs in such performances a revaluation or reconstruction of value, one disruptive of the oppositions of speech and writing, and spirit and matter. It moves by way of the (phono-photo-porno-)graphic disruption the shriek carries out. This movement cuts and augments the primal. If we return again and again to a certain passion, a passionate response to passionate utterance, horn-voice-horn over percussion, a protest, an objection, it is because it is more than another violent scene of subjection too terrible to pass on; it is the ongoing performance, the prefigurative scene of a (re)appropriation—the deconstruction and reconstruction, the improvisational recording and revaluation—of value, of the theory of value, of the theories of value.[13] It's the ongoing event of an antiorigin and an anteorigin, replay and reverb of an impossible natal occasion, the performance of the birth and rebirth of a new science, a phylogenetic fantasy that (dis)establishes genesis, the reproduction of blackness in and as (the) reproduction of black performance(s). It's the offset and re-write, the phonic irruption and rewind, of my last letter, my last record date, my first winter, casting of effect and affect in the widest possible angle of dispersion.

It is important to emphasize that the object's resistance is, among other things, a rupture of two circles, the familial and the hermeneutic. The protocols of this investigation demand the consideration of that resistance as we'll see Douglass both describe and transmit it. More precisely, we must be attuned to the transmission of the very materiality that is being described while noting the relay between material phonography and material substitution.

Impossible, substitutive motherhood is the location of Aunt Hester, a location discovered, if not produced, in Hortense Spillers's improvisational audition of sighting, non-sight, seen; of the heretofore unheard and overlooked (overseen) at the heart of the spectacle. Spillers explains what Douglass brings in his prefigurative disruption of and irruption into a fraternal science of value that emerges in a "social climate" in which motherhood is not perceived "as a legitimate procedure of cultural inheritance":

> The African-American male has been touched, therefore, by the *mother*, handled by her in ways that he cannot escape, and in ways that the white American male is allowed to temporize by a fatherly reprieve. This human and historical development—the text that has been inscribed on the benighted heart of the continent—takes us to the center of an inexorable difference in the depths of American women's community: the African-American woman, the *mother*, the daughter, becomes historically the powerful and shadowy evocation of a cultural synthesis long evaporated—the law of the Mother—only and precisely because legal enslavement removed the African-American male not so much from sight as from *mimetic* view as a partner in the prevailing social fiction of the Father's name, the Father's law.
>
> Therefore, the female, in this order of things, breaks in upon the imagination with a forcefulness that marks both a denial and an "illegitimacy." Because of this peculiar American denial, the black American male embodies the *only* American community of males which has had the specific occasion to learn *who* the female is within itself, the infant child who bears the life against the could-be fateful gamble, against the odds of pulverization and murder, including her own. It is the heritage of the *mother* that the African-American male must regain as an aspect of his own personhood—the "power" of "yes" to the "female" within.[14]

Listen to the echo of Douglass's performative reproduction of a performance inextricably bound to his attempts to repress the learning that Spillers describes. But note that this attenuated covering of the maternal mark in Douglass is itself part and parcel of a kind of counterinscription before the fact, a prefigurative rematerialization constitutive of his recitation that returns as an expansive, audio*visual* discourse on music. Meanwhile, note the indistinctness of the conditions of "mother" and "enslavement" in the milieu from which Douglass emerges and which he describes and narrates. This is to say that enslavement—and the resistance to enslavement that is the performative essence of blackness (or, perhaps less controversially, the essence of black performance) is a *being maternal* that is indistinguishable from a *being material*. But it is also to say something more. And here, the issue of reproduction (the "natural" production of natural children) emerges right on time as it has to do not only with the question concerning slavery, blackness, performance, and the ensemble of their ontologies but also with a contradiction at the heart of the question of value in its relation to personhood that could be said to come into clearer focus against the backdrop of the ensemble of motherhood, blackness, and the bridge between slavery and freedom.

Leopoldina Fortunati puts it this way: "The conflicting presence of value and nonvalue contained within individuals themselves obviously creates a specific and unresolvable contradiction."[15] She is speaking of a certain dematerialization that marks the transition from precapitalist to capitalist production and that works analogously to a dematerializing operation animating the movement from slave labor to "free" labor. These transitions are both characterized by

> the *commodity*, [as] *exchange value*, taking precedence over *the-individual-as-use-value*, despite the fact that the individual is still the only source of the creation of value. For it is only by re-defining the individual as non-value, or rather as pure use-value, that capital can succeed in creating labor power as "a commodity," i.e. an exchange value. But the "value-lessness" of free workers is not only a consequence of the new mode

of production, it is also one of the preconditions, since capital cannot become a social relation other than in relation to the individuals who, divested of all value, are thus forced to sell the only commodity they have, their labor power.

Secondly, under capitalism, *reproduction* is *separated off* from *production;* the former unity that existed between the production of use-values and the reproduction of individuals within precapitalist modes of production has disappeared, and now the general process of commodity production appears as being separated from, and even in direct opposition to, the process of reproduction. While the first appears as the *creation* of value, the second, reproduction, appears as the creation of non-value. Commodity production is thus posited as *the* fundamental point of capitalist production, and the laws that govern it as *the* laws that characterize capitalism itself. Reproduction now becomes posited as "natural" production.[16]

Fortunati joins Marx in a minute but crucial declension from use-value to nonvalue. The individual, enslaved laborer is characterized as use-value that, in the field of capitalist production, is equivalent to no-value, which is to say operative outside of exchange. But if this theoretical placement of the enslaved laborer outside of the field of exchange positions her as noncommodity, it does so not by way of some rigorous accounting but rather as a function of not hearing, of overlooking. This is despite the inescapable fact of the traffic in slaves. And because neither Marx nor Fortunati is able fully to think the articulation of slave and commodity, they both underestimate the commodity's powers, for instance, the power to speak and to break speech. And yet, Fortunati, in her analysis of reproduction and in her submission of Marxian categories to the corrective of feminist theory, sees, along with and ahead of Marx, that the individual contains value and nonvalue, that the commodity is contained within the individual. This presence of the commodity within the individual is an effect of reproduction, a trace of maternity. Of equal importance is the containment of a certain personhood within the commodity that can be seen as the commodity's animation by the material trace of the maternal—a palpable hit or touch, a bodily and visible phonographic inscription. In the end, what I'm interested in is precisely that transference, a carrying or crossing over, that takes place on the bridge of lost matter, lost maternity, lost mechanics that joins bondage and freedom, that interinanimates the body and its ephemeral if productive force, that interarticulates the performance and the reproductive reproduction it always already contains and which contains it. This interest is, in turn, not in the interest of a nostalgic and impossible suturing of wounded kinship but is rather directed toward what this irrepressibly inscriptive, reproductive, and resistant material objecthood does for and might still do to the exclusionary brotherhoods of criticism and black radicalism as experimental black performance. This is to say that this book is an attempt to describe the material reproductivity of black performance and to claim for this reproductivity the status of an ontological condition. This is the story of how apparent nonvalue functions as a creator of value; it is also the story of how value animates what appears as nonvalue. This functioning and this animation are material. This ani*mater*iality—impassioned response to passionate utterance—is painfully and hiddenly disclosed always and everywhere in the tracks of black performance and black discourse on black performance. It is both for and before Marx in ways delineated by Cedric Robinson's historical analysis of "the making of the black radical tradition." This book is meant to contribute both to the aesthetic genealogy of that line and to the invagination of the ontological totality whose preservation, according to Robinson, inspires a tradition whose birth is characterized by an ancient pre-maturity.[17]

Here, then, is one such disclosure, famously and infamously made by Frederick Douglass in his 1845 *Narrative*. By way of a set of resonant nodal points along the massive trajectory it extends, I want to think about this disclosure as an unavoidable anticipation, the prefigurative response to an epochal counterfactual, the always already belated origin of the music that ought to be understood as the rigorously sounded critique of the theory of value.

I have often been awakened at the dawn of day by the most heart-rending shrieks of an own aunt of mine, whom he used to tie up to a joist, and whip upon her naked back till she was literally covered with blood. No words, no tears, no prayers, from his gory victim, seemed to move his iron heart from its bloody purpose. The louder she screamed, the harder he whipped; and where the blood ran fastest, there he whipped the longest. He would whip her to make her scream, and whip her to make her hush; and not until overcome by fatigue, would he cease to swing the blood-clotted cowskin. I remember the first time I ever witnessed this horrible exhibition. I was quite a child, but I well remember it. I shall never forget it whilst I remember anything. It was the first of a long series of such outrages, of which I was doomed to be a witness and a participant. It struck me with awful force. It was the blood-stained gate, the entrance to the hell of slavery, through which I was about to pass. It was a most terrible spectacle. I wish I could commit to paper the feelings with which I beheld it. . . .

Aunt Hester had not only disobeyed his orders in going out, but had been found in company with Lloyd's Ned; which circumstance, I found, from what he said while whipping her, was the chief offense. Had he been a man of pure morals himself, he might have been thought interested in protecting the innocence of my aunt; but those who know him will not suspect him of any such virtue. Before he commenced whipping Aunt Hester he took her into the kitchen, and stripped her from neck to waist, leaving her neck, shoulders, and back entirely naked. He then told her to cross her hands, calling her at the same time a d——d b——h. After crossing her hands, he tied them with strong rope, and led her to a stool under a large hook in the joist, put in for the purpose. He made her get upon the stool, and tied her hands to the hook. She now stood fair for the infernal purpose. Her arms were stretched up at their full length, so that she stood upon the ends of her toes. He then said to her, "Now, you d——d b——h, I'll learn you how to disobey my orders!" and after rolling up his sleeves, he commenced to lay on the heavy cowskin, and soon the warm, red blood (amid heart-rending shrieks from her, and horrid oaths from him) came dripping to the floor. I was so terrified and horror-stricken at the sight, that I hid myself in a closet, and dared not venture out till long after the bloody transaction was over. I expected it would be my turn next. It was all new to me. I had never seen anything like it before. . . .[18]

Now consider that passage's relation to an almost equally well-known one that closely follows it:

The slaves selected to go to the Great House Farm, for the monthly allowance for themselves and their fellow slaves, were peculiarly enthusiastic. While on their way, they would make the dense old woods, for miles around, reverberate with their wild songs, revealing at once the highest joy and the deepest sadness. They would compose and sing as they went along, consulting neither time nor tune. The thought that came up, came out—if not in the word, in the sound;—and as frequently in the one as in the other. They would sometimes sing the most pathetic sentiment in the most rapturous tone, and the most rapturous sentiment in the most pathetic tone. Into all of their songs they would manage to weave something of the Great House Farm. Especially would they do this, when leaving home. They would sing most exultingly the following words:—

"I am going away to the Great House Farm!
Oh, yea! O, yea! O!"

This they would sing, as a chorus, to words which to many would seem unmeaning jargon, but which, nevertheless, were full of meaning to themselves. I have sometimes thought that the mere hearing of those songs would do more to impress some minds with the horrible character of slavery, than the reading of whole volumes of philosophy on the subject could do.

I did not, when a slave, understand the deep meaning of those rude and incoherent songs. I was myself within the circle; so that I neither saw nor heard as those without might see and hear. They told a tale of woe which was then altogether beyond my feeble comprehension; they were tones loud, long, and deep; they breathed the prayer and complaint of souls boiling over with the bitterest anguish. Every tone was a testimony against slavery, and a prayer to God for deliverance from chains. The hearing of those wild notes always depressed my spirit, and filled me with ineffable sadness. I have frequently found myself in tears while hearing them. The mere recurrence to those songs, even now, afflicts me; and while I am writing these lines, an expression of feeling has already found its way down my cheek. To those songs I trace my first glimmering conception of the dehumanizing character of slavery. I can never get rid of that conception. Those songs still follow me, to deepen my hatred of slavery, and quicken my sympathy for my brethren in bonds. If any one wishes to be impressed with the soul-killing effects of slavery, let him go to Colonel Lloyd's plantation, and, on allowance-day, place himself in the deep pine woods, and there let him in silence analyze the sounds that shall pass through the chambers of his soul;—and if he is not impressed, it will only be because "there is no flesh in his obdurate heart."[19]

What does it mean to move in the tradition of these passages, a tradition of devotion both to the happy and the tragic possibilities embedded in passionate utterance and response? Passionate utterance and response together take the form of an encounter, the mutual, negative positioning of master and slave. This encounter is appositional, is shaped by a step away that calls such positions radically into question. In this sense utterance and response, seen together as encounter, form a kind of call wherein Hester's shrieks improvise both speech and writing. What they echo and initiate in their response to the oaths—that must be heard as the passionate utterance or call—of the master helps to constitute a questioning, musical encounter.

Having been called by call and response back to music, let's prepare our descent: let the call of call and response, passionate utterance and response—articulated in the scene Douglass identifies as "the blood-stained gate" through which he entered into subjection and subjectivity; articulated, more precisely, in the phonography of the very screams that open the way into the knowledge of slavery and the knowledge of freedom—operate as a kind of anacrusis (a note or beat or musicked word improvised through the opposition of speech and writing before the definition of rhythm and melody). Gerard Manley Hopkins's term for anacrusis was encountering. Let the articulation of appositional encounter be our encountering: a nondetermining invitation to the new and continually unprecedented performative, historical, philosophical, democratic, communist arrangements that are the only authentic ones.

In the long advent of a movement called "free jazz"—a beginning as long as the tradition it extends—Abbey Lincoln, Max Roach, and Oscar Brown Jr. collaborated in making a recording/performance called "Protest." Lincoln hums and then screams over Roach's increasingly and insistently intense percussion, moving inexorably in a trajectory and toward a location that is remote from—if not in excess of or inaccessible to—words. You cannot help but hear the echo of Aunt Hester's scream as it bears, at the moment of articulation, a sexual overtone, an invagination constantly reconstituting the whole of the voice, the whole of the story, redoubled and intensified by the mediation of years, recitations, auditions. That echo haunts, say, Albert Ayler's "Ghosts" or the fractured, fracturing climax of James Brown's "Cold Sweat." It's the re-en-gendering haint of an old negation: Ayler always screaming secretly to the very idea of mastery, "It's not about you"; Brown paying the price of such negation, a terrible, ecstatic, possessive, dispossessive inability to stop singing; both performing historical placement as a long transfer, a transcendental fade, an interminable songlike drag disrupting song. The revolution embedded in such duration is, for a moment, a run of questions: What is the edge of this event? What am I, the object? What is the music? What is manhood? What is the feminine? What is the beautiful? What will blackness be?[20]

Where shriek turns speech turns song—remote from the impossible comfort of origin—lies the trace of our descent. That place—locus of an ongoingly other recording of event, object, music—is Abbey Lincoln's narrative. This is a recording, an improvisation, of her words, troubled by the trace of the performance of which she tells and the performance of which that performance told.

I was born the tenth of twelve children . . . /I visited a psychiatric hospital 'cause Roach said there was madness in the house. He said it wasn't him, so I figured it must be me/They had me hollering and screaming like a crazy person; I ain't hollering and screaming for my freedom. The women I come from will take something and knock you . . . /Monk whispered in my ear, "Don't be so perfect." He meant make a mistake; reach for something/I didn't think a scream was part of the music/We were riding in the car with my nephew who was eight years old and who said, "The reason I can scream louder than Aunt Abbey is 'cause I'm a little boy/Went all over the world hollering and screaming; it increased my depth as an actress and a singer/I didn't write it, I didn't conceive it; I'm just the singer on it/I got rid of a taboo and screamed in everybody's face/We had to go to court; somebody thought Roach was killing me in the studio/My instrument is deepening and widening; it's because I'm possessed of the spirit/I learned it from my mother—the preacher, that's what they called her/Betty Carter: we came to the stage about the same time; it was a great surprise when she died; she was a year older than me and I've been feeling frail ever since . . . It's easy for me to cry; I'm an actress/You gotta sing a song; you can't sing jazz/When Bird was around he knew he wasn't playing jazz. He was playing his spirit. And I think that's the problem for a lot of the musicians on the scene now. They think that they're playing jazz. But there's no such thing, really/I'm possessed of my own spirit/This is the music of the African muse/I just want to be of use to my ancestors/It's holy work and it's dangerous not to know that 'cause you could die like an animal down here.[21]

Lincoln demands another rethinking, of "Protest" along lines I only thought I knew, lines I never thought I knew. Her relation to Roach disturbingly and rightly echoes Hester's relation to the master and to Douglass. Roach's double identification and desire link him to Douglass and are all bound up with Lincoln's political, musical, and intellectual lingering in a quite specific and brutal kind of horror as Roach's object, accessing and performing, recording, that history, moving in the doubleness of possession, the sexuality of spirituality and the anoriginality of black performances. Not the reduction of but the reduction to phonic materiality where re-en-gendering prefaces and works itself. No originary configuration of attributes but an ongoing shiftiness, a living labor of engendering to be organized in its relation to a politico-aesthesis. It's always going on and has been. Abbey Lincoln starts, in classic (anti-, ante-[slave]) narrative fashion. That black radicalism cannot be understood within the particular context of its genesis is true; it cannot be understood outside that context either. In this sense, black radicalism is (like) black music. The broken circle demands a new analytic (way of listening to the music). So we move with but also out and outside of Douglass's repressive, annular attunement to the secret, the audio-visual materiality of a maternal substitution, identification, and cathexis that he tries to forget, the ongoing re-entry into a vexed self-knowledge that he covers by entering into a discourse on music. Douglass (and, by extension, Roach and Brown and the entire line of mastery's disruptive, oppositional, anoriginal recording) was already sexually cut and augmented, already anticipated and improvised, already re-en-gendered by the sound of the one who comes before him, the one we keep calling on to arrive again, here and now, so we can get to the content of the epigraph.

CHAPTER 1

The Sentimental Avant-Garde

Duke Ellington's Sound of Love

The title comes from a Mingus composition and brings a scene to mind, a triptych, a set of questions concerning the content—the weight and energy in and of sound—of Ellington's life and love, Ellington's eros, (the Ellington) ensemble.

This is about the politics of the erotic and the erotics of sound in Ellington's music, remembering with Ellington's most radically devoted follower, Cecil Taylor, that anything is music as long as you apply certain principles of organization to it. Eros in Ellington is not but nothing other than sexual, moving along lines that Freud lays out in his theory of the drives. This doesn't sanction any strict Freudian analysis of Ellington because Ellingtonian meaning swings in a way that Freud probably can't quite reach. But in this swing there's something that Freud might help to illuminate even as whatever light he sheds is cut and augmented, if not eclipsed, by Ellington's sound. What drives Ellington? How does drive function in Ellington? Swing is given only after the fact of the content—again, the weight and energy in and of sound—of Ellington's drive, which is to say his love. For Freud, eros, life, love, is the drive "to establish ever greater unities and to preserve them thus."[1] This notion of Freud's gives you something to work with in an attempt to appreciate Ellington, to understand at least part of what was contained in what was, for him, the greatest possible compliment: "beyond category."

See, black performance has always been the ongoing improvisation of a kind of lyricism of the surplus—invagination, rupture, collision, augmentation. This surplus lyricism—think here of the muted, mutating horns of Tricky Sam Nanton or Cootie Williams—is what a lot of people are after when they invoke the art and culture—the radical (both rooted and out there, immanent and transcendent) sensuality—of and for my people. It's a lyricism that Marx was trying to get to when he envisioned theoretical senses. It's what that which is called the avant-garde desires whether it accepts or rejects that name. This influence of my people to which Ellington refers, in what it hopes for (a genuinely new universal) and in what it disrupts (that which has heretofore been given as the universal) is the sound of love. But this drive of and for "my people"—who are, for Ellington and according to Ellington, "the people"—is complicated; it continually erupts out of its own categorization like a Cat Anderson hyperclimax.[2] Such blackness is only in that it exceeds itself; it bears the groundedness of an uncontainable outside. It's an erotics of the cut, submerged in the broken, breaking space-time of an improvisation. Blurred, dying life; liberatory, improvisatory, damaged love; freedom drive.

A transcriptive, descriptive triptych from Terry Carter's film *A Duke Named Ellington*:

The voice of Julian Bond attempts to put forward an understanding of what Ellington might have meant by "beyond category," particularly the categories of identity. The voice-over manifests some of the pitfalls of analytic interpretation and in so doing reveals at least some of what's problematic in constant invocations of Ellingtonian elegance and, especially, Ellingtonian universality—mainly the avoidance of what is most truly, deeply, elegantly, and radically universal in Ellington's work. Bond takes Ellington's wonderful performance of the response to one of those questions that so often makes you cringe when you watch sixties documentaries on black folks as a kind of evasion of a particular—most probably racial—identity. But the drive for ever greater unities in Ellington is not animated by the desire for some empty and colorless universality. The cascading and augmentative whole that Ellington constantly achieves, breaks, and exceeds in and with his band, his instrument, is a black whole, a black, brown, and beige whole, even as it is also that which both is and contains "the group of those who admire Beaujolais, those who aspire to produce something fit for the plateau, those who aspire to be dilettantes." More to the point, the beautiful, musical interplay between my people and the people, prefaced by Ellington's jabbing, caressingly disruptive accompaniment of his own utterance, gets at something way more than the appeal to a universality that, in its lack of particularity, could never be a universality at all.

If you thought Ellington's bent response to the call of a question that would seem to oppose blackness and universality straightens out into some simple affirmation of a simple whole, Herb Jeffries, famous not only as a vocalist in Ellington's band but as the Saturday morning movie serial black cowboy, the Bronze Buckaroo, gives you a clue. "Duke was only after your confidence," communicating, arranging his orchestra that is you. He's choreographing, writing a dance with his utterance and conveying a desire for some movement that is divergent and in unison, a position that envelops and breathes.

Like Ellington arranged at the piano surrounded by his instrument as they played without—which is to say outside—music, their arrangement signifying (their knowledge of the) arrangement: Ellington would sing the parts, forging the preparation of the music beside writing, the orchestra's change of motion driven, given, proportional to his motive force or drive. That drive, again, is love.

Where's swing come from? What drive? My People: the rhythm of this performance, a resistance to the question that is erotic. Yet he was black, he did have and was in a band, inside the band that invaginatively envelops him, his comping marking that rhythmic disruption that animates swing, out of which swing emerges, before meaning. Is the freedom drive conservative? Is there some Aristophanean return to a prior unity? Is that which is before swing also before eros, that drive "to establish ever greater unities and to preserve them thus" to which cannot be applied the formula that has the drives tend "towards a return to an earlier state"?[3] Since that origin must have been a prior unity, eros is figured as the drive whose origin is unavailable. At the same time the positing and the fact of eros is unavoidable since it necessarily works in tandem with its other, the destroyer of connections and undoer of things, whose final aim is to lead things into an inorganic state, toward a return, therefore, to death, which is, for Freud, figured as an available origin where origin can only be figured as inanimate and fragmented (which is to say that, for Freud, the inanimate precedes the animate logically).

All this, too, so that we can understand the drives as working in tandem, against, or with each other across the cut of a ruptured and im/possible origin. "The sexual act is an act of aggression with the purpose of the most intimate union. This concurrent and mutually opposing action of the two basic drives gives rise to the whole variegation of the phenomena of life."[4] Yes, but the problem is that we here neither admit to an originary unity (given the necessary logical impossibility of the logically necessary return) nor justify an originary difference (if every drive—including eros—must instantiate a return to an originary state). What justifies eros's breaking of the law of the necessary return of the drives to their originary state?

Freud puts forward an asymmetrical, syncopated, off notion of the duality of the basic drives where each is reducible to the other's origin and one is irreducible to its own. And yet, he says, "Modifications in the proportions of the fusion between the drives have the most tangible results. A surplus of sexual aggressiveness will turn a lover into a sex-murderer, while a sharp diminution in the aggressive factor will make him bashful or impotent."[5] He seems, then, to require a kind of balance in a structure that is originarily asymmetrical, where there seems to be an originary surplus located at the site of the unlocatable origin of eros, the anteoriginary or, as Andrew Benjamin might put it, "anoriginal" drive.[6] This asymmetrical, difference producing, anoriginal difference or *différance* of the drives is, however, further complicated by the fact of a spatial indivisibility of the drives that would seem to imply some originary unity—or, more precisely, an originary erotics—where the idea of originary unity had already been rendered impossible as a function of the impossibility of a return to originary unity in its coupling with the law of the necessary return to origin of the drives. Freud must picture an initial state of eros and that state can tolerate nothing prior to it even though it is a law of the drives that they must tend toward something prior, that the drives cannot be spoken of in terms of their initial state. (This is the reason the death drive spawns no term analogous to "libido";[7] and now we understand eros as breaking two fundamental laws of the drives: it cannot be thought in terms of the necessary return to an original state, on the one hand, and it must be thought in terms of a certain reducibility to an initial state, on the other. Now you've got to try to see the massive, asymptotic difference, the miniscule and unbridgeable distance, between the originary and the initial.) (And yet this spatial indivisibility is almost immediately undermined by the notion of the ego as "the great reservoir" of the libido.[8] How is this to be reconciled to the omnipresence of the drives? Perhaps by way of an understanding of a difference between the drive and energy that is of the same problematic structure as that between the origin and the initial.)

> There can be no question of restricting one or the other of the basic drives to one of the provinces of the mind. They must necessarily be met with everywhere. We may picture an initial state as one in which the total available energy of Eros, which henceforward we will speak of as "libido," is present in the still undifferentiated ego-id and serves to neutralize the destructive tendencies which are simultaneously present. (We are without a term analogous to 'libido' for describing the energy of the destructive instinct.)[9]

In *An Outline of Psycho-Analysis,* Freud's exposition of the theory of the drives turns from eros to libido, which he takes to be the initial stance and energy of eros. And, for Freud, the libido emerges from the body. He says:

> There can be no question but that the libido has somatic sources, that it streams to the ego from various organs and parts of the body. This is most

clearly seen in the case of that portion of the libido which, from its instinctual aim, is described as sexual excitation. The most prominent of the parts of the body from which this libido arises are known by the name of *"erotogenic zones,"* though in fact the whole body is an erotogenic zone of this kind. The greater part of what we know about Eros—that is to say, about its exponent, the libido—has been gained from the study of the sexual function, which, indeed, on the prevailing view, even if not according to our theory, coincides with Eros. We have been able to form a picture of the way in which the sexual urge, which is destined to exercise a decisive influence on our life, gradually develops out of successive contributions from a number of component instincts, which represent particular erotogenic zones.[10]

Between origin and initiality, drive and energy, lies the "sexual 'cut.'" Eros. Event. Forgive the perversity of my insistence that Freud's compression and exposition, which is to say not only the form but the content of that exposition, is a wonderful piece of Ellingtonia. The density of the miniatures that make up the suite we call *An Outline of Psycho-Analysis* is rich with the necessity and effect of forming pictures in the terrain in which *there can be no question.* This is the dense erotics of arrangement, the whole of the text working like the whole of the body working like the whole of the orchestra—a miraculously autoexpansive, invaginative, erotogenic zone. The sexual urge of the text, like Ellington's music, like Ellington's sound of love, develops out of successive contributions, out of the asymmetrical differences of individual players, pictures, metaphors that are also sounds and bodies—particular erotogenic zones. But if Ellington moves out of Mackey's "insistent previousness evading each and every natal occasion," Freud operates after the fact of a locatable natality before which there is nothing. What does the sexual cut do to the primal scene? What does it do to the drive structure? What does the drive structure do to it? What I'm really trying to say is this: Ellington's music reconfigures the context in which everything, which is to say music, is read (+ = more). His sound of love infuses rooms, ruptures walls and hallways, collides with the friezes and carved-out names in library facades, building ever greater unities, making his band (featuring special ghost soloists Sigmund Freud and Karl Marx) swing with the force of a new, another, content, the ensemblic, improvisational nature of this sound of love, the human animality of its instruments.

Voices/Forces

Here's the instrument as small band: Beauford Delaney, Antonin Artaud, Billy Strayhorn.

> Time became different—not just an hour by the clock but a mysterious aliveness from the tips of your toes to the top of your head, touching everything and everyone. This began to be Paris for me. The dilemma of the human experience never lost its sorrow or joy; it simply had a way of existing for long periods immune to both, and all as if one was moving along a musical score to the orchestration of a complete poem of the emotions, hearing and living the music of the place called Paris.[11]

> Insane asylums are conscious and premeditated receptacles of black magic, and it is not only that doctors encourage magic with their inopportune
> and hybrid therapies,
> it is how they use it.[12]

> . . . a week in Paris will ease the bite of it . . .[13]

The idea of the avant-garde is embedded in a theory of history. This is to say that a particular geographical ideology, a geographical-racial or racist unconscious, marks and is the problematic out of which or against the backdrop of which the idea of the avant-garde emerges. The specter of Hegel reigns over and animates this constellation. His haunting, haunted formulations constitute one of the ways racism produces the social, aesthetic, political-economic, and theoretical surplus that is the avant-garde. There is a fundamental connection between the (re)production and performance of the surplus and the avant-garde.[14] This connection is bound to others or operates in a cumulative, ruptural unity with other such connections, the most crucial of which is that between fetishization and the avant-garde or, more precisely, between certain reconstructions of the theory of value (more precisely, an irruption of the foundations of the science of value, an epistemological break and sexual cut that arises in the middle of the nineteenth century as the codification of aesthetic and political energies that emerge out of the specific condition of possibility of modernity, namely, European colonialism) and chattel slavery. This relation of fetishization to the avant-garde must be thought with some precision. It must be situated in relation to a universalization of ritual that rears its head in the invocation of roots or of tradition or interculturalism or appropriation, all of which are made possible by the ongoing development of Northern hegemony. Such invocation unsurprisingly occurs in an era imprecisely characterized as post–cold war (where the nature of the cold war has never or only vaguely been thought) or *newly* globalized (where globalization is thought, somehow, as other than what it has actually been up to now, "a strategy for maximum exclusion," as Masao Miyoshi says). This is to say that the conditions necessary for the production of the surplus remain, that the remainder remains and not only in and as the effects of reproduction. Precision demands that in the encounter with a series of graphic reproductions we *listen*.

What I've been specifically interested in here is how the idea of a black avant-garde exists, as it were, oxymoronically—as if black, on the one hand, and avant-garde, on the other hand, each depends for its coherence upon the exclusion of the other. Now this is probably an overstatement of the case. Yet it's all but justified by a vast interdisciplinary text representative not only of a problematically positivist conclusion that the avant-garde has been exclusively Euro-American, but of a deeper, perhaps unconscious, formulation of the avant-garde as necessarily not black. Part of what I'm after now is this: an assertion that the avant-garde is a black thing (that, for the sake of argument, Richard Schechner wouldn't understand) and an assertion that blackness is an avant-garde thing (that, for the sake of argument, Albert Murray wouldn't understand).

For Murray, the avant-garde is fundamentally determined by its expendability.[15] Focusing on the military connotations of the term, Murray understands the avant-garde as continually submitting itself to a sacrificial experimentalism whose value exists only in what it opens for and echoes of what is essential to the tradition. In his case the tradition is a certain convergence of black cultural expression and a Malrauxvian "museum without walls," the location of a distilled, cross-cultural, aesthetic, and political universality that both culminates in and is saved by America, the apotheosis of the West, and blackness, the West's most iconic creation. Meanwhile, Schechner invests in a formulation of the end of the avant-garde, one structured by the absence or impossibility of the new in the face of a technologically induced exhaustion, a malaise brought on by a general inability to escape the strictures of reproduction, of the fetishization and commodification reproduction fosters.[16] And further, in the spirit of contemporary American triumphalism wherein the end of the avant-garde is an effect and echo of the end of ideology, Schechner says, who cares if no other Artaud comes along. One can only imagine that Murray would say amen. I want to think about why it is that we ought to care about the (second or ongoing) coming (upon) of the avant-garde. To do this I need to try to fill in Schechner's outline of the historical avant-garde, disturb the borders of Murray's conception of blackness, and stage an encounter between Artaud and some others that follow and anticipate him.

This requires a trip to Paris. The trip moves by way of Harlem and the Village, by way of the out extension of renaissance. Actually, the trip has an uncountable number of points of embarkation, none of which is originary, and is made on a railroad both aleatory and underground. Finally, the destination is also subject to cut and augmentation. This requires a trip through Paris.

This is when Harlem is no longer a point of arrival. This constellation is initially marked by a particular black modernist response to that capital of national cosmopolitanism-in-primitivism, Paris. But this response is itself understood as the echo or recording of other, earlier migrations, arrivals, or (re)births. This mode of response is exemplified by Delaney and his work, his movement in the multiply sited encounter between the European and African diasporas. In Delaney's case (as in every other), one site of this encounter (in his case Paris, and the exilic or expatriate movement to it) is always prefigured. Similarly, the natal occasion such an encounter represents is always anticipated. Paris and the movement to Paris echoes Greenwich Village and the movement to Greenwich Village, itself the repetition with differences of Harlem, Boston, Knoxville, Tennessee, and on and on, always, finally, before even Delaney himself. In spite of the uncountable instances of such geographic activity, this encounter is most often conceived of as driven by an agency that moves in only one direction. Whereas a powerful strain of postcolonial theory structures itself as *the reversal* of that direction and its gaze, I'm interested in the discovery of a necessary *appositionality* in this encounter, an almost hidden step (to the side and back) or gesture, a glance or glancing blow, that is the condition of possibility of a genuine aesthetic representation and analysis—in painting and prose—of that encounter.

Something in Delaney's Parisian paintings and autobiographical writings helps to illuminate the necessary connection between black political reason, the possibility of a cosmopolitan and/or geopolitical aesthetic and the rehabilitation of the very idea of the avant-garde. This connection is often and most interestingly made at the site of emergence of what he alternatively called voices and forces, the painted sounds of the thought of the outside, the visual manifestation of phonic substance and the content it bears, the disruption of the border between what could be thought as a debilitating psychic, political, and sexual illness, on the one hand, and—with regard to these same categories—an enabling and invaginative health, on the other. I'm interested in how what might be thought as the merely gestural is given as the *appositional force* that manifests itself in Delaney's paintings and texts as irreducible phonic substance, vocal exteriority, the extremity that is often unnoticed as mere accompaniment to (reasoned) utterance. To refer to this exteriority, after, say, Artaud, simply as madness is no longer possible. Madness is, rather, that understanding of Artaud that moves outside of any reference to Delaney, to their mediated, seemingly impossible encounter. Their encounter is one of space-time separated coincidence and migrant imagination, channels of natal prematurity as well as black rebirth, modernism as intranational as well as international relocation, and the politico-aesthetics of a surplus of content irreducible to identity in or for itself, but held, rather, in identity's relation to a general upheaval. So that this is about the force that animates and awaits release from texts and canvases that represent the itineraries and locales of modernism and modernity.

Is Harlem a privileged place in this chain of renaissance? One must consult Billy Strayhorn here. Strayhorn, with a song called "Lush Life" among a good bit of other compositions he'd penned in his hometown of Pittsburgh, arrives in Harlem around 1940, roughly a decade after Delaney exited the train from Boston there before quickly moving down to the Village. And though Delaney's destinations required taking the A-train in the direction opposite to that which Strayhorn famously recommends, their connection is crucial especially at the site of a certain dream of Paris, even if, for Strayhorn, the dream is only of a week, rather than a more permanent sojourn, in Paris. Of course Delaney and Strayhorn—whose name is so suggestive especially when we hear him sing, the outness or uncontrollability of his voice or horn, itinerant, stray like the brass and winds of Ellington's (and Strayhorn's) "instrument"—share (according to their biographers) in the outness of their (homo)sexuality and their movements, on the A-train and more widely, as "Lush Life" suggests, what it is to be driven by the paradoxically hidden extremity and necessary unrequitedness of love.[17] They are driven to and by a fugitivity that, according to Nathaniel Mackey, is disruptively essential to the music that Delaney's paintings will strive to represent, most especially by way of abstraction, most fundamentally in what might be called a kind of glossolalian application of paint to the canvas. One thinks here, too, of a chain of surplus spellings and christenings (De Laney, Strayhorne) that moved in some space-time separated synchrony with that of Artaud, who signed certain letters—like one, for instance, to the doctor who treated him during his long confinement at the mental institution in Rodez, France, Gaston Ferdière, about whom more in a minute—"Antonin Nalpas," the fictional surname here being the maiden name of his mother, given as if somehow more originary, marking something like that final and impossible return that Ellington points to in the title of his tribute album for Strayhorn, *And His Mother Called Him Bill*. Such renaming also marks a propensity to wander or migrate or stray that is always animated by desire. Think of James Baldwin, Delaney's protégé and object of desire, following Delaney's move from or through Harlem to the Village as the prefiguring of Delaney's following Baldwin to Paris; or think of those hushed voices, about which more in a minute, that later, on the road to Istanbul, in the midst of another tracing of Baldwin's steps, Delaney will overhear as he rides in the back seat of a car. Those voices emanate from a car whose path Delaney and some companions crossed somewhere in Yugoslavia. The car sped toward the one in which Delaney was riding and somehow he heard its passengers, always already translated, say, "Look at that little black faggot riding with those two white boys."[18]

Gaston Ferdière was Beauford Delaney's doctor, too. Delaney's biographer, who is also Baldwin's biographer, David Leeming, informs us:

On December 20 [1961] Solange du Closel and her husband drove Beauford to the Nogent clinic where he was placed under the care of the well-known psychiatrist Dr. Ferdière, whose specialty was depression. Ferdière quickly confirmed the diagnosis of acute paranoia and gave Beauford anti-depressant medicine that stopped the hallucinations. He warned Beauford that alcohol would negate the benefits of the treatment. Ferdière spoke English and had a good knowledge of painting and the arts—he had treated the mental disorders of the dramatist Antonin Artaud and had written a book critical of the handling of Vincent Van Gogh's depression.[19]

Delaney, Strayhorn, and Artaud share some transatlantic maternal machinery (as Artaud might say). Forces. Voices. Leeming records them for us in his citation of Delaney's 1961 journals, written, at Ferdière's prescription, as part of Delaney's therapy. I want to refer to two passages from that journal and argue for their interconnection. In the first, Delaney recalls his beloved older sister, Ogust Mae, whom he lost when she was only nineteen; in the second, Delaney thinks the relation between his paintings and black music:

> Sister was older than me and we were very close. As we grew older there were ever increasing needs for money and mama began to go out in service cooking, or nursing, or being a general housekeeper which meant that Sister with our help had to carry on at home. She was very bright and good natured, although her health was frail, and we were devoted to her and tried in our clumsy way to save her, but we did not know how, we were all so young and so unaware of the pain and unspoken intensity of our home and community life. Sister was full of fun and in no way pretentious—she sang beautifully—it was a joy to hear her. Mama being away from home, all her chores fell upon Sister who never complained—but she was always sick. We became alarmed because [from] the first time the doctor came it was always something the matter with Sister. Mama would quit her job and come home, the house became very quiet and we were awake all night [talking] in hushed voices in fear for Sister's recovery. She was strong willed and survived most difficulties and would seem to be well and we would rejoice. So much of the sickness [Ogust Mae's and others] came from improper places to live—long distances to walk to school improperly heated—a walk twice a day [they came home for lunch]—too much work at home—natural conditions common to the poor that take the bright flowers like terrible cold in nature.[20]

> Life in Paris gives me an anonymity and objectivity to release long stored up memories of [the] beauty and sorrows of the difficult work of orchestrating and releasing into a personal form of color and design what seems to me a long apprenticeship to jazz and spiritual songs augmented by the

deep hope given to my people in the deep south at home. I gave myself
to these experiences devotedly.[21]

With gratitude for his recovery of this text, one moves against or
through Leeming's seemingly necessary bracketed interpolations and
the primacy of interpretation, of the imposition of meaning, they imply.
Listen to the sentence break or break down after the invocation of Sister's singing. That breakdown is not the negative effect of grammatical
insufficiency but the positive trace of a lyrical surplus, counterpart to a
certain tonal breakdown heard in Strayhorn's performance of "Lush
Life" when the word "madness" is uttered with some uncontrollable
accompaniment, the internal exteriority of a voice which is and is not
his own. It is the possession of Delaney's text by Ogust Mae and all of
that for which she substitutes. We've got to think, then, what it means
to "lay awake all night in hushed voices," think the political implications and history of the primal overhearing of a phonic materiality
always tied to the ongoing loss or impossible recovery of the maternal.
Leeming will go on to discuss what he records Delaney as sometimes
calling "my forces," pointing out that these voices/forces were in existence as far back as the Knoxville of Delaney's boyhood, but they are
indexed to an already existing kernel of the illness which becomes more
and more insistent in Delaney and which will prompt, finally, the text
above.[22] At the same time, the voices/forces also emerge, according to
Leeming, as the concrete form of and response to a compartmentalization of Delaney's life that became increasingly severe over the course
of his migrations and their punctuation in interracial and homosexual
encounters. But the materiality of these voices not only exists before
any development or decay purely internal to Delaney, it is irreducible
to Delaney's illness as well. This black-advanced surplus is sexual and
paranoid light and multiplied thick color, impasto—the laying on of
color thickly, one possible painterly equivalent of something Mackey,
with reference to Eric Dolphy, refers to as the "multiply tongued,"
something generally thought, in relation to Artaud, as glossolalia. This

music is not only the "last resort" of "wounded kinship," but is also, precisely as that last resort, the emergence from broken matrilinearity of an insistent reproductive *mater*iality. And we know how the long apprenticeship to the black music that the paintings represent is a long apprenticeship to the *mater*iality of voices that the music represents. You should listen to Strayhorn represent right now.[23]

> . . . *not once more will/I be found with beings/who swallowed the rail of life//And one day I found myself with beings/who swallowed the nail of life/—as soon as I lost my matrix mamma,//and the being twisted under him,/and god poured me back to her/(the motherfucker)* . . .[24]

> I used to go to all the very gay places/those come what may places/relaxing on the axis of the wheel of life/to get the feel of life.[25]

Impasto and glossoalia. Hearing the painting, Artaud is not formless. And the surplus in Strayhorn: too much rhyme (as in "Ci-git" but Strayhorn's performance—live, recorded, him now "dead" as if this weren't that very deconstruction of or improvisation through the opposition of life and death, that silent, surplus e) but the voice is all over, strained or fragile till strong g doubles up with and like the bass—the quickened disruption of the irreducible phonic substance, which is where universality lies. Here lies universality: in this break, this cut, this rupture. Song cutting speech. Scream cutting song. Frenzy cutting scream with silence, movement, gesture. The West is an insane asylum, a conscious and premeditated receptacle of black magic. Every disappearance is a recording. That's what resurrection is. Insurrection. Scat black magic, but to scat or scatter is not to admit formlessness. The aftersound is more than a bridge. It ruptures interpretation even as the trauma it records disappears. Amplification of a rapt countenance, stressed portraiture. No need to dismiss the sound that emerges from the mouth as the mark of a separation. It was always the whole body that emitted sound: instrument and fingers, bend. Your ass is in what you sing. Dedicated to the movement of hips, dedicated by that movement, the harmolodically rhythmic body. Artaud's description of torture in Maryland was published in 1845, mama's gone.

What if we understand the geographical history of the New York avant-garde chorographically, by way of the turning point? We could think it choreographically, bringing the aesthetic back on line, by way of a rhythm analysis that would inject some choreographic play of encounter into our analytic, making certain folks meet in the city. Turning point might then become vanishing point, where the absent presence of the performance becomes the absent and structuring center of perspectival urban space. We could think this in relation to the desire for bohemian space and the way that desire is activated in and as the displacement of the ones who had been there. Such displacement is the carryover of those regimes of property from whence certain avant-garde Puritans had fled as the silencing of that internal antinomian difference that will have always been both the renewal, expansion, invagination of the avant-garde and the recrudescence of enclosure and all that cuts it, before the fact of another mode of thinking that might be structured by and as a collaboration with what and who had been there before. This is the spatial politics of the avant-garde. This is to say that the avant-garde is not only a temporal-historical concept but a spatial-geographical concept as well. Again, Hegel would have understood this. Constraint, mobility, and displacement are, therefore, conditions of possibility of the avant-garde. Deterioration is crucial to the avant-garde, as well: as a certain aesthetics, as an effect of disinvestment, as a psychic condition: the decay of form and the internal and external environment of regenerative aesthetic production: turning, vanishing, enclosing, invaginating.[26]

But there's re*mater*ialization of bourgeois space-time that is also what and where the avant-garde is. This avant-garde disrupts the phantasmatically solipsistic space of bourgeois aesthetic production and reception with some brought noise, voices/forces, mobilizing through enforced hermeticisms. And this works with but also outside of Alain Locke's formulation of a black migratory modernity; not outside but past.

And so a second and third move is what interests me here: a certain movement through Harlem and beyond renaissance, a post-maturity of rebirth and removal, to Bohemia, to the Village, to Paris. Beauford Delaney exemplifies not only this move but another, the outest move of all, with and to and through Artaud you might say. This move could be thought as what Billy Strayhorn imagined: lush life as its own antidote, Paris refigured as a kind of bright magic mountain. But all this movement is not simply felicitous. To move further and further into the heart of lightness, the city of light, is to more fully immerse oneself in the vast asylum of the West, "a conscious and premeditated receptacle of black magic." Still, something is given off in these encountering migrations, the gesture in sound or the sound in painting of another liberty awaiting activation, the politico-economic, ontological, and aesthetic surplus. Such production—such radically ensemblic, radically improvisational objection—is the unfinished, continually re-en-gendered, actively re-engendering project of the black (and blue and sentimental) avant-garde.

Sound in Florescence (Cecil Taylor Floating Garden)

No reading[27] of (the words mark a ritual, annular enactment—a fall: the sentence was broken here; a caesura—even, one could say, of the caesura—has occurred. You could bridge the gap with one of many simple denotations supposed to get to the ensemble of what I want you, now, to hear, but that would have already been unfaithful to the truth and attention carried in the name of what, now, I would have you hear. But this will not be a meditation on the idiom of) *Chinampas*.[28]

No reading because the understanding of literary experience which (a) reading implies is exceeded in the enactment of what *Chinampas* is and moves (to), what *Chinampas* demands: improvisation. And so I have been preparing myself to play with Cecil Taylor, to hear what is transmitted on frequencies outside and beneath the range of reading. *Notes* composed in the interest of that preparation: *phrases*:[29]

> Charles Lloyd, asked to comment on a piece of his music by a radio interviewer, answered "Words don't go there."[30]

Words don't go there. Is it only music, only sound, that goes there? Perhaps these notes and phrases will have mapped the terrain and traversed (at least some of) the space between here and there.

Words don't go there: this implies a difference between words and sounds; it suggests that words are somehow constrained by their implicit reduction to the meanings they carry—meanings inadequate to or detached from the objects or states of affairs they would envelop. What's also implied is an absence of inflection; a loss of mobility, slippage, bend; a missing accent or affect; the impossibility of a slur or crack and the *excess*—rather than loss—of meaning they imply.

Where do words go? Are they the inadequate and residual traces of a ritual performance that is lost in the absence of the recording?[31]

Where do words go? Where, into what, do they turn in Taylor's rendering: a generative disintegration, an emanation of luminous sound? The interinanimation of recording, verbal art and improvisation—which *Chinampas* is and enacts—places performance, ritual, and event within a trembling—that *Chinampas* escapes—between words' florescence and the constitutive absence of the book.[32] Nevertheless that trembling raises certain questions, for instance, that of the relationship between words and their phrasing.[33] Changes, like that from word to growl, occur here taking the word to where it does not go but neither to any origin as pure sound nor to the simple before of the determinations of meaning. This change and movement might be at the phonemic level, might mark the generation of or from a lost language and/or a new thing that is, in spite of its novelty, never structured as if the before that is absent and indeterminate had never been or does not still remain there. What is the nature of this "sexual cut," this "*[l]imbo* [that] reflects a certain kind of gateway to or threshold of a new world and the dislocation of a chain of miles," that is evident in Taylor's words and improvisations of words?[34] Is the only rigorous model one that necessitates the elimination of any previousness, any new world? Where do words go?

Where do words go? Where, to what, do they turn in Taylor's rendering? A blur, like the typescript on the cover of the album,[35] meaning lifted by design, slurred by packaging, the rhythmic architecture of text, texture, textile

> *for example the Mande rhythm cloth, where patterns are juxtaposed against each other, several different types of seemingly different patterns that come together and make the ensemble garment. It's acutely apparent on the poetry record here the overdubs, the voices just sliding around and between each other because (sings melody from Pemmican), but because I don't know much music, or I don't know musical terms, it's difficult for me to articulate what it is that I'm hearing.* Good, you have to define for yourself, all the . . . (*Spencer Richards, Cecil Taylor*)[36]

perhaps the blur signifies that everything is (in) Cecil Taylor, is improvisation or, more precisely, that the improvisation of a notion (or, perhaps more faithfully, a phenomenology) of the ensemble heretofore weakly signaled in the sharp edges of words like "everything" is in effect. Note that (in) is always parenthetical, between the opposing words of that structure, between acts or wars, like Woolf and Jones, homologous with the phenomenon of erasure; ~~everything~~ is (in) erasure, the mark of an imaginary structure of homology, the additive and aggregative imposture of an antitotalitarian ensemble. But, with these provisos, the phrase, the broken sentence, holds (everything).

Taylor's phrase will not be read.

Performance, ritual, and event are of the idea of idiom,[37] of the "anarchic principles" that open the unrepresentable performance of Taylor's phrasing. What happens in the transcription of performance, event, ritual? What happens, which is to say what is lost, in the recording? I am preparing myself to play with Taylor. What is heard there? What history is heard there? There is one which is not just one among others

> I'm really quite happy, or becoming more comfortable with the conception that Ellington, after all, is the genius I must follow, and all the

methodological procedures that I follow are akin, more closely aligned to that than anything else.[38]

the history of (an) organization, orchestra(tion), *construction*. The essence of construction is part of what that phrasing is after; the poem of construction—geometry of a blue space, geometry of a blue ghost—is the poem that is of the music

> So, actually, last year for the first time since the seventies I felt more like a professional musician. I never want to be, nor do I consider myself one. You say you don't consider yourself a professional musician? I would hope never to be a professional musician. So, if one has to, how would you classify yourself? Ha, Ha, Ha ... I've always tried to be a poet more than anything else, I mean, professional musicians die. (Phone rings)[39] /Then the music, the imagination from the music led into the words ... So that the music is primary, but everything is music once you care to begin to apply certain principles of organization to it. So that I imagine there is ... people have told me they see a certain relationship between the word and the music ...[40]

A poetry, then, that is of the music; a poetry that would articulate the music's construction; a poetry that would mark and question the idiomatic difference that is the space-time of performance, ritual, and event; a poetry, finally, that becomes music in that it iconically presents those organizational principles that are the essence of music. The thing is, these organizational principles break down; their breakdown disallows reading, improvises idiom(atic difference) and gestures toward an anarchic and generative meditation on phrasing that occurs in what has become, for reading, the occluded of language: sound.

Let Taylor's "musicked" speech and illegible words resonate and give some attention to their broken grammar, the aural rewriting of grammatical rule that is not simply arbitrary but a function of the elusive content he would convey: what's going on is either in an interstice or of the ensemble, either between professionalism and its other—music and poetry—or in the holism of a kind of everyday ritual.[41] Taylor's poetry: the geometry of a ghost? The physics of remembrance? The architecture of the archétrace? Is there a continuity to be written here or is the continuity in the cut of the phrase? I am preparing myself to play with Cecil Taylor: what is the proper form of my endeavor? Perhaps the transcription of an improvisational blurrrring of the word; perhaps an improvisation through the singular difference of the idiom and its occasion; perhaps an *a*calculation of that function whose upper limit is reading and whose lower limit is transcription—an improvisation through phrases, through some virtual head and coda. Taylor says to his interlocutor, "I'm listening."[42] Perhaps he will have said this to me or to the word: I'm listening, *go on*. Then perhaps the ensemble of the word, Taylor and I will have veered off into the silence that is embedded in the transformation, the truth that is held in the silence of the transformation, a truth that is only discernible in transformation.

Sound: suspended brightness, unrepresentable and inexplicable mystery of (music is the improvisation of organization) ritual is music: principled *(archic)* (spatial) organization that constitutes a kind of nonverbal writing: transparent or instrumental, uninflected by the transformations of a buzz-growl extension, bending whistle, hummm—

> ... there are and we experience the fact that there are *several* philosophical idioms and that this experience alone cannot not be lived by a philosopher, by a self-styled philosopher, by whoever claims to be a philosopher, as both a *scandal* and as the very *chance* of philosophy.[43]

but an improvisation (an*archic*) of those principles that sees through: infinite divisibilities and irreducible singularities; sites of communications never to be received; rites of affliction, tragedies, bodily divisions; spatial/social arrangements that constitute a kind of philosophical writing enacted and reenacted in the annular rememberment and dismemberment of community; nation and race; the imposition and maintenance of hierarchical relations within these units; the vexed and impossible task of a reconciliation of one and many via representation? Here it is if I could work through expressive singularity, the im/possibility of direct communication, the ideas of writing as visible speech and writing as independent of speech. Here it is if idiom becomes the site where an improvisation of/through these might occur: not in the name of an originary creativity or a grounded and telic liberty, but of a free, which is to say anarchic and atelic, generativity; a reconceptualization or out-from-outside reinstrumentalization of idiom that allows an improvisation through rather than a deconstructive oscillation within the *aporia* of philosophy.

Improvisation through the opposition of reading and transcription—precondition and effect of preparation to play with Taylor: the preparation is the playing, the trace of another organization; it starts like and away from a reading and ends like and beyond transcription but is neither homage to indeterminacy nor objectifying rendering nor reduction to a narrow sense of "writing"; not about the hegemony of the visual in reading, nor the suspicion of a singular vision; at the same time not about the etiolation of a capturing picture.

In reading, Taylor's performance—the prefatory dance, the gestures at the instrument which produce/emit sound—along with his sound—independent, though it is, of the reduction of the word to verbal assertion—are too easily subordinated to the visual/spatial and the pervasive occularcentrism, structured around a set of obsolete temporal, ethical, and aesthetic determinations, which grounds it. Nevertheless, Taylor's poetry, the geometry of a blue ghost, is full of spatial and directional renderings.

        a curve having rotation in three dimensions cutting spiral elements at a constant angle

        These are improvised in his sounding of them that I won't read and can't transcribe.

Though the visual/spatial binds, its occlusion distorts the undifferentiated but unfixed ensemble (ensemble) the remembrance of the aural gives. The echo of what is not but nothing other than unremembered is a wound in Derrida (for example), confounding the dream of another universality, conflating that dream with the vision of an old song, old-new language, homely sound, naïve or idiomatic writing. Here it is remedied in Taylor moving out from the outside, out from the paradoxes of idiom to offer up idiom's re-sounding, one which avoids philosophical nationalism without devolving into transparent instrumentality, one that is not a reconceptualization but an improvisation of idiom in its relation/opposition to ritual via suspended luminescence, floating garden. That improvisation is activated in a sound which holds information in the implicit graphics of its rhythm, a spatial orientation affecting a spatial representation that is sound become dispersive sensuality. So, in a kind of holosensual, holœsthetic reversal, one hears music in Taylor's visual-spatial description and sees gestures and spaces in an aurality that exceeds but does not oppose visual-spatial determination.

In Taylor float/drift/linger/cut are fresh in the improvised parlance of another architecture, another geometry. The recording gives the trace *of* performance in the product or artifact, is a constative vessel of information maintaining the question of the product as determinate sign; yet it also marks a temporal/ethical problem that can be solved only by way of a radical movement through certain questions: of the trace *as* performance, of sound, of the rending of the opposition of aurality and spatiality, of the opposition of speech and writing within verbality, of the question of the gestural in literary style, of the question of silence and the absence of the break. . . .

"Rhythm is life, the space of time danced thru"[44] the cut between event and anniversary where sound, writing, ritual lie all improvised. Two passages (of David Parkin and Claude Lévi-Strauss) to the crossing of rhythm and ritual:

> Ritual is formulaic spatiality carried out by groups of people who are conscious of its imperative or compulsory nature and who may or may not further inform this spatiality with spoken words.[45]

> The value of the ritual as meaning seems to reside in instruments and gestures; it is a *paralanguage*. The myth on the other hand, manifests itself as *metalanguage*; it makes full use of discourses, but does so by situating its own significant oppositions at a higher level of complexity than that required by language operating for profane ends.[46]

In these passages ritual is primarily defined by distinctions between itself and forms of aural/verbal activity—most importantly, myth—in which ritual is seen as impoverished or by distinctions between itself and other forms of nonverbal activity that, in their mundaneness, remain untransformed by any ceremonial aura. Parkin focuses on the *silent* communication of propositions in ritual as that which matches or even exceeds verbal assertion through spacing, position, or the visual-graphic architectonics that oscillate between fixity and contestation. According to Lévi-Strauss, however, words *do* go there, arriving under the motive force of "a higher level of complexity" than that afforded by the instrumental or gestural in ritual. If one thinks, though, of a poetry reading—which may very well be (for) a "profane end"—one confronts that which requires that we take into account the ways ritual consists of physical action (in time) that may *be*, as well as emit or transmit, the kind of meaningful aural expression that improvises through the distinction between the paralinguistic and the metalinguistic. And if words that had been thought of as the elements of a purely constative expression are radically reconnected to their essential sonic performance by eccentric physical action, by an excess of the physical (trill-making vibration of tongue or vowel-lengthening squint) that deforms the word conceived of as a mere vessel of meaning, then that requirement becomes even more urgent. The attempt to read ritual as it is manifest in the sound of such words or the attempt to transcribe myth transformed by gesture and meaningful positionality might be better thought in terms of the improvisation of ritual, writing, sound, idiom, event.

The spatio-temporal constitution of ritual raises ambiguities as well. On the one hand ritual is durative. The structure and dance of its positions is ongoing, part of an annulus that seems unopposed to the uninterrupted process of the everyday against which it would be defined. But what of the punctuality of the endlessly/daily repeated event? This punctuality is, too, of ritual, and ritual thus lends punctuality the aura of ceremony: the *special* occasion. There is, then, a temporal contradiction in the opposition of ritual and nonritual, one that activates in both terms a juxtaposition that is manifest as the traumatic/celebratory and obsessional rhythmic breakage of the everyday and that implies a directionality of time—a spatio-temporal constitution—that transforms rhythm into a double determination: of position or movement, on the one hand, and syntagmic order on the other. Thus Parkin's focus on "the use made . . . of directionality—of axes, cardinal points, concentric zones and other expressions of spatial orientation and movement"[47]

on the outside circumference flushed
toward slant intersecting new reference point moves clockwise

and
his interest in the random and contingent effects of contestation as a kind of reading-in-performance, a shifting and reshifting of spatial conventions and temporal order determined by a radical break as when, for instance, the community *cuts* the body in an interinanimation of affliction and renewal, the fragmentation of singular bodies and the coercive reaggregation of community.

Escaping the in/determination of the opposition or sacrificial synthesis of rites of affliction and renewal requires working through the logocentrism of Lévi-Strauss, the occularcentric, spatio-temporal determinism of Parkin and their interrelation in a discursive field grounded in a notion of singularity that I want to move through in my preparation. In Taylor's, the spoken words, the speaking of the words, are not an arbitrary feature but are instead constitutive of that which is not but nothing other than (the improvisation of) ritual, writing, ritual as a form of writing. There, the words are never independent of gesture, but the gesture is never given priority over the words-as-sound. For gestures (and spatial direction) are given there as the sounded, re-sounded (which is to say transformed, bent, extended, improvised) and resounding (which is to say generative) word.

> We then can define writing broadly as *the communication of relatively specific ideas in a conventional manner by means of permanent, visible marks.*[48]

Here Elizabeth Hill Boone moves in the direction of a redefinition of writing in anthropology in general and in the study of Mesoamerican and Andean graphic systems in particular. That movement is critical of notions of writing as the "visible speech" that marks a techno-spiritual difference between cultures capable of graphic-verbal presentation and those before or outside of the historico-temporal frame of the advanced or enlightened. That direction would lead to a more inclusive definition of writing, one able to acknowledge the rich constative capacities of nonverbal graphic systems, one that explicitly acknowledges the insistently unbridgeable gap separating the spoken word from any visual representation. This direction, seen in conjunction with Parkin's attempt to think through the constative/performative opposition that grounds Lévi-Strauss's notion of the difference between myth and ritual, would also lead to an indelible connection between ritual, on the one hand, and writing, on the other hand, if writing is defined in the broader way that Boone lays out. Ritual and nonverbal graphesis would both be seen as constative, and both would be subject to prejudices that end in the denial of that constativity. There is another similarity between Boone's and Parkin's projects that we'll arrive at shortly (the primacy of the visual-spatial), but these are enough to allow us to follow, for a bit, one of the paths this connection implies.

What kind of writing is *Chinampas*? Taylor presents no graphic system—if *Chinampas* is writing, it is so in the absence of visuality. Under what conditions, then, could *Chinampas* be called "writing"? Perhaps within an understanding of writing more broadly conceived as nonverbal, as well as verbal, systems of graphic communication. Yet, since what we have there is nongraphic *verbal* communication, the legitimacy of its claim to writing is not self-evident. Nevertheless ideas of and about graphic systems are presented in *Chinampas*, sound distorting vision in the improvisation of another writing; and image, position, and direction are so encoded—the visual-spatial so embedded—in the poem that what we have is something more complex even than some newly included Outside of writing. Rather, *Chinampas* is out from the outside of writing as it is conventionally defined or redefined in what have become conventional redefinitions. Writing is, in *Chinampas*, a visual-spatial-tactile improvisation of system that activates the aural resources of the language. The poem is an improvisation of writing not to be appropriated by, not proper to, an older and somehow more inclusive graphesis: it is not a valorization but an improvisation of the nonverbal; not an abandonment but a (re)sounding of the visual-spatial.

A possible formulation based upon the inclusive redefinition of writing: it's not that Taylor creates visible speech; rather his is an aural writing given an understanding of writing that includes nonverbal graphic resources. This would almost presuppose that Taylor is interested in grounding the aural in an originary writing (the "older and somehow more inclusive graphesis" referred to above) that corresponds—as spatial, rhythmic organization—to ritual. Ritual here is implicitly conceived as Parkin explicitly describes it: a form of nonverbal graphic (visual/spatial) communication for which spoken words are merely supplemental. We could say, then, that Taylor's refers to an originary writing that is neither hieroglyphic nor pictographic but geometric, positional, directional. In that referent, if not in Taylor's reference, spoken words are not only nonoriginary, they are not even seen in terms of a reversal of traditional, conventional views of language in/and its relation to writing.

But this formulation doesn't go there. Rather, what is required is a further reconfiguration of Parkin, one that moves beyond the idea of constative ritual and beyond the idea of ritual as a form of graphic, nonverbal writing to the extent that in such writing priority is given to, originarity is assumed for, the visual-spatial constellation of gesture, position, movement. That reconfiguration is opened by Taylor's aural improvisation of, rather than (un)silent adherence to, an originary writing-as-ritual and his infusion of the diagrammatics/diagraphesis of ritual with sound. For spoken words, especially when infused with the buzz hummm of the metavoice, are not a neutral (as Parkin implies) but a *dangerous* supplement to ritual-as-writing.[49] Thus, on the one hand, "words don't go there" marks the inadequacy of verbal representation of sound while at the same time signaling the excessive, out-from-the-outside motion and force with which sound infuses the verbal. Words don't go there; words go *past* there. Bent. Turned. Blurrrred.

The picture is text, the image is writing, *sounded and not visible* though of a brilliant luminescence in the ensemble of the graphic, the (non)verbal, the aural. That ensemble is what the floating garden is: word lifted from stone or cloth; *quipu* (an article composed of colored and knotted strings used in Andean cultures to recall various categories of knowledge that are specified by an interpreter; an article whose aesthetic is related to the tactile and to the tactile's relation to rhythm)[50] or rhythm cloth; text/ile, tactile. There meaning is held not unlike a talking drum holds meaning in tone and rhythm; meaning held, for instance, in "eighty-eight tuned drums," independent of any simple, sentence-relational form, given only in phrasing and bent words. In that phrasing Taylor moves, crucially, past whatever in/determination, whatever singularity, the paradoxical interinanimation of ritual and idiom puts forward as if it were or could be The Event.

Perhaps something has occurred in the history of the concept of structure that could be called an "event," if this loaded word did not entail a meaning which it is precisely the function of structural—or structuralist—thought to reduce or suspect. Let us speak of an "event," nevertheless, and let us use quotation marks to serve as a precaution. What would this event be then? Its exterior form would be that of a *rupture* and a redoubling.

. . . up to the event which I wish to mark out and define, structure—or rather the structurality of structure—although it has always been at work, has always been neutralized or reduced, and this by a process of giving it a center or referring it to a point of presence, a fixed origin. *The function of this center was not only to orient, balance, and organize the structure—one cannot in fact conceive of an unorganized structure—but above all to make sure that the organizing principle of the structure would limit what we might call the play of the structure. By orienting and organizing the coherence of the system, the center of a structure permits the play of its elements inside the total form. And even today the notion of a structure lacking any center represents the unthinkable itself.*

Nevertheless, the center also closes off the play which it opens up and makes possible. *As center, it is the point at which the substitution of contents, elements, or terms is no longer possible.* At the center, the permutation or the transformation of elements (which may of course be structures enclosed within a structure) is forbidden. At least this permutation has always been *interdicted* (and I am using this word deliberately). *Thus it has always been thought that the center, which is by definition unique constituted that very thing within a structure which while governing the structure, escapes structurality. This is why classical thought concerning structure could say that the center is, paradoxically, within the structure and outside it. The center is at the center of the totality, and yet, since the center does not belong to the totality (is not part of the totality), the totality has its center elsewhere . . .*[51] [my emphasis]

The event of which Derrida speaks, the putting of the structurality of structure, the center itself, into play, is the moment "when language invaded the universal problematic, the moment when, in the absence of a center or origin, everything became discourse ... a system in which the central signified, the original or transcendental signified, is never absolutely present outside a system of differences." Derrida writes of an event, a rupture, which is also a circle, a circle of thinker-writers but also a circle "unique" in its description of "the form of the relation between the history of metaphysics and the destruction of the history of metaphysics." Here he places the event within a narrative. Part of what I would argue is that this placement of the event within narrative is The Event of the event, the rupture or caesura of the event that occurs within a paradoxical duration or contextualization or montagic-dialectical temporal mapping of the event. This self-rupture of singularity is precisely the geometric precondition of the circularity that Derrida diagnoses and to which he succumbs: the self-deconstructive singularity of the event is the axis on which the circle turns—the one that is not central, the center that is not one. Restructuring could be seen, then, as the process by which structure is placed into play, which is to say into narrative, into the circularity and tension of a narrative that is composed of and that turns on elements or events.

Now we might easily be speaking of the song form as that de/centered structure that Taylor radically reformulates, if not abandons, precisely by rethinking its status as the singular site of order in improvised music.[52] For the point here is that in his aesthetic Taylor deals in what has truly been the unthinkable of the event-determined circularity of the history/narrative of the West and its thinking: the structure or totality that is un(de)composed by a center or its absence, by the event or The Event and their absences. This is a possibility given in ensemble tone, in the improvisation through a certain tradition of temporization and tympanization, through that tradition's injunction to keep time in a simple way, on the beat (of the event), in that simplest (mis)conception—excusable because of the terminology (and we could all see why Plato would be misled by James Brown in the first place)—of the one. Am I saying that Taylor or The Godfather or the music in general is not trapped within the circle that is (the history of) metaphysics as the slide away from the ensemble it would propose? Am I saying that there is access to the outside of this circle or that, somehow, we (who? we.) are always already outside it. Yes. I'm talking about something free of the circle, free of the *event*ual tension/tensing of (this) narrative. Other things are also free.

What is immediately required is an improvisation of singularity, one that allows us to reconfigure what is given beneath/outside the distinction between the elements of the structure and its total form. Because what I'm after is an asystematic, anarchic organizing principle (I note the oxymoron), a notion of totality and (ensemble-)tonality at the conjunction of the pantonal and "that insistent previousness evading each and every natal occasion." But wait: the point here is not to make an analogy between the deconstruction of the center and the organization of the jazz ensemble: it's to say that that organization is of totality, of ensemble in general. Among other things, this music allows us to think of tonality and the structure of harmony as it moves in the oscillation between voice and voicing, not in the interest of any numerical determination (the valorization of the multiple or its shadow), not in the interest of any ethico-temporal determination (the valorization of the durative or of process), but for a kind of decentralization of the organization of the music; a restructuring or, if you will, a reconstruction. Taylor is working through a metaphysics of structure, working through an assumption that equates the essence or structurality of structure with a center. What I'm interested in in Taylor is precisely the refusal to attempt a return to the source: one that is not, on the one hand, forgetful of what is lost or of the fact of loss; one that is forgetive, on the other hand, in the Falstaffian sense of the word—nimble and full of fiery and delectable shapes, improvisatory and incantatory when what is structured in the mind is given over to the mouth, the birth, as (that which is, finally, way more even than) excellent wit.

In "Structure, Sign, and Play" Derrida goes on to quote Lévi-Strauss's *The Raw and the Cooked:*

> But unlike philosophical reflection, which aims to go back to its own source, the reflections we are dealing with here concern rays whose only source is hypothetical.... And in seeking to imitate the spontaneous movement of mythological thought, this essay, which is also both too brief and too long, has had to conform to the requirements of that thought and to respect its rhythm.[53]

Lévi-Strauss and his differentiated echo in/as Derrida go on to think this complex copresence of the question of center and origin in terms of myth and music:

> Thus the myth and the musical work are like the conductors of an orchestra, whose audience becomes the silent performers. If it is now asked where the real center of the work is to be found, the answer is that this is impossible to determine. Music and mythology bring man face to face with potential objects of which only the shadows are actualized.[54]

Here the musical becomes a sign for the absence of center by way of an all-too-facile assumption of some correspondence between myth and music. What happens when we begin to think music in its relation to ritual? Myth and text (myth as the written text of the music, betraying a musical rendition of a certain logocentric assumption in Lévi-Strauss) operate in Lévi-Strauss as the agents of a structural fixity whose submission to the law of supplementarity Derrida would always enforce. In this sense, for Derrida, there is a correspondence between myth, text, and totality that is troubled by a form of musical organization like Taylor's. Now we are dealing in precisely that absence of the center that Lévi-Strauss and Derrida both read and comment upon. Both deal, Derrida more knowingly or self-consciously, with the tension in their work between structure—that which is unthinkable without a center— and the absence of center. This tension is productive; it constitutes or produces something, namely, philosophy. But I'm interested precisely in the unthinkable of philosophy in Taylor's work. For the unthinkable, as we can easily show, is not structure in the absence of the center (for we see all the time that this absence is constitutive of structure; this is what Derrida shows); rather, the unthinkable is structure or ensemble thought independently of any tension between itself and some absent origin. The unthinkable is a tone. That tone is to be thought neither as or in its absence (atonality) nor as/in its multiplicity or plenitude (pan-tonality): it is rather an ensemble tone, the tone that is not structured by or around the presence/absence of singularity or totality, the tone that is not iterative but generative. (Note that Lévi-Strauss insists on a certain iconicity, insists that discourse on myth must itself become mythic, must have the form of which it speaks. Certainly Derrida fol-lows this formulation to the extent that the old-new language may only be spoken of from within, that it constitutes its own true metalanguage, thereby driving Alfred Tarski and his definition of truth as the relation between object- and meta-language crazy such that the old-new lan-guage is not only its own metalanguage but its own truth.)

Taylor's is a voice in the interruption of race and nation, just as it is a voice in the interruption of the sentence and, indeed, in the interruption of the word itself. He works the anarchic irruption and interruption of grammar, enacting a phrasal improvisation through the distinction between poetry and music in the poetry of music, the programmatic manifesto that accompanies the music, that becomes music and turns music into poetry. These things occur

between regions of partial

shadow and complete illumination

in the cut.

Taylor's also bears the trace of (the peculiar) institution and its organi-zation—its deconstruction and reconstruction. This in connection to the continuous or anniversarial, the institutional-durative: marriage-birth-death-seasonal change; the temporal difference within ritual that corresponds to ritual's temporal difference from, on the one hand, myth and, on the other hand, the mundane since rituals "involve a liminal phase, a betwixt and between element and so presuppose an initial phase of separation and one of reaggregation."[55] But let's enact and reenact the *separation* of separation and reaggregation: rather, let's linger, float in the limbo of that cut, in order to mark nothing akin to an initial phase or prior singularity, but, instead, to mark "the insistent previousness evading each and every natal occasion." The trauma of separation is marked here, but not the separation from a determinate origin: rather the separation from the improvisation through origin: the separation from ensemble. How could we have heard the sound of justice called in/by the long duration of the trauma if it hadn't been improvised?

Parmenides is, as far as we know, the first among many to "recognize" an essential connection between thinking and being: his poem is the originary text of that harmony, the originary written moment at which the shadow of what must be conceived of as a more fundamental formulation, a more elemental and singular form, is revealed. One wonders what the relation is between the writing of the poem—within which the trace of a sound remains to be discerned or at least reconstructed from its shards—and that harmony. One wonders whether the harmony upon which Western metaphysics is founded is not itself founded on—or most clearly manifest at—the intersection of music and poetry, which itself seems to signal a prior and barely available unity of the two in *mousike*: the singularization of the muses' art, the distillation of the ensemble of the aesthetic.

Only the trace of *mousike* is available to us and only by way of a tracing of the history of its dissolution. Under the heading "Music and Poetry," *The New Princeton Encyclopedia of Poetry and Poetics* makes a brief survey of that history, moving from "the Egyptian 'hymn of the seven vowels,' [which] appears to have exploited the overtone pitches present in the vowels of any language" to the first disjunctions (through which Taylor improvises) between systems of linguistic pitch, on the one hand, and systems of quantitative meter, on the other; from the technical origins of alphabetic writing-as-musical notation to the hegemonic excess of the visual-written and the differentiation of the arts it helps to solid-ify; from elemental *mousike* to its division/reaggregation as poetry and music to its fourfold fragmentation into poetic and musical performance and musical and rhetorical theory within which can be located that opposition between *praxis* and *theoria* that is never not connected to the harmony of thinking and being that constitutes philosophy's origin and end.[56] What becomes clear is a historical movement from the prior-ity of sonic gesture to the hegemony of visual (which is to say theoret-ical) formulation. The written mark—the convergence of meaning and visuality—is the site of both excess and lack; the word-supplement—only theorizable in the occlusion of its sound—endlessly overshoots its destination; words don't go there. Perhaps it is now possible to give a more satisfactory understanding of this claim, one that is concerned not only with where words do go, but with the nature and position of the "there." First, though, it is necessary to think the effect of that dual spa-tialization/visualization of the word—its placement within an economy determined by movement, instrumentalization, position and theoriza-tion—which troubles any distinction between ritual and myth.

"*Chinampa*—an Aztec word meaning floating garden."[57] This image moves toward what is made even closer by the conjunction of the image (of the title or name) and the sound (of the saying of what it marks or holds). It signals a suspension that is free or that frees by virtue of the contagion of its movement: when one sees a floating garden or is con-fronted with the sound that stems from the word-image, one lingers above or below surface and in what is open there. The surface or topog-raphy upon which a spatio-temporal mapping depends is displaced by a generative motion. One imagines the possibilities inherent in that float-ing, the chance of a dropping off or an extension of certain of those sounds that require a vibrating surface: the n, m, p are put in motion, deepening and rearranging the sound of the word. This loosening is part of Taylor's method: of the word from its meaning, of the sounds from the word in the interest of a generative reconstruction, as if all of a sudden one decided to refuse the abandonment of the full resources of language, as if one decided no longer to follow the determining, structuring, reductive force of law.

There is a piece of musicpoetry by Taylor entitled "Garden" whose words have been collected in *Moment's Notice*, a set of texts that mark the hope or call of a destination for words and for writing.[58] Reading "Garden" raises questions concerning its difference from *Chinampas*, one of which I'd like to address in passing. It is, perhaps unavoidably, a question of spacing or position, a question always shadowed by immaterial visualization: what is the *floating* garden? Perhaps this: the garden that floats is the one that lingers in another, improvisational sense of the aesthetic ensemble that is no simple return to an imagined and originary singularity. Instead the floating garden marks the unprecedented present within which the aesthetic is "ongoingly" reconfigured and reconfiguring, bent and bending; within which the illusion of any immediacy of sound is re/written and the overdetermined and deferred fixity of writing is un/written by the material and transformative present of sound.

It's like when Coltrane, having been shown a transcription of his solo on "Chasin' the Trane," was unable to sight-read what he'd improvised. The beautiful distance between sound and the writing of sound requires a kind of faith that could only be measured, for instance, in Taylor's inability to read

Chinampas #5′04″

ANGLE of incidence
    being matter ignited

one sixtieth of luminous intensity

                                 behind wind

     beginning spiral of two presences

   shelter

    ~~light *drum*~~
angle of incidénce   observant of sighns

be's core based fiber conducting impulses flattened spirals of spirit
            prompting letter per square centimeter of   *three*
dimensions
swept cylinder and cone
        cutting shape   of drying bodiesNow pulverized
                           having fed
on cactí

arranged service of *con*stant spiral elements of floating *cocineal* and
                          kaaay and kaay and kaay
and   agité an-agité and kaay
                         and kaay and
    yyeeagiye yoa,
     ya yoa
deposits of hieroglyphic   regions
womb of continuing   *light*
preexisting blood per square centimeter of aBlaack bhody
a curve having rotation in three dimensions
    cutting spiral elements at a constant angle
behind wind
the inexpressssible inclusion
of one within another
    a lustrous red, reddish brown or black natural *fill* compact or
    attacked
      POINT fixed on circumference
curve about red
does in fact alter regions of contact as a *rooase*
      on the outside circumference   flushed toward slant
intersecting new reference point
moves clockwise
representing a frequency's
    distribution
each bend of ordinan equals the sum in singular
                    youas youas youas

proceeding enclosure engulfing unending spiral
                                   undulation

there floating amidst aliana and overhead
                          romela romelaya romela romelaya a ceeia

invisible expressions of warmed *snake*wood soothed by exudation
of sloed balsam
scent
is arielroot elixir   is knowing circle crossed at oiled extremity
in center of wing burring
creates fire in air
serpent is preexisting light   light   yeah
the meter maintained is ôpen yet a larger *whorl*
describing orbit of earth
eaters incisors   as omniscient
pochee aida aida huelto   aida aida huedo
uniting of three astral plains/planes corresponding to a   serpent
synthesis

altering the sliii'de
               disengage'd ecliptic traveling
                              due north

                       skip through at least two successive meridians
diagonal shear
uniting as macrocosm five heads degrees of   tangiBle *ahhb jects*
graded ascension of floor levels
     suspended voice
                                        vibrations
held within concretized mur'eau de perfume *breath*
                       again *floating*
'tween lighted mooon///soar
and silent cross of bird sensing cold   at base
invisible to source of satyrial/siderial turn   Between regions of
partial

shadow and complete illumination.

omnipotence
omnipotence the florescence of the perpendicular
omnipotence
the floresce of the perpendicular pentamorphic
the florescence of the perpendicular pentamorphic
perpendicular pentamorphic

(kiss, silences, rhythm)
. . .

Praying with Eric

The title comes from a Mingus composition and requires some meditation on the brilliant proliferation of Eric Dolphy's sacred, unknown
tongues. This is a preface on improvisation and it will move toward
Dolphy and his destinations by way of an ambivalent transport from
Ralph Ellison to Nathaniel Mackey, from "the music of invisibility" to
"optic utterance."

Improvisation is located at a seemingly unbridgeable chasm
between feeling and reflection, disarmament and preparation, speech
and writing. Improvisation—as the word's linguistic roots indicate—is
usually understood as speech *without foresight*. But improvisation, in
whatever possible excess of representation that inheres in whatever
probable deviance of form, always also operates as a kind of foreshadowing, if not prophetic, description. So that the theoretical resources
embedded in the cultural practice of improvisation reverse, even as
they bear out, the definition that etymology implies and the theoretical
assumptions it grounds. That which is without foresight is nothing
other than foresight. And if improvisation is to be thought other than
simply as action or speech without provision, you need to look ahead
with a kind of torque that shapes what's being looked at. You need to
do so without constraints of association, by way of a twisted epoché, or
redoubled turn, in the prescription and extemporaneous formation and
reformation of rules, rather than the following of them. Extemporaneity

is often associated with not looking ahead, the absence of forethought, a lack of planning, preparation, and also an absence of prescriptive vision: but improvisation in the music allows another transcription of previousness. Improvisation is already an improvisation of improvisation: through the oppositions implicit in the etymology, through the proscriptive and differential temporality of those oppositions; on the one hand, anarchic and ungrounded, opening a critique of traditions and Tradition, and on the other hand, no simple and naive, unplanned and nonhistorically driven, inscription; on the one hand, the very essence of the visionary, the spirit of the new, an organizational planning of and in free association that transforms the material, and on the other hand, manifest in and as the material. Thus improvisation is never manifest as a kind of pure presence—it is not the multiplicity of present moments just as it is not governed by an ecstatic temporal frame wherein the present is subsumed by past and future. Improvisation must be understood, then, as a matter of sight and as a matter of time, the time of a look ahead whether that looking is the shape of a progressivist line or rounded, turned. The time, shape, and space of improvisation is constructed by and figured as a set of determinations *in and as light*, by and through the illuminative event. And there is no event, just as there is no action, without music.

Now I have one radio-phonograph; I plan to have five. There is a certain acoustical deadness in my hole, and when I have music I want to *feel* its vibration, not only with my ear but with my whole body. I'd like to hear five recordings of Louis Armstrong playing and singing "What Did I Do to Be so Black and Blue"—all at the same time. Sometimes now I listen to Louis while I have my favorite dessert of vanilla ice cream and sloe gin. I pour the red liquid over the white mound, watching it glisten and the vapor rising as Louis bends that military instrument into a beam of lyrical sound. Perhaps I like Louis Armstrong because he's made poetry out of being invisible. I think it must be because he's unaware that he *is* invisible. And my own grasp of invisibility aids me to understand his music. Once when I asked for a cigarette, some jokers gave me a reefer, which I lighted when I got home and sat listening to my phonograph. It was a strange evening. Invisibility, let me explain, gives one a slightly different sense of time, you're never quite on the beat. Sometimes you're ahead, sometimes behind. Instead of the swift and imperceptible flowing of time, you are aware of its nodes, those points where time stands still or from which it leaps ahead. And you slip into the breaks and look around. That's what you hear vaguely in Louis' music.[59]

So under the spell of the reefer I discovered a new analytical way of listening to music. The unheard sounds came through, and each melodic line existed of itself, stood out clearly from all the rest, said its piece, and waited patiently for the other voices to speak. That night I found myself hearing not only in time, but in space as well. I not only entered the music but descended, like Dante, into its depths. And *beneath the swiftness of the hot tempo there was a slower tempo and a cave and I entered it and looked around and heard an old woman singing a spiritual as full of Weltschmerz as flamenco, and beneath that lay a still lower level on which I saw a beautiful girl the color of ivory pleading in a voice like my mother's as she stood before a group of slave owners who bid for her naked body, and below that I found a lower level and a more rapid tempo and I heard someone shout.*[60]

"Brothers and Sisters, my text this morning is the 'Blackness of Blackness.'"

And a congregation of voices answered: "That blackness is most black, brother, most black . . . "

. . . "Black will make you . . . "

"Black . . . "

". . . or black will un-make you."

"Ain't it the truth, lawd?"

And at that point a voice of trombone timbre screamed at me, "Git out of here, you fool! Is you ready to commit treason?"

And I tore myself away, hearing the old singer of spirituals moaning, "Go curse your God, boy, and die."

I stopped and questioned her, asked her what was wrong.

"*I dearly loved my master, son,*" *she said.*

"*You should have hated him,*" *I said.*

"*He gave me several sons,*" *she said,* "*and because I loved my sons I learned to love their father though I hated him too.*"

"*I too have become acquainted with ambivalence,*" *I said.* "*That's why I'm here.*"

"*What's that?*"

"*Nothing, a word that doesn't explain it. Why do you moan?*"

"*I moan this way 'cause he's dead,*" *she said.*

"*Then tell me, who is that laughing upstairs?*"

"*Them's my sons. They glad.*"

"*Yes, I can understand that too,*" *I said.*

"*I laughs too, but I moans too. He promised to set us free but he never could bring hisself to do it. Still I loved him . . .*"

"*Loved him? You mean . . . ?*"

"*Oh yes, but I loved something else even more.*"

"*What more?*"

"*Freedom.*"

"*Freedom,*" *I said.* "*maybe freedom lies in hating.*"

"*Naw, son, it's in loving. I loved him and gave him the poison and he withered away like a frost-bit apple. Them boys woulda tore him to pieces with they homemade knives.*"

"*A mistake was made somewhere,*" *I said,* "*I'm confused.*" *And I wished to say other things, but the laughter upstairs became too loud and moan-like for me and I tried to break out of it, but I couldn't. Just as I was leaving I felt an urgent desire to ask her what freedom was and went back. She sat with her head in her hands, moaning softly; her leather-brown face was filled with sadness.*

"*Old woman, what is this freedom you love so well?*" *I asked around a corner of my mind.*

She looked surprised, then thoughtful, then baffled. "*I done forgot, son. It's all mixed up. First I think it's one thing, then I think it's another. It gits my head to spinning. I guess now it ain't nothing but knowing how to say what I got up in my head. But it's a hard job, son. Too much is done happen to me in too short a time. Hit's like I have a fever. Ever' time I starts to walk my head gits to swirling and I falls down. Or if it ain't that, it's the boys; they gits to laughing and wants to kill up the white folks. They's bitter, that's what they is . . ."*

"But what about freedom?"

"Leave me 'lone. Boy; my head aches!"

I left her, feeling dizzy myself. I didn't get far.[61]

Then somehow I came out of it, ascending hastily from this under-world of sound to hear Louis Armstrong innocently asking,

What did I do
To be so black
And blue?

At first I was afraid; this familiar music had demanded action, the kind of which I was incapable, and yet had I lingered there beneath the surface I might have attempted to act. Nevertheless, I know now that few really listen to this music.[62]

Ellison knows that you can't really listen to this music. He knows, before Mackey as it were, that really listening, when it goes bone-deep into the sunken ark of bones, is something other than itself. It doesn't alternate with but *is* seeing; it's the sense that it excludes; it's the ensemble of the senses. Few really read this novel. This is alarming even though you can't really read this novel. That's why it calls for and tries to open a new analytic way of listening and reading, an improvisation attuned to the ensemble of work's organization and production, the ensemble of the politico-economic structure in which it is produced and the ensemble of the senses from which it springs and which it stimulates. This would be something like a channeling—in and through history—of something more fundamental than the mark of locality: localized movement, extremely determined dream of a specific genius, the novel is not about the delineation of the unitary and singular trait, even if that trait is absolute singularity itself. This is to say—in the invocation of cut, channel—that the novel is about the structures and æffects of race.

The mark of invisibility is a visible, racial mark; invisibility has visibility at its heart. To be invisible is to be seen, instantly and fascinatingly recognized as the unrecognizable, as the abject, as the absence of individual self-consciousness, as a transparent vessel of meanings wholly independent of any influence of the vessel itself. Ellison phonographs this problematic paradox, bringing the noise to in/visibility. The question is whether aurality ever actually exerts an improvisational force in, against, and through the ocularcentric structuration of recognition. *Invisible Man* narrates and describes a certain habitation of this paradox; its prologue records the theoretical particulars implied in such an attempt. The prologue would set the specifically musical conditions for a possible redetermination of the ocular-ethical metaphysics of race and the materiality of the structure and æffects of that metaphysics. But there is a question concerning the noise's resistance to such fatal envisioning. How to activate the noise's transcendence of the ocular frame? Such questioning is not in the interest of replacing the ocular with the aural, not in the interest of putting another metaphysics forward. Rather, one is interested in what the noise carries—not that it's something figured as other than the ocular, just that it's critically easier to discern while remaining, paradoxically or not, so profoundly avoided. What there is in the music is irreducible to music; meanwhile, racialization is given in a visualization of music that forestalls the enactment of what the music holds.

If the prologue of *Invisible Man* holds all that is played out in and much of what happens beyond the novel, then the epilogue is a frightened attempt to retreat into the etiolated metaphysics of America—where the ends of philosophy, history, and man converge; where the unworkable telos of one and many, the radical segregation of prophecy and description, is carried out. The novel's body presents episode after iconic episode, each given as a particular frame of black identity and writing. The prologue holds not only the content but the form of such revelation. It opens the very possibility of the framing of the novel according to the opposition of continuity and succession and always already holds the deconstruction of this very structure—which is constitutive of our understanding of narrative—as a possibility. The prologue imagines a depth that holds out both the frightening chance of a descent into ethnocentric and separatist identity (the sons of the moaner, violent laughter and scream) and the hope of a radical improvisation by way of the music and what it holds for action. The novel is driven by this opposition—by the inability to linger and the rationalization of that inability. That rationalization demands that the music's transgression of the very laws of being and time to which Ellison finally submits must also be domesticated. This domestication is a kind of nationalist reconfiguration wherein the music is presented as the trope of a certain understanding of totality as America, of representation as America, of democracy as America, of the future—which is to say the end—as America.

One way to get through this Ellisonian invocation of what Jacques Derrida calls the "onto-theology of national humanism"[63] is something like what Eve Kosofsky Sedgwick calls a "queer performative."[64] We'll see how Amiri Baraka, for instance, in both approach and avoidance, enacts such a cut interpellation. But maybe all such resignifications or redeployments bear this active, if muted, infelicity, this unhappiness of nomination or incomplete christening. And think the relation of convention to repetition, think the way convention's dependence upon repetition is the condition of its in/security. So that if we imagine a space between repetitions then we imagine something impossible to locate. The moment between moments presents massive ontological problems, like the attempt to establish the reality of pure mathematical objects (for instance, a set, an ensemble). Perhaps political upheaval is in the nonlocatability of discontinuity. Art tries to fictionalize and/or redeploy such location among other things—but now we speak of the artificiality or artifactuality of every rupture in the same way that we would speak of the forgiveness (a cool slip of the finger, speeahh: I meant to write "fictiveness") of some absolute durative stability. What one begins to consider, as a function of the nonlocalizable nature or status of discontinuity, is a special universalization of discontinuity, where discontinuity could be figured as ubiquitous minority, omnipresent queerness.

The tragic and happy (in/felicitous) universality of absolute (temporal-ontological-performative) singularity is what Derrida might say. Anyway, this is just meant to trouble, by disseminating, the break or cut.[65]

What is needed is an improvisation of the transition from descent to cut, an audition of the ancient prefiguring trace of the cut in the depths, an activation of lingering by and in the cut (and of the possibility of action in lingering and the promise of freedom in action). Ellison's figuration of "the blackness of blackness" opens certain things up: what would be broached in that section is the impossibly originary black moment, the maternal origin of this universal doubleness. The claim to that origin is already late; its coherence is a function of some irreferable thing that came before it and whatever comfort it gives bears the very structure of attenuation. Its reference to the knowledge of and action for freedom occurs as an ironic affirmation of freedom's etiolation and in the denial of freedom's connection to the individual voice. The doubleness (blackness) of blackness is given as the aftermath of a determined, durative, fleshly, sexual encounter: the symbolic is cast in reference to the materiality of the miscegenative natal occasion.[66] The moaner, the singer of gospel music, puts this forth: that we love the devil because he is us. He gives us (and, implicitly, we give him) identity: this has the fundamental belatedness, ambivalence, and persistence of the dialectic.

In the blackness of blackness, the doubleness of blackness, the fucked-up whiteness of the essence of blackness, there is an instantiation of a kind of dialog between knowledge of in/visibility and the absence of that knowledge, between improvement and the vernacular. The vernacular, in the figure of Armstrong, is the one who lacks the knowledge of his own in/visibility. This is a geographico-class dynamic—played out, for instance, already on the pages of *The Souls of Black Folk* as fore-shadowing description of *The New Negro*—wherein modernity and migration are the elements of an uplifting convergence. But there is a sexual dynamic as well that remains to be played out. Why is the moaner's vernacular voice—moaning trombone (or trumpet) always on the verge of an unwording, inseparable from the lumpen, violent, hypermasculine laughter that it spawns—not edited from within or without but supplemented such that the knowingly invisible interlocutor, the one who assumes the need for or prior presence of a supplement, is quickly revealed to be at a loss when seen against the anoriginal knowledge of freedom this woman has?[67] Finally, the opposition between the vernacular and the modern, the black and the white, is to be thought precisely in that they are both, if they are real, the product of a miscegenative encounter that exists as a function of the difference between the actors and the internal difference of the encounter. Indeed, it would be more precise to say that we are dealing, again, with structure and æffect, doubled and redoubled. But the deep-down love, the bone-deep love, convergence of death and love, memory and narrative (that's what recognition is), that accompanies the miscegenative origin of black/American identity is exceeded by another love: that of/for freedom. And freedom, here, is not the etiolation that comes as the emergence of individual voice; it is, rather, the ensemblic improvisation that evades the encounter of the others as natal occasion and its pharmacoepic oscillation. Something irreferable—before the ongoing exchange of poisonous gift and available only by way of the disconnection such exchange enforces and, as connection, undermines—lies in wait in cut, augmented, instrumentalized speech like a depth charge.

Redoubled blackness is determined in the encountering time of a caesura, in a dialectic of recognition and abjection, enlightenment and unconcealment; but its condition of possibility lies before this. Accessing this before is, at least in part, accomplished in the improvisation through in/visibility, the interinanimation of light and music, vision and sound. This interinanimation must exceed any mere juxtaposition: it requires some sustained thinking in the music that, again, is excessive of any analytic. It requires some methodological investigation of the problematics of "really listening," of, for instance, the problematic sensual-cognitive reduction whose trace is borne by that phrase.

Invisible Man represents the dialectic of improvement, the transition from the vernacular to the modern, but it also offers a quite devastating critique of that progression while fatalistically clinging to the hope of a purification of the principles and categories that would ground it. Here a kind of revolutionary enlightenment contains revolutionary unconcealment as a particularly special moment or potent and problematic possibility: the imaginary violent rebirth, the screaming laughter of the sons of the moaner/mourner, where the possibility that freedom lies in hating remains to be sung as, say, "BLACK DADA NIHILISMUS."[68] We could say, then, that the novel between its ends, between the prologue and the epilogue, between the sexual cut and the emergence, submergence, and reemergence of the individual subject in and from out of the depths, is about the supposed transition from vernacular to modern, from in/visibility (as unreflective expression, an unarticulated juxtaposition of light and sound) to knowledge of in/visibility (as the conjugation of light and sound as if they were ever two in the first place), from a jook joint in some outlying parish to Minton's Playhouse, from whatever Armstrong echoes to whoever replicates Charlie Christian. Still, at the end, *Invisible Man* awaits what only the cut can give and what is prefigured in its prologue. As Houston Baker might say, whatever manifests itself as modernity was embedded in the vernacular all along. Meanwhile, the sexual cut keeps the question of the ontological constitution of the vernacular open despite all attempts at closure.

The rhythm of in/visibility is cut time: phantasmatic interruptions and fascinations. Stories are propelled by this formation of inhabitable temporal breaks; they are driven by the time they inhabit, violently reproducing, iconizing, improvising themselves. The break that drives and is *Invisible Man* constitutes the continuity and the incommensurability of the prologue and the epilogue, which is to say the continuity between and the incommensurability of the intimation of the improvisational and affirmative agency of ensemble and its etiolated calculation as the synthesis of one and many, individuality and collectivity, difference and universality. The visionary force of the prologue succumbs, in the break, to a pure description: from an awareness (though admittedly, conventionally privatized) of the imperatives of improvisation—"this familiar music had demanded action, the kind of which I was incapable, and yet had I lingered there beneath the surface I might have attempted to act"—through an interpretive but faithful rendition of "the invisible music of my isolation" (always already overdetermined by the individualism of that originary understanding of improvisation's ethical imperative) to the nonimprovisational (because formed within the opposition of individual and collective, race and humanity) re/capitulation of that imperative: "Our fate is to become one, and yet many—This is not prophecy, but description."[69] A certain understanding of totality is given as a possibility in the improvisatory break, even in that break's regrammatical irruption into Ellison's erstwhile sentence. The dash produces what Mackey's N. remembers as "the feeling I've gotten from the characteristic, almost clucking beat one hears in reggae, where the syncopation comes down like a blade."[70] The image given in the sound the dash produces is "one of a rickety bridge (sometimes a rickety boat) arching finer than a hair to touch down on the sands at, say, Abidjan."[71] See, when we check the sexual cut—"an insistent *previousness* evading each and every natal occasion"[72]—it speaks of a beginning whose origin is never fully recoverable, never operative as the end of any imagined return, and moves in the almost impossible demand of an embrace of the bridge's double figuration as both connection and disconnection. There is no inactive suspension between any rendering of the reading subject undecidable and any simple revalorization of some old and singular version of that subject. Rather, the bridge becomes, precisely in its doubleness, something other than itself that is yet to be determined. It will not compensate for a re-en-gendering rupture that the fineness of its arch renders unavoidable; the distance to Abidjan is asymptotic but unbridgeable and is no more so than that to any (thankfully) unapproachable America. The bridge is something other. In/visible music, "seen-said belief," will lead us, eventually, to the question of the bridge.

Cecil Taylor offers the following formulation concerning improvisation:

> The player advances to the area, an unknown totality, made whole thru self-analysis (improvisation), the conscious manipulation of known material . . .[73]

What is self-analysis? What is the direction toward unknown totality? Talking cure, the verbal interruption of the innerview, "The new black music is this: find the self then kill it."[74] This is the strenuous play of the new thing, this incalculable set of black singularities. It will never be possible to think this set outside of the theme of sexual difference, a theme now inseparable from psychoanalysis. Let's extend the record of some out improvisations; this is the record of an out confrontation, a Derridean mode of transport or transfer between Ellison and Mackey, an engaged and demure, sounded and silent, carrying on.

I should try to answer or perhaps to carry on.

But I will tell you that I indeed feel disarmed. This evening I have come as disarmed as *possible*. And disarrayed. I did not want to prepare for this session, I did not want to prepare myself. As deliberately as possible, I have chosen—which I think has never happened to me before—to expose myself to the course of a debate, and must also be said of a show, without any defensive or offensive anticipation (which always somewhat amounts to the same). In any event with as little anticipation as *possible*. I thought that if something was to occur tonight, by hypothesis the event would be on this condition, to wit, that I come without preparation, neither on display or on parade, as without ammunition as *possible*, and if it is possible.

Therefore I have come, if, at least, I have come, saying to myself: something will happen tonight only on condition of your disarmament.

But you might suspect me of exaggerating with this agonistic language: he says that he is disarmed in order to disarm, a well-known device. Certainly. Therefore, I immediately add: I have not come, I did not want to, I still do not want to, I have not come naked.

I have not come naked, not come without anything.

I have come accompanied by a small—how to put it, a small phrase, if it is one, only one, very small.[75]

If something is to happen you have to come unprepared, unarmed; but you don't come with nothing. You've got to bring something that adorns you even if it doesn't arm you. Just a very small phrase, the noise of a small phrase if it is one, just the spirit of some phrasing, the soft racket of a small accompaniment. You've got to be adorned with the smallest augmentation. Derrida's strange amalgam of foresight and disarmament—occasioned by a foray into that foundation or fortress of psychoanalysis called "confrontation"—makes necessary and real what had otherwise been sheer fantasy: "So there was a movement of nostalgic, mournful lyricism to reserve. Perhaps encode, in short to render both *accessible and inaccessible.* And deep down this is still my most naïve desire."[76] For Derrida the naïve and the idiomatic converge at that which is nothing other than improvisation, than an otherwise always interdicted being-prepared-to-improvise, by way of an extended, indirect, circular migration.

> JACQUES DERRIDA: . . . I feel as if I've been involved, for twenty years, in a long detour, in order to get back to this something, this idiomatic writing whose purity I know to be inaccessible, but which I continue, nonetheless, to dream about.
>
> LE NOUVEL OBSERVATEUR: What do you mean by "idiomatic"?
>
> J.D.: A property you cannot appropriate; it somehow marks you without belonging to you. It appears only to others, never to you—except in flashes of madness which draw together life and death, which render you at once alive and dead. It's fatal to dream of inventing a language or a song which would be yours—not the attributes of an "ego," but rather, the accentuated flourish, that is the musical flourish of your own most unreadable history. I'm not speaking about style, but of an intersection of singularities, of manners of living, voices, writing, of what you carry with you, what you can never leave behind. What I write resembles, by my account, a dotted outline of a book to be written, in what I call—at least for me—the "old new language," the most archaic and the newest, unheard of, and thereby at present unreadable. You know that the oldest

synagogue in Prague is called the Old-New? Such a book would be quite another thing; nonetheless, it would bear some resemblance to this train of thought. In any case, it is an interminable remembering, still seeking its own form: it would be not only my story, but also that of the culture, of language, of families, and above all, of Algeria. . . .[77]

The idiomatic is an inalienable property yet to have been accomplished, a quality both always already present and achieved only by way of an impossible return. And how do we reconcile the necessities of both return and detour? No. More precisely, how do we deal with their inter-inanimation? In this case return is accomplished by way of a rerouting structured by properly philosophical refusals to improvise, proper valorizations of writing over speech, given, in this instance, in relation to Freud's incalculable achievement, an achievement that is, at least, aligned with the theme of sexual difference, that is, at least, aligned with the encountering form and time of the improvisational interview.

> We must study the texts. Is the theme of sexual difference the achievement of Freudian thought? I do not know. I do not even know if Freudian thought—or any thought there is—achieves or completes itself somewhere. And should we think sexual difference in terms of *différance* in general or the inverse? I do not know. I suspect this question is badly formulated. I cannot go on by improvising. . . .[78]

Derrida's words are of (the) ensemble though he cannot, in the wake of an ill-formed question, improvise. The question, that it might be deconstructed, must be well formed. But the music of which he dreams, the writing to which he is drawn, bear the trace and, even, the hope of improvisation.[79] They bear ensemble's sound, its extension and reformulation, in supplemented line and clustered sentence. But Derrida would move slowly and deliberately from the well-formed question even as he hears the call of the sound of Algeria; indeed he hears the distinction in the sounds, sees the trajectory after the question as a detour, hopes, finally, for something that is, somehow, both more and less than a synthesis, but mutes the improvisational quality of his philosophical tradition. So we must study the texts in order to break the pursuit of encountering speech that psychoanalysis ambivalently gives as a kind of impossible dream. The road twists so because inalienable speech, even inalienable accent, is given back only by way of their return. What one receives as a result of indirect, interminable returning to what one already had is a language of feeling that is broached in an emotionally charged, personal, and politico-historical insistence:

> I insist on improvising. For the last two months, I have not stopped thinking in a quasi-obsessional fashion about this, but I preferred not to prepare what I am going to say. I think it is necessary this evening that everyone tell us, speaking personally and after a first analysis, what he or she thinks of these things. On the other hand, I wanted to tell you what my own *feeling* is.[80]

It's as if at the end of philosophy, brushed all up against a range of other phantasmatic ends—of man, of history—one returns to the dark matter or continent of philosophy's unconscious to shed some light. Psychoanalysis is not this unconscious though it might be said to operate in that process through which one is given back (to) what one already has, that to which one is always and never returning. This unconscious, or, more precisely, this thing of darkness that philosophy has seemed incapable of acknowledging as its own, is improvisation. By briefly and inadequately tracing the trajectory of this disappearing bridge or dematerialized romance in Derrida's phonography (the "discography," if you will, of his recorded speech), one sees how even in the most radical—which might, in this case, be taken to mean the blackest—of philosophers improvisation remains a problem, the problem of feeling. This is the question concerning philosophy's color line. How does it feel to be the problem of feeling? Derrida's brilliance lies precisely in his sounding of that question.[81]

On the other hand, in certain circles, broken romance, the dangers of unbroken romance always about to be broken and re-en-gendering, and broken speech have always been understood—though this understanding has never been peaceful—as the constituting intoxication of the most radical political and aesthetic reason. Here are the multiple covers(-without-origin) of another phonographed encounter:

> Mingus' solo is subtle and yet strongly assertive. Dolphy's bass clarinet continues the free-speaking momentum of the performances until he and Mingus engage in a conversation that should not be too difficult to follow in its literal argument. It begins with Mingus swearing at Dolphy on the bass as a similar musical conversation actually did begin on the stand of the Showplace several months before. The conversations gathered in intensity when Dolphy said he was going to leave the band and continued in this piece night after night. On the record Mingus again criticizes Dolphy for leaving; but Dolphy explains why he has to, urgently asks Mingus to understand, and at last Mingus does. The final return to the melody is, therefore, resigned—and leads to the quick goodbye.[82]

The importance of communicativeness and the ability to hear is underscored by another type of language metaphor used by musicians: "to say" or "to talk" often substitutes for "to play." In explaining what Tony Williams plays for a ride cymbal beat, Michael Carvin stated:

> That wasn't the limb keeping time ... Tony would say [see musical example 9 in Carvin's chapter 2], but his foot was talking about [straight quarters].

Aesthetic evaluations frequently include this usage. To suggest that a soloist "isn't saying anything" is an insult; conversely, to say that he or she "makes that horn talk" is very high praise. The perception of musical ideas as a communicative medium in and of themselves can be most effectively understood against the background of aural recognition of elements of musical tradition. . . . A secondary meaning of the talking horn image relates to the ability of the horn players to mimic a vocal quality through articulation, attack, and timbre. A very literal imitation of arguing voices can be heard on Charles Mingus's "What Love" (1960). Eric Dolphy on bass clarinet and Mingus on bass sound as though they are having a very intense verbal argument. The musical image of the talking horn personifies the horn, once again refusing to separate the sound from the person who makes it.[83]

I don't want to fall in love with anybody in the business because—because, well, a situation like this. Fall in love with George Tucker and Joe Farrell and they're gone. See, so you can't fall in love with them, but you can enjoy playing with them and reaching [musical] excitement with them.... Oh, you're getting me into some *heavy, heavy* stuff.... That's one of the main reasons why after these guys passed away—Eric [Dolphy], Booker Ervin, Joe Farrell, George Tucker, and a drummer named J. C. Moses ... All these guys are *tremendous* musicians, and we had a ball playing with each other, you know. Now when I hear that, I say "Oh, I feel so sad that he's gone." But he did document this, thank the powers for electricity.[84]

_____17. VII. 82

Dear Angel of Dust

The balloons are words taken out of our mouths, an eruptive critique of predication's rickety spin rewound as endowment. They subsist, if not on excision, on exhaust, abstract-extrapolative strenuousness, tenuity, technical-ecstatic duress. They advance the exponential potency of dubbed excision—plexed, parallactic articulacy, vexed elevation, vatic vacuity, giddy stilt. They speak of overblown hope, loss's learned aspiration, the eventuality of seen-said formula, filled-in equation, vocative imprint, prophylactic bluff. They raise hopes while striking an otherwise cautionary note, warnings having to do with empty authority, habitable indent, housed as well as unhoused vacuity, fecund recess.

The balloons are love's exponential debris, "high would's" atmospheric dispatch. Hyperbolic aubade (love's post-expectant farewell), they arise from the depth we invest in ordeal, chivalric trauma—depth charge and buoy rolled into one. They advance an exchange adumbrating the advent of optic utterance, seen-said exogamous mix of which the coupling of tryst and trial would bear the inaugural brunt. Like Djeannine's logarithmic flute, they obey, in the most graphic imaginable fashion, ocular deficit's oracular ricochet, seen-said remit.

The balloons are thrown-away baggage, oddly sonic survival, sound and sight rolled into one. They map even as they mourn post-appropriative precincts, chthonic or subaquatic residua come to the surface caroling world collapse. They dredge vestiges of premature post-expectancy (overblown arrival, overblown goodbye), seen-said belief's wooed risk of inflation, synaesthetic excess, erotic-elegiac behest. The balloons augur—or, put more modestly, acknowledge—the ascendancy of videotic premises (autoerotic tube, autoerotic test pattern), automatic stigmata bruited as though of the air itself.

Such, at least, was the insistence I heard coming out of Dolphy's horn. "The Madrig Speaks, the Panther Walks" was the cut. I sat down to listen to it only minutes ago and found myself writing what you've just read. Never had Eric's alto sounded so precocious and multiply-tongued, never so filled with foreboding yet buoyant all the same, walk (panther) and talk (madrig) never so disarmingly entwined.

Listening, more deeply than ever, bone-deep, I knew the balloons were evanescent essence, fleet seen-said equivalence, flighty identity, sigil, sigh. This was the horn's bone-deep indenture, wedge and decipherment rolled into one. This could only, I knew, be the very thing whose name I'd long known albeit not yet found its fit, the very thing which, long before I knew it as I now know it, I knew by name—the name of a new piece I'd write if I could.

What I wouldn't give, that is, to compose a piece I could rightly call "Dolphic Oracle." It would indeed ally song (madrig) with speech, as well as with catlike muscularity and sinew—but also with catlike, post-expectant tread, oxymoronically catlike post-expectant prowl, post-expectant pounce, an aroused, heretofore unheard of, hopefully seen-said panther-python mix . . .

Yours,

N. [85]

when you hear music

after it's over

it's gone

in the air

you can never

capture   it again[86]

What's it mean to speak of the literal here? Nat Hentoff is attuned to the shattered erotics of the situation and this is cool to the extent that it links the sound of the horn and bass—shriek and boom—to ancient departures. But the imposition of a literal meaning seems problematic given the uninterpretable status of such ruptural aesthesis. The point, however, is that some voices are here, even and especially within a discursive frame that asserts the propositionality of the instruments.

Dolphy's syntax, yes, but also that even in his outness he insisted upon some reference to the chord, that in his mind there was an insistence of the chord, that it had been there and remained in its irruption. So that an analytic of phrasing is required in order to hear music after it's over. After its performance is over is when music is heard. Air returned to air, aspire, expire. Music lies before and up ahead of its performance as subsistence, persistence, lingering, and sounded remainder in the breach, in the movement, from and between. The recording is the remainder as well as the rupture, where rapturous sounds stay even in the declaration of their inevitable disappearance, like words. There is no performance in the absence of the recording.

Rigorously un/captured, captured but you can't capture it again, heard after the fact of its disappearance, the music—organization in the improvisation of principles, nonexclusion of sound in the improvisation (through the relation and opposition of the generation and subversion) of meaning—lies before us. "'The Madrig Speaks, the Panther Walks' was the cut. I sat down to listen to it only minutes ago and found myself writing what you just read"/"The mere recurrence to those songs, even now, afflicts me; and while I am writing these lines, an expression of feeling has already found its way down my cheek."[87]

When Dolphy died he was preparing himself to play with Cecil Taylor, that necessary submergence. You wonder how to play without a bridge, how to navigate what is no longer song but carries song, to do your thang underwater, bone-deep in the deep of bones, ghost-ship risen sunken ark of bones, out and cut of the (radically excluded middle) passage. You've got to move from the extended interruption of the un-bridged, the chance of the synaesthetic and what it marks and unmarks in the cut, what it leaves and opens to the senses like a subject broken and abundant in some kitchen, field, or studio of representation, of securing and capturing: but the descent beckons toward a rewinding of invention, of (the hope of) composition, of positing, of contrivance and disclosure—of the condition of possibility of predication. Beneath the surface of the waters of nothing but interstice "I might have committed an action," might have acted out in group formation, neither invention nor securing, neither composition nor predication, neither constitu-tion nor performance, of the Real, of the whole, outside, public in the orchestration of every uncapturable and long-awaited letter. Mean-while, I work my way back to come upon some black performances by way of the effects (texts/recordings) that mark their ongoing production and invention, the improvisation of ensemble.

So that an analytic of phrasing is required in order to read unwrit-ten lines and these pauses from and between: a/ cut spirit
b/ floating warning and submerged peril (buoy, depth charge/saving power, danger)
"in lovely blue"
c/ hope and misunderstanding (the interruption or modular-ization that is caution)
d/ ... rigorous enrapture
(the eruptive critique of the ascribed become the appre-hended, the created become the discovered). Doubleness of invention. Complexities of before. Slice.

Writing, expression, rolls: the cut, recording, the remainder, and the rupture in which rapturous sounds (words) remain, disseminate, mark, and stain even in declarations of their necessary disappearance.

What I wouldn't give to speak of, not speak for, speak from, what I wouldn't give to compose, invent (in the place of "discover" hear "come upon") that which has been come upon, doubleness of invention, to ascribe what has been apprehended, captured, secured, you cannot capture it again. What I wouldn't do, if I ever thought I'd lose you.

You better know that the bridge collapsed. Don't just enter the music, but descend into its depths. A bone-deep listening, a sensing of the unbridgeable chasm, seen-said, seen cry unheard but for that bone-deep listening, improvisational vision of invisible performance, that descent into the music, descent into organization, the ensemble of the senses, unexcluded in the cut, excision of the unit, out in the ensemble, in preparation of the necessary sound. From a double anchor to anchor-lessness, from anchorless floating to weighted descent, the descent beckons, the fall no mere suspension, no rickety or rackety oscillation if the bridge is out and the cut beckons, beckoning of the "rolled-into-one," of the "seen-said," the "post-expectant," an insistence as insistent previousness, like the insisted upon in-sists of Lacan, like some "specific prematurity of birth" as the field of play or troubled depths of a "phylogenetic heritage," the extended interruption of the unbridged, the chance of the synaesthetic and what it marks and unmarks in the cut, what it leaves and opens to the senses. "[E]ruptive critique of predication's rickety spin," of the attribution of properties to the subject, of representation, of securing and capturing: but the descent beckons toward a rewinding of invention, of (the hope of/for) composition, of positing, of contrivance and disclosure—of the condition of possibility of predication. Maybe hope is always overblown, but the overblown produces unprecedented sound, overtones of the heretofore unheard (of), laughter outside the house, "unhoused vacuity"; nevertheless, hope is not quite on the bridge. The rackety bridge collapsed under the weight of its own unsustainable oscillation, vibrations that are too demanding. Hope is in the beckoning of descent, where what is made possible in the synaesthetic is not undermined by its totalizing excess, by what exceeds or is excised or is excluded in any such totalization, by what time still leaves out, by how time still takes you out from what's collected in "premature post-expectancy," otherwise known as mourning. To record this insight is an Ellisonian imperative: not just an impossible and impolitic staving off of invisibility, which after all has hypervisibility at its heart; rather, in the hope of an ensemble of the senses and, after the fact of its ongoing deferral, an emergence of radical orchestration. You descend into the depths of the music and linger there, dancing in the hoped-for shadow of a bridge, unfathomable ocean song, uncrossable river suite, sentimental avant-garde, subjunctive-sentimental mood. This is an Ellingtonian imperative.

CHAPTER 2

In the Break

Tragedy, Elegy

Amiri Baraka's work is in the break, in the scene, in the music.[1] This location, at once internal and interstitial, determines the character of Baraka's political and aesthetic intervention. Syncopation, performance, and the anarchic organization of phonic substance delineate an ontological field wherein black radicalism is set to work, and in the early sixties Baraka is situated—ambivalently, shiftingly, reticently—at the opening of that field. His work is also situated *as* the opening of that field, as part of a critique immanent to the black radical tradition that constitutes its radicalism as a cutting and abundant refusal of closure. This refusal of closure is not a rejection but an ongoing and reconstructive improvisation of ensemble; this reconstruction's motive is the sexual differentiation of sexual difference. The trajectory of Baraka's work in this period moves from the resistant embrace to the repressive transfer of this motive, and that trajectory is often discernible within individual works that emerge all along that trajectory. I want to trace this movement in the interest of amplifying the work's radical force while recognizing that this desire goes against the grain of Baraka's own assessment of the period I describe. What he sees as a transitional phase of his development—ground simply to have been covered or passed through—is a very definite seizure and advent, a musical caesura that demands precisely that immersive lingering that, according to Ralph Ellison, is a necessary preface to action.

As in Ellison, the occasion for such lingering is the entrance into that scene where the question of being and the question of blackness converge. As in Ellison, they converge as sexual questions. As in Ellison, they require a politico-economic response. This convergence is, of course, a point of divergence between Ellison and Baraka. They diverge precisely by way of the figure of transition, development. Baraka would say that Ellison moves through nationalism and Marxism to a devolutionary aesthetic individualism. Ellison would decry Baraka's migration from precisely that aesthetic individualism to nationalist and Marxist vulgarity. The extremity of both positions is, of course, problematic, but the positions remain instructive to the extent that their crossing marks a spot. That spot is the location of the interplay between nationalism and Marxism wherein the two are continually cut and abounded by the sexual differentiation of sexual difference. For Baraka, this spot exists between 1962 and 1966 even though neither he nor his commentators would characterize this moment as occurring within either his black nationalist or Marxist-Leninist "phases." Baraka's lingering in the broken rhythms of the field where blackness and black radicalism are given in and as black (musical) performance, in and as the improvisation of ensemble, amounts to a massive intervention in and contribution to the prophetic description—a kind of anticipatory rewriting or phonography—of communism that is, as Cedric Robinson has written, the essence of black radicalism. Such prophetic description is the project of a sentimental, criminal, proletarian, (homo)erotic, impossibly maternal avant-garde that works by way of a disruptive doubling of certain other theoretical hallmarks of "our modernity" as well. Attunement to the placement of these forces, of this vicious modernity, in Baraka's body of work, even if he would reject or disavow them, is the opening onto an understanding of the placement of these forces in the black radical tradition in general. This work is meant to contribute to the aesthetic genealogy of that tradition.

Of course, such a genealogy could never be simple, and the complexity of Baraka's out modernity is always on the verge of a lyrical scandal:

The wide open ensembles, the working friezes … the attempts at total definition are exciting and beautiful. It all works. The whole music seems less "bound" (by charts, by reading, by contracts, by spurious attentions) than before.[2]

The richness of this passage lies in the fact that the "wide open ensembles" it invokes and extends are shadowed by the threat of closures both internally and externally determined. It is not a coincidence that the very specific concerns with the animative object, with performative totality, that drive this passage are asserted at around the same time that Martin Heidegger was moving toward the end of a long techno-anxiety over the fact of everything functioning;[3] that Derrida and others were moving in the beginning of an extended assault—driven by and in avoidance of Heidegger, among others—on the very idea of total definition that, according to Philippe Sollers, for instance (updating and diagnosing another nausea), was shaped and plotted, as if a piece of Black Art, against a backdrop of sound: a horn, a trumpet, whatever voice there was or body animating it from the open music of vernacular, sentimental avant-garde and appositional encounter. Now these can be seen as detached Euro-intellectual echoes unheard underneath the shattered upheaval of fucked-up, funked-up, post-'65 Newark, itself called into being by the actively forgetful description of a returning exile, prophetic descriptions of destruction and rebuilding, *destruktion* and reconstruction, *deconstruire* and (urban) renewal, removal, foreshadowing descriptions of some out improvisations. But I will try to amplify them while plotting the course of a particular trajectory of transfer between certain musical performances and various modes of their reproduction, and between different moments and strains in the history of that reproduction, and toward the future of that history and what it might engender, whatever liberatory possibility it might hold and activate, the drives by which it's animated and punctuated. Part of what I'd like to get to is whatever generative forces there are in the asymptotic, syncopated nonconvergence of event, text, and tradition. That convergence emerges in and as a certain glancing confrontation—of Africa,

Europe, and America, of outness, labor, and sentiment—that is both before and a part of the material preface to the theoretical and practical formulation of a black public sphere.

Baraka thinks the possibility of such a public montagically, musically, and at the locus of the overlapping of these fields—mechanical reproduction. At a certain moment in the trajectory of his career he found the work of Wittgenstein useful to his meditations. Here is a small collection of Wittgenstein's formulations by way of which we might proceed.

> 4.014 The gramophone record, the musical thought, the score, the waves of sound, all stand to one another in that pictorial internal relation, which holds between language and the world. To all of them the logical structure is common.
>
> (Like the two youths, their two horses and their lilies in the story. They are all in a certain sense one.)
>
> 4.0141 In the fact that there is a general rule by which the musician is able to read the symphony out of the score, and that there is a rule by which one could reconstruct the symphony from the line on the gramophone record and from this again—by means of the first rule—construct the score, herein lies the internal similarity between these things which at first sight seem to be entirely different. And the rule is the law of projection which projects the symphony into the language of the musical score. It is the rule of the translation of this language into the language of the gramophone record.[4]

> 5. "But doesn't one *experience* meaning?" "But doesn't one hear the piano?" Each of these questions can be meant, i.e. used, factually or conceptually. (Temporally or timelessly.)
>
> 494. Doesn't it take imagination to hear something as a variation on a particular theme? And yet one is perceiving something in so hearing it.[5]

> 22. Think, for example of certain involuntary interpretations that we give to one or another passage in a piece of music. We say: This

interpretation forces itself upon us. (That is surely an experience.) And the interpretation can be explained by purely musical relationships:— Very well, but *our* purpose is not to explain, but to describe.[6]

I contemplate a face, and then suddenly notice its likeness to another. I *see* that it has not changed; and yet I see it differently. I call this experience "noticing an aspect."[7]

783.   We can say that someone doesn't have a "musical ear," and "aspect-blindness" is (in a way) comparable to this sort of inability to hear. 784.   The importance of the concept "aspect-blindness" lies in the kinship of seeing an aspect and experiencing the meaning of a word. For we want to ask: "What are you missing if you do not *experience* the meaning of a word?"—If you cannot utter the word "bank" by itself, now with one meaning, then with the other, or if you do not find that when you utter a word ten times in a row it loses its meaning, as it were, and becomes a mere sound.[8]

Montage renders inoperative any simple opposition of totality to singularity. It makes you linger in the cut between them, a generative space that fills and erases itself. That space is, is the site of, *ensemble:* the improvisation *of* singularity and totality and *through* their opposition. For now that space will manifest itself somewhere between the first lines of tragedy and the last lines of elegy. Lingering in that space is not but is of deconstruction, the oscillation between ghostly poles. We can begin, perhaps; perhaps not begin but move on; naw, we can linger in and over a formulation of Derrida's: "what is happily and tragically *universal* is *absolute singularity*."[9] There, here, the "not but of" that haunts here and there, the resonant sound and flashing light, the emergence of the ensemble of the senses, dawns on us iconically, but in a way that is always touched by, or bears the trace of, the fullness of the sign.

We could think of this dawning in many ways, by way of many questions. What is the use or structure of iconicity? What's the relation between iconicity and that fullness of the sign (the richness that Peirce located at the intersection of the symbolic, the iconic, and the indexical) that we might call *semioticity*?[10] What is the relation between iconicity, semioticity, and the experience that exceeds normal conceptions of temporality and ontology and that is, according to Stephen Mulhall, "characterized by the observer's felt need to employ a representation which might otherwise refer to subjective ... experience—to one way of seeing the figure—as if it were the report of a new perception" and that we call (after Wittgenstein) *noticing an aspect* or aspect-dawning or aspect-seeing or (my favorites) hearing or having a musical ear or phrasing?[11] What is the relation between this experience and the experience of the poem? What are the internal relations within that experience between the intellection of the poem's meaning and the sensing of its visuality and/or aurality? What are the relations between versions of or variations on the poem, manifestations of the eye and ear that raise the too deep question of the ontological status of the poem itself? What has this constellation to do with the phenomena of singularity and totality and their improvisation? What has this constellation to do with tragedy and/or elegy and/or (their) improvisation? And what have all of these to do with utopian aspiration and political despair?

Part of what I'm interested in, part of what I'd like to use in order to orient myself, is what could be called the (or, more precisely, Wittgenstein's) way to (or around or against) phenomenology. More specifically, I'm after the way concern with perception and cognition (of the things themselves) leads to the deconstruction of ontology; the way deconstruction generates riffs and rifts, odds and ends, of philosophy and of the intersection in philosophy of semiotics and phenomenology; the way we move beyond such productive cuts and eccentric arrivals to something more intense—like an "active forgetting" embedded in *the improvisation of the things themselves* whose broadest sense and implications deconstruction spurns and craves. What I'm after depends upon thinking through the question of the relation between semiotics and phenomenology *by way of the phenomenon or experience of noticing an aspect* (which is, I think we can say, again after Wittgenstein, the experience of meaning or of an insistent interpretation). It will be well, here, to remember a (para)phrase ('cause every phrase is a paraphrase) of Wittgenstein's—there is no phenomenology, only phenomenological problems—and to notice in passing that noticing an aspect—a phenomenological problem that, as we shall see, demands *description* in light of its exceeding of *explanation*—is in the aftermath or wake of this formulation: not but of not but of not but of

So another big part of what drives these fragments is interest in what is given in or emanates from the movement from the harmony of thinking and being, thought and reality (formations from the musics of Parmenides and Wittgenstein), to that harmony's figuration in signs. We could think this also as the movement from "logical structure" to iconicity and beyond. Think about logical structure or its variations, "pictorial internal relation" and/or "internal similarity": these formulations of the Wittgenstein of the *Tractatus* have an almost Peircean ring, coming as close as they do to Peirce's notion of iconicity. In Wittgenstein "logical structure" is shared between two objects (one a proposition about the other) in much the same way that for Peirce a "diagrammatic sign or *icon* ... exhibits a similarity or analogy to the subject of discourse."[12] We must keep in mind two things: (1) this similarity occurs in the context of a struggle between sight and sound or, more precisely, in an insistence of music in Wittgenstein's visual/spatial metaphorics; (2) Wittgenstein became increasingly dissatisfied with the nature and implications of this notion of logical structure perhaps in part because of a certain restrictiveness embedded in the philosophical conceptualization of the phenomenon of likeness. Indeed, *phenomenon* is probably a misleading word since the strictures of likeness are bound to the insistence of its noumenality, a noumenality marked by the resistance of likeness to explanation or to, more precisely, employment in the task of explanation. Something slips through the cracks or cuts of iconicity, likeness, metaphor, such that thinking operates in the absence of any real correspondent and translational manipulation of the concept of internal similarity or pictorial internal relation. In that absence or cut, in the space between expression and meaning or between meaning and reference, remains an experience of meaning that Peircean or what I'll call *first* iconicity doesn't get to and to which Wittgenstein would get.

The question, then, is how to describe that experience, and bound up in this question is the assumption (pointed to above, bitten off Wittgenstein) that description, rather than explanation, is the task with which we must now be concerned. More precisely, we must attempt a description of an experience whose provenance or emergence is not reducible to logical structure, pictorial internal relation or internal similarity; it is an experience of the passage or cut that cannot be explained because those formulations upon which our explanations must be grounded—spooky actions at a distance; communication between space-time separated entities; rigid, naturalized, but anti-phenomenal samenesses—are themselves so profoundly without ground. Like the strange correspondence between distant particles, like the mysteries of communication with the dead (or with tradition), the paradoxically elective and imperative affinities of and within ensemble are to be described within a radical improvisation of the very idea of description (in and through its relation to explanation), one that would move us from hidden and ontologically fixed likeness to the anarchization of variation, variation not (on) but of—and thus with(out[-from-the-outside])—a theme. At the constellation of meaning, understanding, music, phrase, feeling, variation, and imagination, we might speak again of iconicity, a *second* iconicity, not as the signification of shared logical structure but as a kind of noticing of an aspect, one that allows a temporal as well as ontological sense, a sense outside the temporal and the ontological, where we see—both factually and conceptually, statically and transitionally—entity and variation, each without theme. Perhaps this second iconicity, this semioticity or fullness of the sign, is the mechanism through which ensemble is made available to us as phenomena. Perhaps it is the supplement of description that allows description; for description of the phenomenon or experience of ensemble is only adequate if it is also itself the phenomenon or experience of ensemble.

Now, if you allow me to present some axioms *in the context of an imprecise but necessary conflation of the philosophy of the end of philosophy (of which phenomenology is not just one element among others) with modernism and with Enlightenment; and if you allow me to suggest the shadow of a parallel declension, trajectories whose essential points are passed through in a silence only the occasion justifies; then I'd trace the genealogy of iconicity from Plato through Peirce through Wittgenstein: from a representational formulation of* eikon *as likeness or image—the spectral, phantomic emanation of some absent essence that places us in the systemic epistemological and ontological oscillation between sameness and difference; through the semiotic structuration of a system of likenesses that subsumes questions of difference and absence in a pragmatic consideration of our absolute remoteness from the noumenal; through, finally, the reconsideration of the spooky dynamism of objects that attempts to validate what could be called "the changes" that an object (for instance, the jazz ensemble and its sound or the poem and its sound or their interinanimation and political implications) enacts and demands. By paying particular attention to the "grammar" and metaphorics of Wittgenstein's formulations on noticing aspects, keeping always in mind the necessary and, if you will, cinematically holistic logical form of his texts (the interplay of the aphorism and its collection), we might begin to experience and describe the organization of things*: (1) there's something tragic about the end (of philosophy); (2) Baraka is in the tradition of that end continually played out, played outside like a "vicious (rather than post-) modernism"; (3) the tragic in Baraka is political despair.

Have you ever suffered from political despair, from despair about the organization of things? What does it mean to suffer from political despair when your identity is bound up with utopian political aspirations and desires? How is identity reconfigured in the absence or betrayal of those aspirations? What's the relation between political despair and mourning? In the face of the problem this constellation of questions forms, what is required is an anarchization of certain principles so that an improvisation of Enlightenment might become possible. The unsayable claims of black utopian political desire, an unrequited love imaged after the fact, its sexuality violently reconfigured (and this is in and shapes the tradition, the phantasmagoric image/desire/fear on both sides of the raping of the daughter) is posited: what happens to that desire—and the identity that goes along with it—when faith is lost, when prayer is no longer possible or is unheard over the beautiful, screaming, fractured music that precedes it? What happens when the improvisation of Enlightenment or modernism or (the philosophy of) (the end of) philosophy—as predicated on the eradication of a certain obsession with differentiated, representative, and representational identity—is lost? What chance does music, the music of the poem, the music that prompts the poem, the music that is prompted by the poem, give us to arrive at such an improvisation? How is such an improvisation to be recalled if its source grows more and more remote, separated from us by the death, by the distance, of Miles?[13]

The tragic in any tradition, especially the black radical tradition, is never wholly abstract. It is always in relation to quite particular and material loss. This is what "BLACK DADA NIHILISMUS" is about: the absence, the irrecoverability of an originary and constitutive event; the impossibility of a return to an African, the impossibility of an arrival at an American, home. "BLACK DADA NIHILISMUS" is a response to political homelessness and this is the sense in which it is tragic; and this is also why Baraka, between 1962 and 1966, became America's great tragic poet by way of an improvisation through the opposition of the existential and the political, which extends and improves, say, the formulations of "Sartre, a white man."[14]

The tragic political despair of "BLACK DADA NIHILISMUS" is a function of the weakness of its relation to ensemble and to ensemble's condition of possibility, improvisation. Perhaps we'll come to understand tragedy as an absence of light (*Lichtüng* or *Aufklärung*) and breath (*Geist, anima*), the nothing that does not come to stand against them (or, more precisely, their effigies). If so, that understanding will have only been possible by way of the activation of the trace of improvisation and ensemble that, though dormant, is in the poem always and everywhere like the spirit of elegy, like every bit of what "the spirit of elegy" means.

Here are the first lines of tragedy.

> Against what light
> is false what breath
> sucked, for deadness.[15]

Slippage from question to assertion: question concerning absence, nothing, the hope or trace of what is not there that would stand against, that could never fully stand against, light and breath and the constellation of their meanings and associations, most especially, Enlightenment, revelation, spirit, song, and the vast and paradoxical network of liberatory and oppressive political implications they contain, reduced here, despairingly, in negative assertion, to the false and the dead. The intellect demands an analog—in the absence of symmetry between form and content, in the absence of what might be called a kind of iconicity (what I've referred to as first iconicity, a conflation of likeness and pictorial internal relation: perhaps that absence of symmetry or iconicity is what I referred to earlier as a kind of dormancy)—to the visual and aural tools a poetic reading can bring to bear on the changes Baraka plays: from question to assertion, from line to line (spatial reorientations), from sight to sound.[16] The recording, as such and here, brings a whole other ensemble of changes, versions and their slippages, noticings of aspects or improvisations, through the opposition or conflation of objective and subjective experience by way of modes of variation that are organized within another understanding of poem or theme and without ground such that "the paradoxical air definitive of aspect-dawning experiences—the paradox manifest in our saying of a figure we know to be unchanged: 'Before I saw something else, but now I see a [rabbit].'"— must be heard again in the light, if you will, of a description of a phenomenon that philosophy will have not quite been ready for: the improvisation through the opposition of stasis and dynamism, object and experience of the object.[17] This is the paradoxical and definitive air of an accompaniment and it allows us to say that the poem—which is to say the music, the ensemble marked by the interinanimation of poem and music among everything else in Baraka's work—"refreshes life" so that this phenomenon (something akin to but more than what Wallace Stevens calls "the first idea") is given us.

Perhaps all we know is that in the absence of what stands against, in the absence that is the dead and false, a poem is generated. It represents these absences, projecting into the future of their structures and effects from which, it would appear, only a god can save us.[18] But a poem is generated, like a transcendental clue for that in which faith has been lost. Think of Baraka's sound as the sound of a belief in the dialectic: that sound extends a powerful strain in the African American tradition that desperately holds to utopian (re)visions of Enlightenment formulations of universality and freedom. But in and after the fact of the realization that these things are not for us comes the chance of a tragedy. When that hold is loosened, under the pressure of catastrophic and durative loss, a hard critique like a multiphonic scream or "slide away from the proposed"—from the propositions encoded in the philosophical instrument that sounds your death and birth and death and birth—is opened.[19] At the point where and when all you can do is appeal to "a lost god damballah" to "rest or save us against the murders we intend," something else kicks in against all the determinations of freedom; a lived, *sounded* philosophical lingering in the cut between the dangers and saving powers of (the refusals of) totality and singularity; an improvisation of (the) ensemble. Then, here, we ask: what if we let the music (no reduction to the aural, no mere addition of the visual but a radical nonexclusion of the ensemble of the senses such that music becomes a mode of organization in which principles dawn) take us?

And don't let any artificial hierarchy of the senses keep you from the mysterious holoesthetic experience of ensemble Baraka's poems approach. One must have an ear and eye, skin and tongue, to perceive the poems' publication, aural reproduction, and their effects. We see the poem, read it, hear it, feel it—is it, in the midst of these various experiences, the same? Does it change? Where is the poem? Is the entirety of the poem ever present to us in any of its manifestations?

The relation between a musical score and the music is like the relation between the page and the poem. That which appears on the page is not the poem but a visual-spatial representation of the poem that would approximate or indicate its sound and meaning, form and content, and the particular sculpted manifestation of language as their interinanimations, the orchestration or arrangement of the body: voice and eye, the instrument upon which that music is played, the locus of the senses that must, in the face of all pressure, not allow itself to be reduced either to eye or voice and that must not allow the occlusion of the other senses and the correspondent exclusions that would follow.

So the spatial representation, the visual-ritual embodiment of the poem on the page, is supposed to indicate how it sounds, *how you sound*. But does it? Can it? Do the visual/spatial/ritual enactment or positioning or dance on the page of "BLACK DADA NIHILISMUS" adequately indicate how it's supposed to sound, thus sanctioning the commerce between eye and ear through which we must go in order to arrive at a description of the poem and that broader understanding of music to which I just referred and that notion of politics for which music is a transcendental clue?

But it's wrong to speak here of the poem as if it were the function of relation, of some determined mode of interaction between elements—rather, we might want to think of the poem as the entire field or saturation, flood or plain, within which the page, sound and meaning, the live, the original, the recording, the score exist as icons or singular aspects of a totality that is, itself, iconic of totality as such. Would this happily tragic formation, the mark, for Derrida, of "this strange institution called literature" of which nothing can be said, be adequate to the music that emanates from that peculiar institution whereof everything, all, the whole, ensemble, remains to be said and whose trace is the object of an unnamed seer/singer/sayer's deepest political desire?

Let's return for a minute to Wittgenstein's metaphorics. Noticing an aspect was, for Wittgenstein, a holoesthetic phenomenon or experience: not to be described by way of a exclusive reference to the visual-spatial but by reference to the aural as well. Thus the ability to notice aspects is (like) having a musical ear. Thus noticing an aspect is what I have been calling second iconicity, though semioticity, again, might be a better term because a kind of holism is implied, one that would correspond to that fullness or richness of the semiotic in which Peirce was interested and to which I earlier referred. Wittgenstein's work gets us to the point at which it is no longer possible to deny that semioticity is an object of the philosophy of psychology; he also gets us past that point to the extent that his work, part of the philosophy of philosophy's end, must also think the end of the philosophy of psychology. Finally, semioticity is nothing more than the ability to experience, understand, describe, generate, imagine, improvise, ensemble. It is not a kind of totalistic substitute or cipher for individuality or singularity; it is rather the mechanism by way of which we understand singularity and totality to be phenomena within the larger phenomenon of ensemble.

I want to think of this in much the same way Bakhtin thinks of the novel: as a force that reveals the limits of a systemic mode of thought, namely, that thinking in the spirit of system that has heretofore been called metaphysics, that thinking of the whole that is continually interrupted by temporal and ontological differentiation.[20] I want to show the novel, the new, the improvisational, at work in ensemble—which is to say in music, in utopian desire, in institutions strange and peculiar, and in their echoes and aftermaths, deconstructions and reconstructions—through both the despair of tragedy and the joy of (elegiac) resurrection.

Elegy is related to tragedy to the extent that it mourns for that which is the condition of possibility of the tragic: (a desire for) home. But what is the relation between tragedy, elegy, and improvisation? Perhaps this: that what animates the tragic-elegiac is something more than home(lessness) and (the absence of) singularity and totality: perhaps also there is a certain constellation that exceeds them, that exceeds the structure of their oscillation between happiness and despair, resurrection and mourning. What I'm talking about is ensemble and the improvisation that allows us to experience and describe it. It is our access to "the sexual cut," that "insistent previousness evading each and every natal occasion," and it allows us to move beyond either the simple evasion of the abyss or the spatio-temporal discontinuity that impedes our direction (home) or the narcotic belief in some spectral reemergence from its depths: rather we might look at that temporal-spatial discontinuity as a generative break, one wherein action becomes possible, one in which it is our duty to linger in the name of ensemble and its performance. That break allows, indeed demands, a fundamental reorientation that we might call novelty, that always exists at the heart of tragedy and elegy, which is there in Baraka's poetry and is there as that poetry would enact—through the opposition of description and explanation—the free music and politics, the free mode of organization it moves within and points to and whose logical structure it shares. Such enactment occurs by way of an improvisation through the very idea of logical structure in a way that is way past any normal ontology or time: so that what I'm into here is the anarchronic improvisation of ensemble that exists in the tragic and elegiac Baraka. Part of what one might say, then, about singularity is that it is tragic and that it always points to a kind of despair or inevitability or to an endless dialectical struggle with despair as inevitability; to remain within its grasp requires a powerful faith in resurrection, ghosts, spirits, specters, a powerful faith in the possibility of some mystical and therefore totalizing force rising from the abyss that blocks any notion of continuity, fate, destiny, any notion, more specifically, of progress or perfectibility. You must have faith, in short, in some animus that allows the continual projection of discontinuity, the persistence of a certain structure of life in which final judgment—in which justice—is always deferred, to come, up ahead. Thus we can say that totality is elegiac; that in some sense elegy is the necessary reaction to the tragic state of affairs that singularity imposes: singularity always implies an end, a break, a radical interruption. Elegy is the response to that interruption, it is the mechanism by which hopelessly fragile singularity, after the fact of the inevitable end it is and brings, is regenerated in the form of a call to the spirit of a totality that is no longer, that has perhaps never been, one. The elegiac response to the end that is of singularity is the invocation of totality's ghost.

If *first* iconicity is the idea of logical structure that grounds the relations between tragedy and elegy, singularity and totality—and is that which keeps the time of their rhythmic, deconstructive, timeless oscillation—then *second* iconicity offers an improvisation of that structure and through its effects. That second iconicity—noticing an aspect—that we must transform first into a less exclusionary semioticity and finally into a more radical, out-from-the-outside improvisation, is all throughout Baraka and resides especially in the cut between the beginning of "BLACK DADA NIHILISMUS" and the end of a piece we'll arrive at momentarily, "The Dark Lady of the Sonnets," a cut that is filled, erased, by our lingering in what animates it. That lingering, of course, would be musical. The passage I'd like to take you to is music. "So What?" you might ask . . .

"So What," the most famous tune from Miles Davis's most celebrated album, *Kind of Blue*, is in that it changes both from the point of view of the observer/listener and by way of the actions of the ensembles that generate it. Its paradoxical, anti-ontological status is a function of a form that de-emphasizes harmonic variation—the dominant "grammar" of jazz improvisation from Armstrong to bebop—by focusing on movement between tonalities, thereby allowing music to be generated out of the heretofore unthought locus of a multiply centered or decentered structure, namely, modal composition/improvisation. Though "Milestones," a 1958 cut from Miles Davis's album of the same name, and Eddie Harris's "Freedom Jazz Dance," a tune recorded by Davis for his 1966 album *Miles Smiles*, are most often cited as the first experiments in this new form of jazz composition, "So What" (1959) marks the full emergence of the era of modal improvisation in jazz and is considered "the modal composition par excellence," the bridge linking and separating the severe stricture's of bebop's harmonically based improvisational model to the more melodic, even anarchic, reconstructions of or improvisations through the song form itself that the music known as free jazz enacts.[21]

"So What" defies the opposition between object and experience upon which Wittgenstein relies both in his first and second reconfigurations of iconicity. Neither the kind of likeness that would be explained by way of the idea of logical structure or pictorial internal relation nor the kind of likeness that would be described by way of reference to noticing aspects are evident in "So What" (i.e., in the "internal relations" that exist between the theme- or song-as-object and its variations, either as perceived by an observer, enacted by a participant in its making or interpreted by some reverentially reconstructive artist or critic). Indeed, and as I have tried to point out earlier with regard to some of the other things we've examined here, the opposition between theme and variation is no longer operative after the fact of the music's organization and the residual effects of that organization, across various disciplinary and/or cultural boundaries marking domains that were never, in their own right, devoid of the improvisational motion which The Music celebrates and philosophy represses. We can see Wittgenstein's second iconicity, his noticing of aspects and valorization of description, as an attempt to repress that improvisational motion even as it also would embrace it, even as the aphoristic and deeply improvisational form of Wittgenstein's work embodies it (as any reading of his work suggests; as Monk's—Ray's not Thelonius's [though you know that "Light Blue" was the story of both their lives, Thelonius Sphere's and Ludwig's I mean]—biography of him moves to confirm).[22]

"So What" is reducible neither to its near nonexistent score nor to some imaginarily definitive initial recording nor to any other of the myriad renditions of this improvisation that Miles's ensembles played almost every night, coincidentally, during the years of what I temporarily call Baraka's tragic period.[23] So that "So What" is the unheard music that is the background (and here I mean something like a Searlean background—[a production of] the ensemble or "set of nonrepresentational ... capacities that enable all representing to take place") of tragedy returning by way of the rough echo of its name in elegy.[24] It is an object whose objectivity *is* in that it transforms; it is what Stevens would call, if he could ever have recognized it, in a phrase more precise than the one ("the first idea") I echo above, "a supreme fiction": abstract, pleasure-giving, changing, yet material enough to bear the exultant mournfulness of the blues, the high and essential pleasure of repetition encoded in all the possible experiences of meaning that the sound and title offer us, the infinity of whatever follows the absent loss that the title implies, absent loss paralleling the absence that would stand against that other manifestation of itself with which "BLACK DADA NIHILISMUS" begins, echoing what comes in the aftermath of loss in an ending in which Baraka's voice becomes Miles's, in which voice becomes metavoice, shadowed and deepened by mourning, moaning, growl,[25] at which the textual citation only gestures:

> I know the last few years I heard you and saw you dressed up all purple and shit. It did scare me. All that loud ass rock and roll I wasn't into most of it, but look brother, I heard *Tutu* and *Human Nature* and *D Train*. I heard you one night behind the Apollo for Q, and you was bashin like the you we knew, when you used to stand coiled like a blue note and play everything the world meant, and be in charge of the shit too. I'll always remember you like that Miles, and yr million children will too. With that messed up poppa stoppa voice, I know you looken up right now and say (growl) So What?[26]

That growl bears the trace of what I would imagine of each manifestation in these poems of joy and pain. Don't describe. Don't explain.

The Dark Lady and the Sexual Cut

Leon Forrest refers (soon after the cutting auto-interruption of his own text's beginning, the one in which he calls himself out for being unfaithful to the literary muse, seduced by Lady, by music, by what abounds the literary in the sounded word, by what he then would deny by surrendering to the lyric, by having Lady so surrender, by invoking the literary as a category for her work) to the story in *Lady Sings the Blues* regarding Billie Holiday's one-time husband Jimmy Monroe and the origins of the song "Don't Explain."[27]

> One of the songs I wrote and recorded has my marriage to Jimmy Monroe written all over it. I guess I always knew what I was letting myself

in for when he married me. I knew this beautiful white English girl was still in town. He didn't admit it, of course. But I knew. One night he came in with lipstick on his collar. Mom had moved to the Bronx then, and we were staying there when we were in New York.

I saw the lipstick. He saw I saw it and he started explaining and explaining. I could stand anything but that. Lying to me was worse than anything he could have done with any bitch. I cut him off, just like that. "Take a bath, man," I said. "Don't explain."

That should have been the end of it. But that night stuck in my crop. I couldn't forget it. The words "don't explain, don't explain," kept going through my damn head. I had to get it out of my system some way, I guess. The more I thought about it, it changed from an ugly scene to a sad song.[28]

There's a record in which Gilbert Millstein recites these ghost-written, haunted words before "Don't Explain" is performed by Lady Day.[29] What's the status of such reading? Forrest might try to claim that he has all along thought Billie's singing as a reading, of romance, let's say, or romance's distantiation, and that what she reveals at the microphone is revealed in just such a reading of "Don't Explain." On the other hand, here Forrest offers a reading of her writing as a kind of reading since somebody tells the story of the song's provenance in the autobiography. In this case another augmentation interrupts when Millstein delivers this celebrated passage from the downstage shadows at Carnegie Hall. Was Forrest listening to this reading, a reading both by Billie and of her and neither of these? Did he work in the midst of such a free, incalculable transfer?

What's it mean to speak of her "wisdom-cutting literature"?[30] The laugh ain't funny. She cuts literature like St. Theresa, with muteness and grain. Is muteness an attribute of wordlessness or of the word? To mute, to distort, augment or abound, divide or add to the sound, to the instrument's range, breaking the signifier's logic, very softly right up against the microphone. What does it mean to surrender to the lyric? It's not only an abstract reaching, this going for, this willingness to fail.

Something is reached for, an unprecedented communication (cuts literature, literature is cut and cuts) possible only when language is not reducible to a means of communication, when the sounded word is not reducible to linguistic meaning. "Billie just mesmerizes the English language, that's how exacting she was."[31] What about this intoxication? Who's afraid? Whose suffocated desire? They act out arrestment. Such held breathing, abrupt cancellation. Billie Holiday sings at the locus of a massive transference; the (literary) interpretation of Billie Holiday operates as a massive acting out. She resists such interpretation, is constantly reversing and interrupting such analytic situations, offering and taking back that mastery, finally reaching radically around it. Therefore, motherfuckers are scared. Got to domesticate or explain the grained voice. Got to keep that strange—keeping shit under wraps even though it always echoes. But why is her lipstick ingrained on your temple?[32] She wrote on it, "know your self!" Check yourself in the midst of an explanation that could only reveal the trace of what can't be explained—both in the actions of a dark lady and in her grained voice. Don't explain what they already know. She didn't seduce you. You played yourself. The grained voice engrains, the sign of the mouth, which is the birth, the sign of a kiss, reading you like an analyst reads the signs; here that reversal, where the listener oscillates between the analytic positions, is now such that the listener is without knowledge and waiting on Lady to lecture, to free-associate. So Lady interprets. She reads. But what she reads exceeds and undermines any coercive anticipatory idea; it's not all about the regime of love within which Forrest operates, reanimating his authorship to a large ensemble. He imagines her reading what he already knows, but her wisdom, as he knows and would actively repress, cuts that wisdom. She's on another thing, another register of desire. And that grained voice elsewhere resists the interpretation of the audience when the analytic positions are exchanged. This imaginary kiss marks a voice that resists reading and writing when the audible is forgotten in the interest of a repetition of suffocated desire and lost object, of transference and drive, that would tell the audience what they want to hear and what they already know. But this is the site of a self-analysis in Cecil

Taylor's sense of the term: an improvisation, an abundant internal trans-ference, a drunken, doubly sexual cut. When the narrator and the inter-preter enter the text and when the ghostwriter haunts it, the conditions for such transference, such unprecedented analysis and communication, are optimal. These interventions or mediations allow her replicative, inaugurative power. Muted, mutated, bent; muting, mutating, bending these words that are hers and before her

like now, as Billie reads, at the microphone

she comes in a bit too quickly after Millstein's strange recitation before his beat, in interrup-tion or too-quick cessation of his rhythm, established in the opening phrases of the text, establishing an implied narrative timing, that of the *Bildungsroman* and its way to tragedy. We are prepared for the sorrows of young Billie by caesurae that are meant to be hers but the rhythm they instantiate is interrupted by the poverty and richness of the one who lies before this instant, now at stage center, riding and bursting the gramophone right now.

> Mom and Pop were just a couple of kids when they got married. He was eighteen, she was sixteen, and I was three.[33]

This is the ghostwritten anacrusis of an anti-slave narrative, a narrative after slavery, narration of the ante-slave. Carry it and start it, initiate it, an ongoing or too-long-running tale she cuts and cuts off, cutting off "her" words and their recitation by a musical abundance. "Lady Sings the Blues" cuts *Lady Sings the Blues*. Beginning dissonantly, anarchroni-cally, in the interruption of a narrative we already know, in abundance of a tragedy foretold, seen, her phrasing abounds.

Two phonographies: the violence she does to words when sing-ing is duplicated in her writing. A letter, for instance, or her book, the letter to Dufty that is without punctuation. In anticipation of some beat, she will have sent that letter on up ahead so that it can be read, so that she can read it, phrase it, deform it, recollect it:

When I get to New York I will read this letter for you I am at the St Clair
Hotel please write or call me Miss you love you

Billie Holiday

PS ... Now you know why I don't write i can't[34]

One wishes for the tapes, that she would hurry up and come to New
York so she could read this book to me, but then Millstein reads downstage, the location of the text is downstage, the location of the text is
in the phonograph. She has come to read this book to me, only someone else stands in. The voice is present but off to the side, augmented
and divided or differed by the presence of someone else. The presence
implied by the voice is a haunted, ghostly striation, repeating lies that
turn out to be true when they get phrased like that. The presence is a
performance starting now, resistance in transference on stage.

Resistance to imposed and repressive racial/sexual regimes and
to specific events of repression, but further: these events, regimes, institutions to which she replies are not originary; nor is this resistance
interminable, nor can we simply say that the reply is paradoxically inaugurative. Sometimes this resistance comes in the form of a laugh that
serves to resist both the saddest interpretation and the more differentiated reading of an oscillation between tragic heroine and macho slut,
the turn to Miss Brown from My Man. There's a barely suppressed laugh
in "My Man," a laugh resistant in both political and psychoanalytic
terms. It's an abundant laugh that opens up by disturbing another convergence of Millstein's and (her ghostwriter, William) Dufty's rephrasing. The very line that ends the text, that seems to solidify her position
within a tragic and falsely hopeful economy of dependence upon a man.
Note these transfers: the performer of someone else's lyrics and of her
own becomes the composer whose intentions are rendered unavailable
by others' rephrasing; but at the point at which they would incorporate
lyrics she reads, and Millstein would incorporate her own reconfigured
lyric about the way she reads the lyric, the way she says "hunger" and
"love," into the always already constructed narrative of the tragic woman,

at the point of a condensation in Millstein's reading that would rework the very occasion of that reading as the echo of a trauma, the only time she ever fainted was at Carnegie, some laughter lets you know that there's another story before that one: "Tired? You bet. But all that I'll soon forget with my man."[35] Millstein's conclusion, converging with the conclusion of the autobiography, is opened by her, just like she interrupts what is initiated by the Millstein/Dufty ghosted and reghosted beginning. She cuts Millstein and Dufty, cuts her own words by dividing and fulfilling and abounding them. Reading them a lecture she reads everything just like that.

Lady in Satin is the record of a wonderfully articulate body in pain. It works in the way, or in the field, of a new ethics, perhaps even a new morality. The ancient tension between product and process, technologized into a new strife between the live and the recording, is smoothed by sound that emerges from, among other things, massive loss and massive resistance, only in order to reproduce agony as pleasure differently with every listening. That tension is smoothed by a sound that is anything but, however, so that what the sound carries has itself been roughened, so that an irreducible pattern of wear, a disruptive and augmentative pattern of content, alters the surface of meaning. So that "You've Changed" is an iterable event of joy and pain, the extension of an event whose instantiation ruptures origin every time.

The lady in satin uses the crack in the voice, extremity of the instrument, willingness to fail reconfigured as a willingness to go past, though the achievement or arrival at the object is neither undermined by partiality or incompleteness nor burdened by the soft, heavy romance of a simple fullness. The crack in the voice is an abundant loss, the strings a romance with what she don't need and already has. The crack is like that laugh in the voice of "My Man"—trace of some impossible initial version or inaugurative incident and effect of the resistance and excess of every intervening narrative and interpretation. Those last records, when leaned into, into the depth of the grain, grain become crack or cut (you can lay your pen in there; upon what is this writing before writing inscribed? what temple?), undermine any narrative of life and art that would smoothly move from a light business (busyness) to spare tragedy. Willingness to fail goes past; new coefficients of freedom.

The lady in satin says come, she announces herself, before the suppression of that call—as it coincides with the transformation of the name—in a text, by Baraka, called "The Dark Lady of the Sonnets." The call arrives like a response to some earlier cry in Baltimore, in the echo of some traveling song on the Eastern Shore, through recordings, Armstrong and Bessie Smith redoubling the echo of the work songs from upstairs at the house where Eleanora Fagan started listening. In turn, Baraka responds—an open response that carries with it a trace he'll never lose even when response begins to turn away toward some smooth, false interinanimations of manhood, nation, race.

And I'm interested in the concept of race. I'm interested in the opening of its differentiation and in the differentiation of its categorization. I'm interested in the frame, in framing, in the frame's rupture, and in the invention of the frame's hidden internal corners. Such reconstructions would mark the full ensemble of the determinations and indeterminations of race and the frame, their interinanimations and interruptive encounters. Then we might step outside and laugh at a surprising range of things: an identification of the sonnet's subjectivity that exceeds all methodological transformation by way of a marked racialization (Shakespeare offers a critique of the arrest of the frame and its durative yet artifactual by-product in the course of an iconic framing practice, a technical reinvention of the frame, a restructuring of the sonnet/stanza, and its sequencing and a reformation of the subjectivity that the form and content of his sonnets demand and imply); the held line of another absolute alterity, the singularity of breath's serrated edge (in Baraka the frame is spirit—a deep, paradoxically artifactual valorization of elemental and durative breath—the ongoing held within a fundamental, local, even national *anima*); a reduction of film to an effect of an effect of the photographic apparatus, a reduction that will also have been understood as a kind of racialization (Eisenstein gives us the spirit of the frame, which would have been outside, the originary dynamics of relation). At the place where Shakespeare, Baraka, and Eisenstein do not meet, not in between but outside and home, race cuts race and frame cuts frame. In order to understand how such cuts are sexual cuts, we'll need to deal with what marks and forms that place, a sensuality represented by textured satin, the Dark Lady Day. The sonnet-as-frame and the montagic sequencing of sonnets appear in conjunction with Shakespeare's enactment of a technicistic subjectivity. Here I would both extend and contradict Joel Fineman's *Shakespeare's Perjured Eye* on the "new" subjectivity Shakespeare constructs in his sonnets: if Shakespeare instantiates a new subjectivity, it is both the opening of a quintessentially technicistic poetical subjectivity and the beginning of the end of that subjectivity, formed, allowed, and endowed by the double encounter (discovery and expulsion, desire and revulsion) with the epideictic other.

Fineman argues that Shakespeare's sonnets rewrite epideictic poetry—a form whose name joins a root that means to show, bring to light, reveal, point or point out to a prefix that signals both the supplemental and the self-reflexive thereby marking epideictic poetry as that which is directed toward the description and exaltation of another while also containing surplus effects that are self-directed.[36] Fineman begins his reading of Shakespeare's sonnets indirectly, by way of the opening sonnet from Sidney's *Astrophil and Stella*, in order to provide a background against which we can see this Shakespearean rewriting and the revelatory event at which it arrives.

> Loving in truth, and fain in verse my love to show,
> That the dear she might take some pleasure of my pain,
> Pleasure might cause her read, reading might make her know,
> Knowledge might pity win, and pity grace obtain,
> I sought fit words to paint the blackest face of woe:
> Studying inventions fine, her wits to entertain,
> Oft turning others' leaves, to see if thence would flow
> Some fresh and fruitful showers upon my sunburned brain.
> But words came halting forth, wanting Invention's stay;

Invention, Nature's child, fled step-dame Study's blows,
And others' feet still seemed but strangers in my way.
Thus great with child to speak, and helpless in my throes,
    Biting my trewand pen, beating myself for spite,
    "Fool," said my Muse to me, "look in thy heart and write."

Fineman reads Sidney's sonnet as a fairly straightforward mode of epideixis in spite of the struggle to praise that the poem represents: for
when all is said and done, all the poet need do is look at the engraving
or framing of the object of praise and desire on his heart and, in an
imaginary ecphrastic reversal, turn that picture into words. This implies
the possibility of a direct correspondence between the visual and the
verbal that empowers one simply to write what one sees; it also implies
that one has easy access to a language that adequately represents what
one sees; indeed, it suggests that what one sees seems almost to generate that language. What Sidney speaks of and prefaces is a kind of automatic writing, a revelatory writing, one in which "the dear she" who
both prompts and receives the dual passion of vision and love is easily
and directly revealed, uncovered, disclosed; no impediment is admitted
to the marriage of what is seen, loved, or esteemed and what is said
about what is seen, loved, or esteemed. For Sidney the language of the
sonnet is, in fact, a pure physical language and, to the extent that it is
epideictic and thus reflects both the process of praise and the passions
that allow it, a pure phenomenological language as well, one descriptive
of both the object and event of sight and desire.

What is new and both cool and scary about Shakespeare, according to Fineman, is precisely his admission of impediments to the marriage of the visual and the verbal. Shakespeare shows that the visual
object of praise cannot be praised directly since language and the visual
are unheld by any absolute convergence. Immediately, however, there's
a deepening of this problematic because Shakespeare's revelation regarding the impossibility of praise occurs in and as praise and because his
opposition of language and vision is always doubled by their relation to
the extent that the language that reveals its opposition to vision is also

about vision. This paradox is thematized, according to Fineman, by way of the (dis)connection of the primary objects of praise in the sonnet sequence, the fair young man and the dark lady to whom the young man's revelatory truth and beauty is opposed—not because of any absolute verbal falsity and ugliness but because she is both true and false, both beautiful and ugly.[37] What Fineman observes, in short, is "a poetics of a double tongue rather than a poetics of a unified and unifying eye, a language of suspicious word rather than a language of true vision" that comes about as a function of "a genuinely new poetic subjectivity that I call, using the themes of Shakespeare's sonnets, the subject of a 'perjur'd eye.'"[38] Fineman thereby provides a myth of origin for the anxious affect and effect of modern subjectivity through a differential calculation of the subject. What I'd like to move toward, however, is a representation of the incalculable that stems not from any judgment on the etiolated verbal force of the subject but results, rather, from and in an improvisation through the interinanimation of singularity and subjectivity that Fineman's reading assumes and that the form and the content of the sonnets both affirm and deny. Such a representation would work in the interest of a new and complex understanding of the *present* and presence of the object.

The work of Stephen Booth, particularly his extended note on the greatness of Shakespeare's sonnets, is here both instructive and revelatory.[39] Booth clearly places himself in the position of the epideictic poet by supplementing his praise of the sonnets with a self-reflexive discourse on the praising of the sonnets. Not surprisingly, the gist of his argument is that they're so great because they exceed calculation, because they give us a visionary, revelatory experience that cannot be accounted for when we break the poem down into component parts in order to attempt a calculation or a reaggregation—i.e., a reading—of it. Yes, Shakespeare's poems show the impossibility of a truthful declaration— of a real poetic fidelity—in the midst of a declaration of truth, and yes, they thus exhibit what appears as a strikingly divided subjectivity: this is made evident to us as we break the poem down. Nevertheless, the truth of the poem, its fidelity to its object, is what is revealed to us in our experience of the poem. There are, then, a couple of things going on: we understand the poem and we do not understand the poem; we know something in spite of the convoluted and contradictory evidence that is the poem and, at the same time, we are required to try and figure out what that contradictory and convoluted evidence means and what it means seems to be precisely the opposite of what it is that we know.

Shakespeare produces certain effects, then: a continual figuring of the position of the reader and the dynamics of reading along with a foreclosure of the possibility of pure epideictic response that simultaneously produces that response and reproduces the demand for that response by demanding that we respond to him and allowing us to do so. He continually does that which upon closer analysis he proves he cannot do. And in so doing he forces us to accomplish the same feat. These sonnets are all intelligible to us in their general direction and thematics yet they become less intelligible the more we look at them, the more we know about them, the more we know. For the myriad of effects contained in a given sonnet, its multiple facets, when counted, added, collected in literary analysis, never add up to the sonnet itself. But the effect here is more than just the cliché of the whole as more than the sum of its parts. Here, rather, we have the following paradox: that the whole is undermined as an idea by the fact that it is not the sum of its parts and that in spite of this when we experience the sonnet we experience it as (an icon of) the whole. "Everything is in Shakespeare"[40] is, for example, precisely that epideictic response that reproduces the Shakespeare effect—the extension of that effect that I would here affect, implied by the corollary formulation "Shakespeare is improvisation," would be: Shakespeare is ensemble, ensemble referring to the generative—divided, dividing, and abundant—totality out of which and against which (Shakespearean or post-Shakespearean) subjectivity appears.[41]

The haphazard conditions of their production and reproduction help to maintain the sonnets' status as ideationally and bibliographically problematic. I am thinking here of the publishing of what are generally perceived as lexical or diacritical incorrectnesses that have had a material effect on the meaning that is produced in/from the work and, more importantly, of the magnification of that effect by a sequential ordering of the sonnets that carries the illusion of a narrative but cannot be traced to the singularly ordering subjectivity of an author. This super-imposed narrative works in conjunction with the altogether untraditional structures of address around which the sonnets are built to maintain and disseminate the in/determinations of reading. We can then trace, for example, that "sub-sequence/plot" addressed to a male beloved in which sexual favor is sought for someone who both is and is necessarily other than the male sonneteer and in which sexuality and procreativity as such are given as the (not necessarily linked) epideictic object; or we can analyze the "sub-sequence/plot" that is addressed to a person of the "appropriate"—which is to say opposite—sex who is in every other way unworthy precisely by exemplifying the paradoxically worthy and unworthy essence of woman and in which sexuality and procreativity are described in a "dark" imagery correspondent to a wholly critical scrutiny of their necessary linkage. This second group of sonnets and the protocols of reading they lay out are both addressed to the one who has come to be called the dark lady; they are what I'm most interested in here—partly because I think they allow for a return to the questions of race and spirit in their own right and partly because, even if they didn't, Baraka has constructed from the echoed sound of Billie Holiday a bridge that spans the distance from the trace of Shakespeare's sonnets to the question of these questions. This implied return requires atten-tion to some minute deformations of the texts at hand—birth defects in some cases, in others simply the effects of a new technology. Can I kick it with a missing apostrophe or the typography of the "s" or the accidental duplication of a pair of eyes? What happens in the transition from the fair youth to the dark lady? What is the significance of the truncation of that transition, the absence of the couplet, the change in form from the celebration of the impossible procreation of the sonnet to the fear of a procreative blackness/beauty that has undermined all previous standards? The undermining of standards is both an effect of language and of Shakespeare's intent in the sonnets—to explore the problematics of the object of love and the frame of desire.

The falsity of painting—of the devotion of the eye and its engraving on the heart—is a prominent motif that runs throughout the whole of Shakespeare's sonnet sequence but is reintroduced with redoubled intensity in the dark lady sonnets. There such falsity is ontologically determined in the seen rather than phenomenologically determined in the act, which is to say passion, of seeing. There is no slippage in the process of seeing/writing/engraving/framing or, rather, the slippage inherent there has not been contained, has wrested from beauty its ontological endowment, its name and local habitation. Painting now has a double edge, at the level of the object as such as well as at the level of the seeing/representation of the object. And whereas the possibility of the truth in painting remained in spite of the displacements of representation, that truth seems more problematic when the object to be represented is always already given as painted, its fairness either mere show or absolute absence. This falsity or doubleness—a kind of strange, if not deadly, life or animation—that inheres in the object itself renders the procreativity the sonnets mark and represent problematic: they are gotten in the dark place of an illicit—and not "simply" impossible—verbal-visual concord, one that has its basis in a procreative structure that is lustful and debilitating.

Sonnet 129 ends the transition in a sense: the effect of painting becomes "th'expense of spirit" wholly unmediated by that ethereal and true representation of the object of desire that the earlier sonnets impossibly attain.

> Th'expense of spirit in a waste of shame
> Is lust in action, and till action lust
> Is perjured, murd'rous, bloody, full of blame,
> Savage, extreme, rude, cruel, not to trust,
> Enjoyed no sooner but despisèd straight,
> Past reason hunted, and no sooner had,
> Past reason hated as a swallowed bait,
> On purpose laid to make the taker mad;
> Mad in pursuit, and in possession so,

Had, having, and in quest to have extreme
A bliss in proof, and proved a very woe,
Before, a joy proposed, behind a dream.
   All this the world well knows, yet none knows well
   To shun the heav'n that leads men to this hell.

Still, a narrative is discerned in this transition from an ethereal, idealized, nongenerative, male, homoerotic, literary sexuality to a visceral, heteroerotic, and necessarily illegitimate procreativity that exists as such only as a function of the racialization of sexual difference. Either way Sonnet 129 is an icon of the whole of the sonnets, one that contains allusions to the illusions of plot that take the form of a diagrammatically iconic, internal, temporal constituency that corresponds to a similar effect produced by the unnatural or, more precisely, naturalized sequencing of the sonnets.[42] "Had, having, and in quest to have extreme," perhaps the sonnet's most analyzed line, is iconic of the sonnet's iconicity. Thus numbers 1 through 126 could be read as those sonnets that are in quest to have (the violent and unreasonable quest for the formation of an interiority, a differential integrity, a singular subjectivity that would somehow emerge in an impossible homoerotic procreativity), and numbers 127 through 154 mark fulfilled desire with all the customarily feminized and racialized metaphorics of death and decay, from whence nothing comes except the impossible, tainted residue of art, while somewhere in a gap that fails to show itself, unless we take the "missing" final couplet of number 126 to offer the impossible representation of having, resides the action of which there is no view and whose absence produces the need for a retrospective illusion of "itself."[43] Sonnet 129 would be, in a sense, the embodiment of the extreme experience of the sonnets, the singular framing of their phenomenality, the clearest moment of the Shakespearean difference in poetic subjectivity. That sonnet, that frame, would contain a picture of the arrested or eternally deferred action of the sonnets and would thus also hold within it an image, if you will, of the arrested subjectivity that engenders that action. The doubleness inherent in the phrases' arrested subjectivity or deferred action is figured in the poem by "th'expense of spirit" and by the duality—the dark desirability or Monkish "ugly beauty"—upon which or within whom that spirit is expended. Again, I'm interested in the model of poetic subjectivity that the workings of this poem produce and exemplify and in the provenance of that model—the (hetero)sexualized and racialized encounter with the object of praise, revulsion, desire and the simultaneously enabling and debilitating waste of spirit.

a rush, onset; rapid action; the space or distance between two points;

a natural or inherited disposition; a particular class of wine or the characteristic flavour supposedly due to the soil;

a set of children or group of descendants; a generation; a tribe, nation or people or groups thereof; a class—one of the great divisions of mankind; one of the sexes;

to cut, tear (with regard to weaving), channel, course, line: a row or series;

a peculiar or characteristic style or manner [of writing]: liveliness, sprightliness, piquancy—"I think the epistles of Phalaris to have more Race, more spirit, more force of wit and genius . . ."[44]

NOTHING WAS more perfect than what she was. Nor more willing to fail. (If we call failure something light can realize. Once you have seen it, or felt whatever thing she conjured growing in your flesh.)

At the point where what she did left singing, you were on your own. At the point where what she was was in her voice, you listen and make your own promises.

More than I have felt to say, she says always. More than she has ever felt is what we mean by fantasy. Emotion, is wherever you are. She stayed in the street.

The myth of the blues is dragged from people. Though some others make categories no one understands. A man told me Billie Holiday wasn't singing the blues, and he knew. O.K., but what I ask myself is what had she seen to shape her singing so? What, in her life, proposed such tragedy, such final hopeless agony? Or flip the coin and she is singing, "Miss

Brown to You." And none of you cats would dare cross her. One eye closed, and her arms held in such balance, as if all women were so aloof. Or could laugh so.

And even in the laughter, something other than brightness, completed the sound. A voice that grew from a singer's instrument into a woman's. And from that (those last records critics say are weak) to a black landscape of need, and perhaps, suffocated desire.

Sometimes you are afraid to listen to this lady.[45]

This piece by Baraka, entitled "The Dark Lady of the Sonnets," is an elegy for one whose perfection was of the perfect, of its peculiar temporality, of the valorization durativity invites. Baraka's Billie Holiday exceeds in the way that the perfect exceeds any idea of succession or caesura, precisely in the willingness to move out, in voice, from any prior restraint or rule, to expand the range of the instrument, to move through any shadow of a separation of the voice-as-instrument from the body.

Baraka's sonnet would enact an epideixis of aurality, a move away from the occularcentrism of the discourse of praise. We only see her obliquely, obliquely seeing, "one eye closed, and her arms held in such balance, as if all women were so aloof." Nevertheless, a presence is felt, one that troubles the distinction between transmission and the sensation transmitted, one that reopens the question of sound in writing and the question of fear. Fear because, as Baraka writes, "Sometimes you are afraid to listen to this lady." Sometimes, the ghostly emanation of her sound from his writing instantiates a shuddering affect, a fascination or interruption that is frightening not only in the emotional effect it produces but also in the cognitive disjunction it opens, a disjunction between the perfection of the Lady and the rupture of a dead, recorded voice, between the insistence and the absence her sound marks. Sometimes you are afraid to listen to the voice of the dead, to its palpable, material sound. Sometimes you are afraid to listen to the perfect failure of voice. That perfect failure is not just a function of the cessation—the "dying fall"—that the rhythmic manipulation of the durative voice enacts; it is, too, the phantasm that the mechanical reproduction of the silenced voice emits, the artifact of the recording, the necessary reduction of process to product, the containment and replication of the sense of excess. This is the paradoxical phenomenon that the musical recording, the sonnet and montage demand that we address and improvise.

"The Dark Lady of the Sonnets" (re)writes the music. It is more than a recording in the way that recordings are; not merely an artifact, it transmits, through an improvisational writing, the music as a kind of abstraction directed toward ensemble. "The Dark Lady of the Sonnets" is representation that moves in the absence of representation: not as any simple valorization of process—though such happens in the words—and not just in the ideology and metaphysics of spirit and nation (the expressive manifestation of the blackness Baraka loves, needs, and desires, the blackness whose overdetermined history of [negative] reference he both extends and overturns). It is, rather, an improvisation through the opposition of valorized process (coupled with the loss of sound, air, breath, or "th'expense of spirit") and valorized product (as the artifactual, the presence of the recorded and etiolated sound, another inadequate compensation like the orgiastic and orgasmic screaming associated with the deadly concord of music and audience). It is an improvisation through the complex interrelations of shame, song, and prostitution and their connection to madness, intoxication, bewitchment, and infatuation: formulations past reason, of an apocalyptic tone, held within the expense of a sigh or the frightening, arresting sound a horn or a voice makes in its extension, bound up in the metaphysical connection between jazz, death, race, and spirit.

Something problematic is at stake, though, in what above I called Baraka's "oblique" visual representation of Holiday, in the overdetermined visualization of woman as oblique, vague, malleable, interpretable, assignable in the process of more fixed signification. The vague particularity of woman marks a mystery that signifies origin, the unfathomable site of an imaginary return—to the mother, to Africa—with which Baraka's writing in the 1960s was intimately concerned. Here elegy is determined by the constitutive absence that surrounds it, namely race. What we have in Baraka's text (in the apparent elision of the visual) is yet another "scopic hybridity" in which the music is reduced to something gestured toward in an etymological reduction of "jazz" (one paralleled by a similar reduction of spirit; a bridge connects "th'expense of spirit" and the dissemination of jazz; that same bridge connects sexual and aesthetic procreativity: spirit, sperm, jism, jazz): the fundamental element of another illicit procreativity indexed to and determined by either the literal or figural dissemination of a singular, originary, male substance. The sexualization of racial difference that is thereby enacted is a reversal of Shakespeare's production of the dark lady of the sonnets; but that reversal is nothing more than a highly determined movement within the very structural economy that allows Shakespeare's formulation in the first place.

Nevertheless, a certain phenomenon remains: one parallel to the undifferentiated, nonsingular generativity Shakespeare's sonnets exhibit, one that is perhaps best described precisely as the phenomenon of the remainder as such or, better yet, as the mark of the totality that "everything" (that which is in Shakespeare and Baraka and their "objects") can never capture. This phenomenon raises certain questions that trouble the distinctions between the object of sight and the event of seeing, the heard voice and the event of hearing. Here the question might best be formed thus: what is the relation between the determinate form of the blues (and the particular mode of subjectivity that form implies), the record (as the determined manifestation of a particular technical apparatus) and improvisation? Perhaps it is this: that the recording is a determination that is also an improvisation, one that extends, emanates, holds a trace that moves out of the tragedy the blues holds. Perhaps it is this: that the dark lady improvises through the blues and all that it implies from within its form and in the fixity of the recording. Perhaps it is this: that the tragic-erotic end that the blues seems always to foreshadow is supplemented not only by the transformative effect of improvisation but the ghostly emanation of those last records, the sound that extends beyond the end of which it tells. Perhaps it is this: that the sonic image of a death foretold contains not only the trace of an early and generative beauty but the promise of a new beauty—song coming out of, song for . . .

The blues is what Lady sings and—in singing and in the excess of singing, by way of an improvisation through the overdetermination of the recording and the determination of the blues as tragedy, in the more than illuminative, undertonal expense and expanse of her dark, fantastic laughter—exceeds. The record is the sonnet, (re)written in Baraka's elegiac address to the one of desperate music. The sonnet is the analog of the frame. Sonnet, record, and frame are their own improvisations; this is to say that something held within these forms also exceeds them, that there is a remainder that is not reducible to the technical apparatus that produces them or the technicity that grounds them. That technicity resides in the idea of singularity through which sonnet, record, and frame are constituted and in their origin in a particular kind of technological apparatus, namely, the subjectivity structure to which Shakespeare is given and which Shakespeare writes and rewrites. That structure's essence is a technicity apparent in the oscillation between singularity and difference, singularity and totality. I do not think it would be unfair to think of this principle, this novel subjectivity of the sequence or, deeper still, of the interval, as montagic. And, as Baraka teaches us, "The question of montage is impossible without Eisenstein, whether they know it or not."[46] "[T]hey" refers, let's say, to Shakespeare and Lady Day, both of whom were aware—always and everywhere in their work—of the centrality of the question that Eisenstein (did "they" know him?) makes possible by questioning.

Eisenstein is essential here because of his theoretical exposition of ideas and practices already at work in the forms of things determined by technicistic, proto-mechanical origins. (These forms are no less technical, for all their relative earliness, than those that determine much of contemporary aesthetic production—I'm thinking here of the sonnet sequence—and no less subversive of the technical in spite of their position within the age of mechanical reproduction—I'm thinking here of

Holiday's *recordings* of her improvisations of the blues.) Most important is his pursuit of a theory of montage as nonexclusive totality: thus his movement from the polyphonic to the overtonal and all in the interest (according to Annette Michelson),[47] of a whole art, a *Gesamtkunstwerk*, which would offer, represent, and enact what Trinh T. Minh-Ha calls "the multiple oneness of life."[48] That pursuit is restricted by singularity (the cognitive model or structure of subjectivity or principle of technicity or technical apparatus that produces forms such as the sonnet, the blues, or the frame) in/and its dialectical relation to totality (the synthesis of process and artifact that occurs in and as montage), and by the interval as the structure of that relation, the motive force and form or dynamism that infuses and animates "the ensemble of social relations." Yet Eisenstein begins to put some pressure on that idea of singularity in a critique of the static frame: Michelson argues that in this theorization, in "The Filmic Fourth Dimension,"[49] a radicalizing of montage is brought into effect such that it enters its utmost possibility; but it does so, I would argue, at precisely the moment of the foreclosure of that possibility. For montage comes into its own by way of the deconstruction of the elemental status, which is to say staticity, of the frame. Such a deconstruction cannot not include an improvisation through the idea of the frame as pure singularity: this means not only a theorization of movement in/of the frame but an iconization that acts as an affirmation against the very idea of the frame. When montage comes into its own, it comes into the deconstruction of its singular element and that element's intervalic relation to the set of which it is a member. What remains is a totality or ensemble that is structured neither by relation nor singularity but by the internal differentiation—the sexual cut—of singularity and the new relations, the everything, that differentiation allows.

Montage is the bridge that suspends or denies its transportive function: it's the internal suspension or translation of the syntagmic or, better yet, the phrasal supersession of the sentence. It enacts a dissemination of polyphony and pantonality within its heretofore univocal (time)line: the bridge collapses to an aporetic enduring, though, as I've said, there is already present a movement through these in/determinations of singularity. This dissemination of ensemble, this new animation of the object, this animative improvisation of the old-new thing, is for the cinema to come: it is a pluri-dimensionality, heretofore repressed, of the instant, of the clearing, of the trace of Heideggerian *Lichtüng* or *ekstasis* at work in Eisenstein's formulations, in the context of an appeal to affectivity or to the fact of the film having to be felt. And all we've been thinking of here is feeling—an ephemeral and paradoxical generativity, an expressive procreativity improvising through opposition and relation of cut and suture, the image and the sound of love. This is just to say that there is always something more than what is just to say, an abundance that accrues especially at moments such as these when things sound "edgy, maybe garbled at points," when "ears literally burn with what the words don't manage to say." This is to say + more that the lectural apparatus gives the word, in their inadequacy, something to say + more to and for the cinematic apparatus, performative force deforming and reforming the categories of the audio-visual field. Lady writes this knowledge onto Baraka's heart and writing.

How long can he remember?

German Inversion

What's gained by his dis(re)membering?

Here's the opening of Baraka's essay "The Burton Greene Affair":

THE QUALITY of Being is what soul is, or what a soul is. What is the quality of your Being? Quality here meaning, what does it possess? What a Being doesn't possess, by default, also determines the quality of the Being—what its soul actually is.

And let us think of soul, as *anima:* spirit (*spiritus,* breath) as that which carries breath or the living wind. We are animate because we breathe. And the spirit which breathes in us, which animates us, which drives us, makes the paths by which we go along our way and is the final characterization of our lives. Essence/Spirit. The final sum of what we call Being, and the most elemental. There is no life without spirit. the human Being cannot exist without a soul, unless the thing be from evil-smelling freezing caves breathing high-valence poison gases now internalized into the argon-blue eyes.

What your spirit is is what you are, what you breathe upon your fellows. Your internal and elemental volition.

At the *Jazz Art Music Society* in Newark, one night, pianist Burton Greene performed in a group made up of Marion Brown, alto saxophone and Pharoah Sanders, tenor saxophone.[50]

"The Burton Greene Affair" is a recording of that ensemble. The music that was heard by Baraka that night in Newark resonates through his words even as it is denigrated, idealized, and distorted in the reading, hearing, and composing that forms the essay as name and description. Writing is marked by the possibility of variation; what you sing, read, improvise, *moves* you. Baraka's writing is no exception. The question is whether such movement must be a return. Baraka's affair veers toward a provisional return to the primordial and the question of its meaning. The aim of this return is twofold: being and blackness. Baraka talks about being by way of the music and within what he comes to figure as an "other" tradition (one that values a certain understanding and embodiment of improvisation, one that respects and theorizes totality in the work of art and in the artwork's self-deconstructive relation to the everyday). By the same token, the problem of blackness emerges only by way of an ontological questioning that might be the very essence of the tradition of the "same." This conflict at the heart of Baraka's text demands precisely what it produces: deep sound. Such sound, in turn, requires the kind of listening that activates rather than fragments the whole of the sensorium. One must, therefore, look at the music Baraka makes with his own vicious eye. Adrian Piper might understand this as a parable about the interplay of visual pathology and racist categoriza-tion, but she also knows how hard it is—within a certain continuum of intensity, of aesthetic, political, even libidinal, saturation that black folks call everyday life—to look at what seems only to emerge as the occlu-sion of blackness, the deferral and destruction of another ensemble. In the face of such violent seizure, the temptation to return to an imagined primordiality is massive. We'll have to see whether or not being and blackness are approachable by way of this originary, fragmentary drive. On the one hand, Baraka moves down the broken line of an appositional choreography, a (phono/video) graphic sidestep. On the other hand, Baraka translates the old-new thing's improvisational theory of ensemble into an ontological language whose exclusionary totalizations would shut the gathering down. His translations cross over but only in the sense that would obtain if the design and engineering of the bridge were done in some disruptively excessive hard way (as if the architect were Hardaway). This is the old-new language—tragic, hopeful, fallen—of the broken ensemble, the phenomenal object. Baraka discovers the improvisational, ensemblic nature of the language of ontology in his use of it. He comes upon it by playing it. He invents it in a performance that will not just represent. He improvises, thereby bringing to bear on ontology the tradition of another inscription that renders "the tradition" meaningless or too meaningful, that opens us continually to the value of improvisation even as that value is thought in the spirit of system, even as improvisation renders that spirit meaningless. His improvisation is consumed by the very force upon which it would act. The fantasy of return turns to cold oscillation. The only remaining question concerns what it was that the music that was played that night recorded. Perhaps what was recorded was this: the fantasy of what hadn't happened yet. The questions demand that we turn obliquely, up ahead, to the recording, to what seems and doesn't seem to be there, to what it is (to seem) to be. This is what it is to activate the foresight that is not prophecy but description. This is what it is to improvise.

"The Burton Greene Affair" is a network of desires, a constellation of nonconvergences, the erasure and re-enracure—repetition and variation, passive and active forgetting—of some of modernity's foundational figures (Wittgenstein, Holiday, Eisenstein, Du Bois, Heidegger, Derrida) and of what they resist and repress in the sensing of the temporal and ontological, racial and sexual, other. This resistance and repression is embodied and silently sounded in the music's knowing echo of

shriek and prayer, its reproduction of the out thematics of the transferential ensemble of a known, unknowable origin.

The ensemble of performance that is called "The Burton Greene
Affair" is neither the disappearance of the event nor the disappearance
of any possible product or trace (the record is neither definitive nor
unapparent) nor the dark consciousness—disappearing consciousness or
consciousness of the unapparent or invisible—of the ones who witness
the event: it is, rather, that which disappears the conceptual apparatuses
of identity and difference, singularity and totality. (The *destruktion* of)
that conceptual apparatus is what "The Burton Greene Affair" is after
and is where "The Burton Greene Affair" is at: the turbulent convergence of a deconstruction of the machinery of exclusion and the emergence of a r/evolutionary shift away from that machinery and toward
a radical materialization of spirit whose forces carry Baraka but never
allow in him a divestiture of the exclusionary thinking that he carries.
That thinking is manifest precisely where Baraka establishes an ethos
of violent differentiation by way of essentializing differences—between
east and west, spirit and body, elevation and descent, ecstacy and stasis—
that replicates the (oscillational form of the) ethos and thinking he
would abdure. He does this even while his writing is driven by the
shattering tremble of the improvising ensemble's music. How do we
linger in the ruptural, impossible junction of this reconstructive music
and the *destruktive* lens through which Baraka views it, a ruptural, unbridgeable, asymptotic distance between sight and sound that text
always suspends.[51] Not in the interest of an understanding or adequate
representation of the action whose performance would occur in this
lingering, but in the interest of an enactive invocation, a material
prayer, the dissemination of the conditions of possibility of the action
Baraka's text carries (on and over) by lingering, we need to think a little
bit about improvisation.

Such thinking is opened by an opening movement in Baraka's
work. He has moved on (from here, through that opening), but I want
to call into question the valorization of movement and process, to think
through some of that valorization's more problematic affinities, to

demythologize the durative, to debunk a certain set of transformational wishes, to separate the fact of transition from whatever supposed liberatory significance it is given, to trouble while also pointing out the Euro-philosophical (particularly Heideggerian) parallels to—if not origins of—this valorization of process and to read what will emerge as the valorization of process in the ode to spirit and the ongoing in the blowing of Sanders and Brown with which Baraka's essay concludes.

The critique of the valorization of process is connected to an investigation of the name and author; that critique demands, for instance, that when I refer to the moment and writing and writer of, say, Heidegger's texts, I speak of a particular Heidegger and not of Heidegger in general. Similarly, I must be sure I know whom I mean, which one I mean, when I say, "Roi is dead." I must provisionally honor the Barakan self-portraiture that asserts he was in that place at that time, that particular now, though now he's somewhere else, someplace better, more advanced. I must do so to show that the now and the fact that it is indexed to a particular product and a particular productive persona belie and undermine the valorization of ongoing process. But can we say any more about these moments than we might have said about the trajectory of the career from which they arise? Can I articulate anything about some singular and atomic moment in the history of (what name would I use?) X any more clearly than I give the sense of an ongoing and unfinished project called (again, what name would I use?) X? One could think this all within the context of a certain Wittgensteinian split between phenomenology and physics or an Aristotelian split between *energeia* and *ergon* or a Barakan split between "Hunting" and "Those Heads on the Wall."[52] Finally the impossibility of accurately pinpointing the name of the author and the moment of authorship renders obsolete the temporal arrangements structured around the opposition of the idea of process and the idea of a determinate moment of production in their relation to any possible discernment of the phenomena of text and author, of the experience of transformation, of our access to that experience or to the individual artifacts we might say are artificially thrown off in that process.

Note that even in invoking the specifics of the proper name as a way of marking the internal difference—and thereby undermining the authority—of the author, and even in moving as gingerly as possible through the epistemic field shaped by the punctuated temporality wherein lie the events that correspond with specific names and authors, my work betrays its embeddedness in methods and discourses it would question. I have to hope it goes somewhere out from that questioning's outside. I must confront the strangeness or estrangement of knowing that the project I'm after, which continually projects itself in every temporal and historical direction (like the review or revisioning or envisioned distortion and transformation and extension of an event problematically named "The Burton Greene Affair"), is the project of Enlightenment, "the unfinished project of [a] modernity" taken out or made vicious in the improvisation of ensemble.

"The Burton Greene Affair" bears a dialectical, dialectal stammer.[53] It has a divided articulacy that recalibrates the rhythmic marking of racial difference. We'll note how Baraka sees the ensemble in the interplay of his own representation of Greene's impeded search for materiality (given in the percussiveness of his playing) and Sanders's and Brown's flowing extensions into and of spirit (given in the animation of the horn). The ensemble will have been given in the incompatibilities Baraka projects, in the cut between rhythms, between syntagmic order and eventual break; ensemble will have been heard in the arrhythmia that separates these rhythms. As such it is the entity whose apprehension demands the improvisation through any prior notions of ontology, epistemology, and ethics. That apprehension requires an interest in the nature of improvisation's time and the time of ensemble's organization. These interests have in turn required an attempt to become more aware of the place of ensemble in this very writing, to sustain the desire that you anticipate, that you'll have felt even now, to stop, to look up, to sing the inscription. Something in that desire feels like it might reach the implicate order that holds fragments and ellipses and aphorisms as breaks in a background; that holds things that are neither local nor copresent together so that you don't need to justify any attention—in the name of justice and freedom—to the ensemble that appears as the juxtaposition of traditions, idioms, authors, genres, grammars, sounds. Another kind of rigorous expression of something like feeling.

First Heidegger, then Baraka, then Heidegger again, 1966:

> Everything is functioning. That is precisely what is awesome, that every-thing functions, that the functioning propels everything more and more toward further functioning, and that technicity increasingly dislodges man and uproots him from the earth. I don't know if you were shocked, but [certainly] I was shocked when a short time ago I saw the pictures of the earth taken from the moon. We do not need atomic bombs at all [to uproot us]—the uprooting of man is already here. All our relationships have become merely technical ones. It is no longer upon an earth that man lives today. . . . As far as my own orientation goes, in any case, I know that, according to our human experience and history, everything essential and of great magnitude has arisen only out of the fact that man had a home and was rooted in a tradition.[54]

> In order for the non-white world to assume control, it must transcend the technology that has enslaved it. But the expressive and instinctive (nat-ural) reflection that characterizes black art and culture, listen to these players, transcends any emotional state (human realization) the white man knows. I said elsewhere, "Feeling predicts intelligence."[55]

> Only a god can save us. The only possibility available to us is that by thinking and poetizing we prepare a readiness for the appearance of a god, or for the absence of a god in [our] decline, insofar as in view of the absent god we are in a state of decline.[56]

By the time "The Burton Greene Affair" was written, also in 1966, the structural possibilities of jazz improvisation had undergone a revolu-tion. In *Free Jazz* Ekkehard Jost writes, a new type of group improvisation emerges in which melodic-motivic evolution gives way to the molding of a total sound. For Ornette Coleman the various parts have an intellectual influence on one another, resulting in a collective conversation; for Cecil Taylor the collective is mainly led by one player who acts in accordance with constructivist principles; for the later Coltrane, particularly *Ascension*, the macro-structures of the total sound are more important than the individual microparts.[57]

He adds that

in solos there is a gradual emancipation of timbre from pitch that leads to a-melodic structures delineated by changes in color and register. This kind of playing is more easily connected to a kind of expression of emotionalism.[58]

Jost's final formulation returns, again and again, seemingly eternally, as a critical lens through which black art and thinking have been obscured. For now, it is important to argue again that what occurs in the New Black Music of the sixties—indeed what occurs throughout the short and accelerated history of the music *as the music's historicity*—is the emergence of an art and thinking in which emotion and structure, preparation and spontaneity, individuality and collectivity can no longer be understood in opposition to one another. Rather the art itself resists any interpretation in which these elements are opposed, resists any designation, even those of the artists themselves, that depends upon such oppositions. The primary problems here are that these oppositions can all be indexed to two others that move within a kind of mutual primordiality—that between improvisational composition and that between black and white. The question is whether the discourse that surrounds the music gets to the liberatory space the music opens. These oppositions form the conceptual apparatus Baraka uses to represent the music, but there is something in Baraka's language that remains unbounded by that representational-calculative thinking, something that places it under an immanent critique. That something is improvisation itself. It is, finally, precisely that motion that is free of the systematic oscillation that begins and ends at the illusion of the originary, the primordial—the systematic oscillation that, therefore, never ends.

When Baraka split—from the Village, from the house, from interracial "romance" and (black) "bohemian" lifestyle, from other, former selves (in)to other, new ones—he attempted (by way of a complex "return") to move away from a particular structure of thought. He did so at a time when Third World national liberation was already being engulfed in the emergent neocolonial formations of global capitalism; engulfed, then, in a certain economic world picture in which the dual motion of fragmentation and homogenization, exclusionary differentiation and metaphysical sameness, are evident in the world and in the ideology that informs Baraka's text. Baraka's particular form of nationalism emerges alongside a liberatory consciousness whose decline is already encoded in the particulars of that emergence. Indeed, the nationalism Baraka embraces is, in some fundamental ways, a remnant or trace of the (philosophical) tradition he would abdure. Yet Baraka is not reducible to nationalism and therefore his anachronism is double. He's after and before nationalism as a nascent revolutionary ethics of response (rather than a politics or even a culturalism that bears political resistance only as a legitimizing trace), though this is what he would have the music enact and signify. What Frantz Fanon theorizes in *Black Skins, White Masks* as the encounter with the other as racially resistant fascination is what Baraka hears and would amplify, transmit, or shape from "The Burton Greene Affair." He wants to transform the ensemble and its performance into an internally fragmented reenactment of an originary and tragic encounter that would parallel the dramatic content of recordings that animate his trajectory throughout the early sixties as a set of transitions prefatory to an impossible return. Baraka's black and Heideggerian nationalism comes as response to European technicity's violent forgetting of spirit and origin. The thing is that the music, which would manifest the interinanimation of race, spirit, origin, and freedom along with the exemplary revolutionary ethics of the objectifying encounter with otherness (which is supposed to reverse the direction of fit both between lord and bondsman and within the im/possible consciousness of the bondsman alone), obliterates the ethical, ontological, and epistemological conceptual apparatuses upon which the manifestation of these complexes depends. As we'll see, the music wouldn't do what Baraka wanted it to do; nevertheless he's carried along by it, perhaps in that self-same way that Greene is carried along by it, into a whole other thing, a whole other understanding of the cut between and within which freedom and identity might articulate one another, a cut shaped in the interminable constitution and reconstitution of a kind of knowledge to which conventional philosophies of Enlightenment and opposition to Enlightenment have no access.

So what Baraka says about Burton Greene, that he is being driven by forces that he neither understands nor assimilates, is also true of himself. What occurs in "The Burton Greene Affair" occurs not only with but through Baraka—the improvisational force of ensemble occurs through him, in spite of him. More specifically, what occurs moves by way of some operations given at a specific moment in the development of Baraka's ontology. All the collective and improvisational resources, all the unresolvable contradictions, of modern European ontological language resonate—as the transmission of the sound of the ensemble—in Baraka's philosophical voice, most clearly in the utterance (of "being") that would name, describe, formalize, and therefore obfuscate the ensemble in the spirit of an other tradition, one that would read, reflect, and transcend the interinanimation of being, language, race, and (the crisis of European) humanity. "The Burton Greene Affair" arrives at this moment in the world: when the restructuring of capitalism dislocates nation and origin and when such dislocation is sped along by global and globalizing technicity that secures, finally, the literal formulation of a "world picture" that constitutes the final degradation of the illusory prefigurations of Enlightenment cosmopolitanism. At this moment, in their appeals to nation and origin and in their relative inability to think an alternative world picture, Baraka and Heidegger sound alike even in the sharp differences of their circumstances, motivations, and utterances.

These utterances are sexual. With and against his invocations, the sexual cut still animates Amiri Baraka's "The Burton Greene Affair." The essay is situated where eros meets ontology, and when Baraka's text resonates with what Derrida calls "the vibration of grammar in the voice," we know that an old attraction to the interplay of division and collection is at work as the animating force of a new symposium, an underground set and brokedown gathering, the ensemble of the black avant-garde disrupted by the racial difference that shapes it.[59] This vibration, an improvisational movement, resonance of the sound of (the) ensemble, is neither essentialized nor differentiated, determined neither by the vernacular nor its originary other nor the interminable and systematic opposition and oscillation between the two. Charting that grammar requires more attention to the question of sex—where what appears as the absence of the formulation of sex is thought as in relation to what appears as the presence of the formulation of race—and to the particularities of Baraka's comportment toward that question. Baraka's comportment in "The Burton Greene Affair" is Heideggerian. His refracted and repressed address of the question of sex repeats with differences the method of Heidegger's dismissal of that question.

In "*Geschlecht:* Sexual Difference, Ontological Difference,"[60] Derrida notes the barely incomplete avoidance of sex in Heidegger's analytic, an avoidance unfinished by the presence of a moment in *Being and Time*[61] when Heidegger argues that *Dasein* (the being to whom understandings of being are given and who is not but nothing other than man) "is neither of the two sexes."[62] For Derrida, this is the formulation of an "asexuality [that] is not the indifference of an empty nothing, the feeble negativity of an indifferent ontic nothing. In its neutrality *Dasein* is not just anyone no matter who but the originary positivity and power of essence."[63] This unsexed mode of being that Heidegger decrees is echoed and translated by the more complete silence of (the question of) sex in "The Burton Greene Affair." For Baraka the mode of being of blackness and its expression in the music is heard in the silence of sex's supposed absence. Of course an abundance of work across a wide array of discourses has shown that any absent or indifferent sexuality, any mode of being that is before sexual difference, is, in fact, originarily and rigorously sexed. In the cases of Baraka and Heidegger the opening of the question of being's meaning, truth, essence, is sexed in a way to which they are practically blind though they see quite clearly that opening's racial, cultural, spiritual, linguistic, and aesthetic determinations. That opening is the location of a mode of being determined by (the thinking of) *Geschlecht* (the locus of differences that is itself differentiated, the structure determined by what it occludes—by an absence, an unrepresentable silence, the unheard voice that utters and is uttered by [the question of] sex).

One could say that sex is what lies secret and unheard in the work of Heidegger. In "The Burton Greene Affair" this unheard secret is a threat of difference at the heart of the music—which is to say the mode of being—of blackness. This threat to itself that black music carries is in Baraka's phonography as well. It is, in fact, the very opening, the very condition of possibility, of Baraka's recording, invocation, and analysis of the ensemble. As ante-analytic resonance it resists the deathly fragmentation of Baraka's analysis even as it animates his nothing-other-than-analytic idiom. This opening of (the) ensemble, of that which is neither represented nor unrepresentable but improvised in and as Baraka's grammar and sound, is precisely what is unheard in the oppositional structure of what is, for Heidegger, philosophical truth, *aletheia*, unconcealment. The music, the sexual cut, is what remains unheard by philosophy—by the mode of attention allowed by the philosophical distinctions between essence and contingency, individuality and collectivity, particularity and universality—but the music is also precisely what is heard and improvised in philosophy. It is that which avoids not sex but what Samuel Beckett calls "the spirit of system."[64] It is what Derrida attempts to isolate and describe as that which operates, but is uncontained, within a system of determination and indetermination:

> What is involved in the phonographic act? Here's an interpretation, one among others. At each syllable, even at each silence, a decision is imposed: it was not always deliberate, nor sometimes even the same from one

repetition to the other. And what it signs is neither the law nor the truth. Other interpretations remain possible—and doubtless necessary. Thus we analyze the resource this double text affords us today: on the one hand, a graphic space opened to multiple readings, in the traditional and protected form of the book—and it is not like a libretto, because each time it gives a different reading, another gift, dealing out a new hand all over again—but on the other hand, simultaneously, and also for the first time, we have the tape recording of a singular interpretation, made one day, by so on and so forth, at a single stroke calculated and by chance.[65]

What we have in "The Burton Greene Affair" is not a mechanical recording—nothing so seemingly determined and nothing in which another voice as singularity in and out of the constellation of *Geschlecht* shows up. In what appears as the absence of the recording—which is to say in the field of its resistance—singularity is given over to a division and abundance whose distillate is the sound of the ensemble.

Meanwhile, in *Cinders* Derrida's ensemble writes, which is to say speaks, of the impossible possibility of the mark's copresence with the effacement of the *accent grave* in the letter "a" as it is used in *la*, the "there."[66] This im/possibility is, finally, exactly what the improvisation of (the) ensemble gives us: not the Ellisonian oscillation between the establishment and disestablishment of (the) identity (of the soloist) within a systematic tension between individual and group, individual and tradition; and not as an ensemble immediately foreclosed and fragmented as it is submitted to exclusionary determinations of the social. This dual movement is what Derrida desires, though that desire is exceeded: the motion and structure of a truth whose revelation has at its heart an originary concealment, an originary betrayal; a moment where the voice of an absolute other is unheard so that the voices of the others can be heard is not all that is given.

For this motion is always caught within a philosophical in/determination—the voice of the other and the voices of the others are always, ultimately, only the possibilities of abstract singularities and particularities even when they are to provide a necessary antidote to the abstract generalities of a given Enlightenment. The point, however, is to maintain neither an abstract notion of universal humanity nor the abstract particularity of a racial or gendered other—the point is to develop discursive and practical organizational assaults on the concrete effects of these abstractions. What Baraka's improvisation on the music offers, despite the determination of race and the indetermination of sex, is both attempted closure and initializing embrace, and Baraka's sound and grammar, improvising through the attempt to decompose the ensemble through an interpretation of its anarchic time, is the resonance of an iconic totality to be heard only in the direction of a response to the question of sex. Sex, here, is not the mark of a particular exclusion conceived of as woman or the feminine. What is excluded, ultimately, is not the mark of an abstract other but ensemble. What is opened here is not the possibility of an other voice but the question of sex and the sexuality and generativity of philosophical questioning that inheres in the exclusionary fragmentation of totality. And what is opened in the question of sex and interpretation is the possibility of a total, improvisational and anarchic voicing.

We'll arrive at such voicing by way of an aspectual-ethical paradox:

> And these moves, most times unconscious (until, maybe, I'd look over something I'd just written and whistle, "Yow, yeh, I'm way over there, huh?"), seem to me to have been always toward the thing I had coming into the world, with no sweat: my blackness.

> To get there, from anywhere, going wherever, always. By the time this book appears, I will be even blacker.[67]

Arrival as end and process is articulated along with and through the distinction between being and having, essence and quality. Baraka writes himself as that which he already had, though what he already had is placed on a differential scale as if he could become more of what he already is, as if that movement—totally determined—had no determinate end. In *From LeRoi Jones to Amiri Baraka*, Theodore Hudson quotes the lines above (from the introduction to *Home*, a collection of essays that chronicle Baraka's non/return to "origins" in writing, through writing) but doesn't dwell on the contradiction they embody. We ought to linger in the cut between the "origin" and "end" that is signified by the nominal poles of Hudson's title; in, more precisely, the German inversion placed between LeRoi Jones and Amiri Baraka—"Johannes Koenig," a pseudonym Baraka uses for some texts of his in *The Floating Bear* (a magazine he coedited for a time in the mid-1960s with Diane di Prima) that has an important suggestiveness.[68] For one could make an argument that this is the proper name of the author of "The Burton Greene Affair": the name of the imaginary native of an imaginary return, the provisional name of the real native whose real return will have always been deferred, the name that marks a highly localized habitation as the site of a transition to an unreachable home. Note that this structure of deferral is part of what is shown in "The Burton Greene Affair," though, again, it's not reducible to this internal deconstruction. "Johannes Koenig" is, finally, a signpost that marks a certain position in the history of Baraka's understanding of identity—as well as a certain moment in his own oscillation between identities. From that position, in that moment, Baraka enters and transforms a long, historical meditation on the music and its relation to artistic, emotional, and finally political freedom. That's why it's important to have asked: what is the meaning and the implication of freedom in black music, what will have been the implications of the idea of freedom in the music for Jones/Koenig/Baraka as he changes, and what, finally, will freedom have had to do with (black) identity?

There is ambivalence present in the title of *The Autobiography of LeRoi Jones by Amiri Baraka* and, in a different way, in *From LeRoi Jones to Amiri Baraka*. This ambivalence—rather this nonconvergence of designation—of the name marks a valorization of process, transformation, and motion that signifies much in the political and racial ontologies I want to see ahead of or before; it raises a question—Who is the author of "The Burton Greene Affair"?—that must be placed alongside that which "The Burton Greene Affair" raises and that had been and continues to be a primary guide: What is the agency that activates the text called "The Burton Greene Affair" and that event/performance/ritual that we know only by the name "The Burton Green Affair"? So much of what the essay does is in the interest of denying authority for, in and/or over the event to the one known that night in Newark as Burton Greene, the one in whom authority is paradoxically vested by the essay's act of naming.

So the author of "The Burton Greene Affair" might very well be (named) Johannes Koenig, an identification in between or off to the side of LeRoi Jones and Amiri Baraka under which appears some dense and intense phenomenologico-lyric investigations into the nature of being and its manifestation in poetic language. That name carries the trace of the German in the way that "The Burton Greene Affair" carries the trace of the particular Heideggerian brand of German philosophical nationalism that animates Koenig's brief texts. Perhaps then one could say that Johannes Koenig is the name that marks a cut between names and is the structure that would but doesn't bridge the space between identities. It is not a point of intersection or one-to-one transfer but a generative nonsuspension. It's the mark of an improvisation shaped by the field of nonconvergence that we might call the Amiri Baraka Ensemble, featuring LeRoi Jones. It's the sound heard in the descent into that immeasurable and impossible distance between affairs. If Johannes Koenig were the eponymous recording, echo, or backward sound of an otherwise unavailable Burton Greene experience, then we could place him in another tradition, of the self-analytic improvisation of philosophical nationalism, of a philosophical nationalist auto-critique or self-deconstruction infused with the desire for another freedom. (This is the tradition—wherein certain animative shrieks and moans echo everywhere, in the sound of horns, just as masterful percussive beating marks Greene's time; and Baraka, in a powerful tradition, cannot keep them distinct; the vibrating grammar in the voice is a sexual grammar, a sexual cut, a sexual differentiation of sexual, which is to say racial and national, difference—of the otherwise excluded racial/sexual other shattering the imago of an incomplete and static "universality" given as Universality.)

This is where these explanatory and exploratory identities keep missing each other. But there is something in and where they miss each other. Nevertheless, how do we account for the name change and the change that change would signify? Is it objective or a projection of the subjective experience of a reader (even Baraka as the most privileged reader, the one who looks upon "his" own work retrospectively and with surprise, with both attachment and detachment, always after the fact of the work or the process that engenders or produces it)? Are LeRoi Jones, Johannes Koenig, Amiri Baraka three separate entities or personae or is there an essence or essential mode of being that exists as the condition of possibility of these beings, that gives them to us and to each other? (Note that these are only three of the names by which this phenomenon—interaction of man and work or text—is called.) When I read Baraka, am I *reading* an aspect in a way that is similar to Wittgenstein's noticing an aspect? Is the logical structure of one name, in another Wittgensteinian phenomenon, identical to the others and to that to which they refer? Even if I say that the name of the author doesn't matter, that the author's persona doesn't matter, I still remain intensely and primarily interested in the agency that generates the text; and, of course, the name of the text itself refers to another questionable naming or name. Why "The Burton Greene Affair"? The point is that the importance of the name persists and is unavoidable especially since I am, in the end, deeply concerned not only with the agency that generates but with the author of "The Burton Greene Affair." I've got to improvise through all the names in the ensemble (this is part of the preface, the cut between, the transition from LeRoi Jones to Johannes Koenig to Amiri Baraka and marks, would bridge, that cut; but just like the way home seems to go through Germany, like the way back to the ground of metaphysics is a middle passage, like the way back to Afro-spirit is through *Geist* and *anima* in spite of the invocations of the east, the way back to Euro-spirit is scored with the boom of an other rhythm).

Ensemble is and requires attunement not only to the name but to the phrase.[69] The task of developing that attunement is given to us by "The

Burton Greene Affair"; by the illusion of singularity and the illusion of its plurals' intersections and divergences; by the myth of the crossroads at which would be played the drama of the negative, of differentiation and relation, of an impulse to name and represent. That which would be named—the sound of the structure and agency that is improvisation—is that which the crossroads only figures: the ensemble. Ensemble.

Such attunement requires concern with the uses of a few words and the structures and effects of a few practices in "The Burton Greene Affair." Such concern is shaped by the fact that in attempts to name and describe reality through a particular naming and description of a part of reality, the structure of philosophical thinking intervenes and leads inevitably toward a conceptualization of the interplay of what is and what is not contained in the word "being." To read "The Burton Greene Affair" is to be struck by that intervention and its errancy: description and naming become something wholly other—an effect heightened by the concern with being that marks the work, a concern that carries with it not only something of the history of such concern but something also of the enduring inability to *activate* a forgetfulness of being. Baraka's language prompts that concern, a concern that is of and for language, of and for the proper placement in sound and breath of fundamental questions.

"The Burton Greene Affair" strains toward what Wittgenstein calls "ostensive gestures." Such gestures would perform a showing that—in the very interstices of the verbal naming and description of (an) ensemble and its music—get at what is essential. But this performance gestures toward a performance that its medium—language—cannot capture and therefore improvisationally records. It thereby joins—which is not to say completes but is, rather, to say rupturally augments—this performance of (the) ensemble that is (the) ensemble. This complex, compound performance is not simple though it is unanalyzable; Baraka's corrosive analysis cannot perform the breakdown it intends. It only scars its object, thereby renewing the demand to think again about what kind of object (the) ensemble is. In the meantime, Baraka's performance (phono)graphs what had seemed impossible to say: that the ostensive gesture is not a simple pointing to what is simply present, that it implies no simple relation between word and world. It is, rather, a resonance in language of what is essential to its object. In such a gesture, through its performance, the name and the description disseminate what Baraka sees and hears as the essence of the ensemble. The dissemination occurs by way of open analytic failure (the breakdown of the breakdown) and by way of a kind of recapitulative improvisation (a lingering in the iconic break of this double breakdown). *This resistance to analysis that is carried out in and by the complexity of the object is everything.* It occurs in the break, the sexual cut, between simple naming and complex description, both of which are rendered impossible by the object in its complexity. The distinction between the object that would be named and the musical—which is to say organized—compound no longer performs. This performatively induced nonperformance occurs within and as a chain of differences and modalities—totalizing systems and exclusionary singularities—that are embedded in "The Burton Greene Affair" as both name and description.[70]

In *Philosophical Grammar*, Wittgenstein makes the following formulation regarding ostensive gestures:

> The correlation of an object and a name is generated by nothing but a table, by ostensive gestures at the same time as the name is uttered, or by something familiar.[71]

This formulation, given here in Merril B. and Jaakko Hintikka's slight modification of Anthony Kenny's translation, is quoted just after the following passage in their *Investigating Wittgenstein*:

> Wittgenstein's mysterious-sounding idea of *showing* has to be understood in an almost literal sense. Since the simple objects of the *Tractatus* have to be given to us for our language to make sense, we cannot say in language that some particular simple object exists. Nor can its essence be expressed in language, because that would enable us to get around the impossibility of expressing its existence. For we could then say that it exists by saying

that these essential properties are in fact exemplified. As Wittgenstein puts it in *Philosophical Remarks*, IX, sec. 94:

> There is a sense in which an object may not be described. That is, the description may ascribe to it no property whose absence would reduce the existence of the object to nothing, i.e. the description may not express what would be essential to the existence of the object.

How, then, can we introduce a simple object into our discourse? Wittgenstein's answer is: by showing it.[72]

In short, according to Wittgenstein, simple objects cannot be named and described in language; they must be, by way of some extralinguistic gesture, shown. And yet this showing must not only be introduced into discourse, but constitutes the very foundation of discourse. As the Hintikkas put it, these objects "have to be given to us for our language to make sense."

What I'm after here is this: the linguistic problems that the simple objects of Wittgenstein's *Tractatus* pose are not wholly unlike those that are posed by complex objects such as Burton Greene, the ensemble that bears his name, and the other members of that ensemble. It is already unorthodox to speak of complex objects by way of Wittgenstein. His later work is, in part, an attempt to diagnose that mental state that seems to be manifest as an engagement with the ontologically and temporally complex object *in its impossibility*. But I do so because Baraka is operating within another political and philosophical tradition, one structured by the exigencies of the complex object. Like the simple objects of Wittgenstein's philosophy, the complex objects of this other tradition resist naming and description, but by way, naturally, of a more complex orientation. The task of "The Burton Greene Affair" is framed by and within this other tradition in its encounter with the tradition of the same, in its propriation of the same's tradition's terms and conceptual apparatuses. That task—moving before the one who enacts it, as the trace of an "ontological totality" in excess of this flat description and of any proper or improper name—is to show or record the ensemble by way of failure of language and to encrypt that failure in the text as (the representation of) Greene's failure. Encryption moves by way of a description that is nothing less than ascription. The ensemble, the complex object, bears a property—Burton Greene—whose absence would, rather than reduce the object to nothing, somehow bring the existence of the object fully to itself in something that is not but nothing other than a kind of (racial, spiritual) simplicity. Ultimately, the difference between the impossibility of bringing simple objects into discourse and the achievement of complex objects' irruption into discourse is the difference between ostension and improvisation. Ostension is an enactment on the other side of linguistic failure; improvisation is sounding in linguistic failure.

Meanwhile, Baraka's description of the ensemble and its music oscillates between the languages of the physical and the phenomenal, the punctual and the durative, count and mass; and he falls into the traps of the systemic operations these distinctions delimit. He describes within physical language in order to phenomenalize, differentializes in order to essentialize, systematically reducing the ensemble that it might be atomized. There is at the end of the essay the final abstraction of Burton Greene from the ensemble so that Sanders and Brown will have continued; their sound, become durative in the performance of blackness, will have gone "on and on." The trouble is that the removal (or, perhaps more precisely, the dematerialization) of the object—embodied and enacted in the artifactual aesthetic manifest for Baraka in the playing of Greene—in the name of the phenomenal is part of a designation only to be made in the language of the physical object, a language inadequate to Baraka's own construction of (black) "being's" phenomenality.[73] Meanwhile, the ensemble—the complex phenomenal object—is what asserts itself at the moment when phenomenon and object each appear in and as the eclipse of the other.

Heidegger's determination of "being" comes within the thinking of race, nation, spirit, and tradition and in a language that is echoed with difference throughout Baraka's work of the 1960s. But Baraka's work is much more than either a repetition or an overturning of Heidegger's. Baraka moves along a more than philosophical trajectory "The Burton Greene Affair" precisely because the sound of the ensemble is still to be heard, improvising *through* the motion of ontology, through the same of Heidegger and the repetition and difference of Baraka. That I can call the sound of the music a movement through ontological questioning brings us to an other and overwhelming question: what is the nature of ontology, its structures and effects, in the black radical traditions Baraka inhabits and extends? First, there is the largely unacknowledged fact that the traditions speak ontologically, that is to say, metaphysically. Heidegger's words about what he calls "Occidental-European thought" might easily be applied to Baraka's text and to all of the tradition(s) it voices and pierces:

> But if we recall once again the history of Occidental-European thought, then we see that the question about Being, taken as a question about the Being of the existent, is double in form. It asks on the one hand: What is the existent, in general, as existent? Considerations within the province of this question come, in the course of the history of philosophy, under the heading of ontology. The question "What is the existent?" includes also the question, "Which existent is the highest and how does it exist?" The question is about the divine and God. The province of this question is called theology. The duality of the question about the Being of the existent can be brought together in the title "onto-theo-logy." The twofold question, What is the existent? asks on the one hand, What is (in general) the existent? The question asks on the other hand, What (which one) is the (absolute) existent?[74]

Baraka's dual question in "The Burton Greene Affair" is this: What is the being of the music? What is the highest being of the music? Here we shift again, back to Heidegger, but with this dual realization: that question of black ontology can't be asked as if it were located in the course of a particular or "vernacular" separate from that of the "Occident";

that the question of the nature of Occidental ontology cannot be asked as if that nature were located in a realm in which the sound of the music—of Algeria, say, or Harlem or Tutwiler—is inaudible. Baraka begins by moving in the direction from being to (a mode of) being. How does that move work, what does its motion signify? What is its status with regard to what is seen as a difference in traditions? This is a problematic described clearly by Edmund Husserl:

> [The mathematical disciplines] are "deductive" sciences and that means that in their scientifically theoretical mode of development mediate deductive knowledge plays an incomparably greater part than the immediate axiomatic knowledge upon which all the deductions are based. An infinitude of deductions rests on a very few axioms.
>
> But in the transcendental sphere we have an infinitude of knowledge previous to all deduction, knowledge whose mediated connexions (those of intentional implication) have nothing to do with deduction, and Being entirely intuitive prove refractory to every methodically devised scheme of constructive symbolism.[75]

What does Baraka have to do with these questions? "What is the quality of your Being?" Baraka begins within a certain ontological commitment and within a certain ontological questioning. What is the status, within this commitment and questioning, of Burton Greene? Baraka would use "being" to name something that cannot be named. As Derrida says, "There is no unique word for being."[76] There is, rather, the complex origin of quantification, differences, formalizations. Heidegger and Baraka, however, search for the unique word, the essence, the meaning, the essential quality of "being." What lies between the desire for and the absence of the unique word for being? Does the absence of the unique word for being mean that being is not? The space between the word and what that word would signify is the space of a deferral. In that deferral, Baraka reinfuses being with *anima* and spirit, thus reversing the distinction between *animalitas* and *Geist* that Heidegger deploys. Can we align *anima*, as differentiated from spirit, with improvisation without that differentiation *within the human* of the human from the animal that seems to inhabit Heidegger's and Baraka's particular understandings of spirit? What, then, is the connection between *animalitas* and rhythm? Baraka improvises a holistic understanding of the nondifference of *humanitas* and *animalitas*, but follows, in a Heideggerian vein, with an infusion of *Geist* into *humanitas* that banishes *anima/litas* and differentiates, all in the quest for being's proper name. Baraka uses the discourse of animality to dehumanize Greene, a discourse marked by race and rhythm, though he criticizes that discourse as it applies to blacks in the very same essay.

The performance, for Baraka, is therefore not simply (or even primarily) the existence of the sound, of what he hears as sound; it is rather the unmediated performance of essential blackness (and whiteness) that is made apparent in the difference between sounds (here lies its "meaning" in the semiotic frame). That difference is spiritual, racial, temporal: it is the different silence that occurs when one sound goes on and the other does not go on. Foucault writes that "Mallarmé taught us that the word is the manifest non-existence of what it designates; we now know that the Being of language is the visible effacement of the one who speaks."[77] Baraka would have the being—that is to say the highest being—of the music efface the player who, in his view, is the voice of an outside, an other tradition. But his text does not *do*, his text does not *be*, the effacement of the sound of (any necessarily necessary member of) the ensemble. It would not designate in a way that effaces any aspect of its materiality. What Baraka *would* do is turn the sound of music into meaning and the sound of Burton Greene's playing into absence.

Can Burton Greene—in the reconfigured space between being and beings, Being and its word—be effaced without the effacement of the ensemble in general? Can Burton Greene be abstracted from the music? Perhaps, finally, and to return to the beginning yet again, the answer to these questions is to be found in the question of the name: "The Burton Greene Affair." In that name is the mark of the governance of the empty center, the thought of Baraka's outside. These are questions of history—in the language (of ensemble) and in the music. These are questions of tradition to be sounded and collected within the aurality of a radical vision, as the improvisation *of* Enlightenment and *through* its other.

As trembling, hear the speed of Baraka's narrative, the rhythm— barely regulated by the comma, the bar line, the pause—free most especially at the moment of the most severe quantification, atomizing, and differentialization of "being," that which is done in the name of the phenomenon of "being." What is the motion of our breathing through this passage? How are its rhythms determined and undetermined by the metaphysics of breath, of spirit—note that sound and content here are combined and divergent, for the rhythm frees as the meaning restricts; the rhythm frees what the rhythm would contradict:

> In the beautiful writhe of the black spirit-energy sound the whole cellar was possessed and animated. Things flew through the air.
>
> Burton Greene, at one point, began to bang aimlessly at the keyboard. He was writhing, too, pushed by forces he could not use or properly assimilate. He kept running his fingers compulsively through his hair.
>
> Finally he stood above the piano . . . the music around him flying . . . and began to strike the piano strings with his fingers and knock on the wood of the instrument. He got a drumstick to make it louder. (Green's "style" is pointed, I would presume, in the direction of Cecil Taylor, and I would also suppose, with Taylor the Euro-American Tudor-Cage, Stockhausen-Wolf-Cowell-Feldman interpretations.)
>
> But the sound he made would not do, was not where the other sound was. He beat the piano, began to slam it open and shut slapping the front and side and top of the box. The sound would not do, would not be what the other sound was.
>
> He sat again and doodled, he slumped his head. He ran his fingers desultorily across the keys. Pharoah and Marion still surged; they still went on screaming us into spirit.
>
> Burton Greene got up again. A sudden burst like at an offending organism he struck out again at the piano. . . . he beat and slammed and pummeled it. (The wood.) He hit it with his fist.
>
> Finally he sprawled on the floor, under the piano, shadow knocking

on the piano bottom, on his elbows he tapped, tapped furiously then sub-sided to a soft flap, bap bap then to silence, he slumped to quiet his head under his arm and the shadow of the piano.

Pharoah and Marion were still blowing. The beautiful sound went on and on.[78]

Here is the absolute reification of the difference between breath and pulse, figured in the end of an affair whose beginning cannot be read but through that end. Greene's percussion signifies the fall from spirit to time, from aspect to tense, from duration to punctuation, in "the degradation of an original temporalization into a temporality that is separated into different levels, inauthentic, improper."[79] That sound is overwhelmed by the emergence and endurance of the primordial aspi-ration, "the beautiful sound." Is this Heidegger or Baraka? Baraka, though the sound of "the east" is given its value within a Heideggerian appropriation of the idea of the primordial and within a Heidegger-like integration of aestheticism, nationalism, spirit, and primordiality that reduces the phenomenon of being to a mode, a case, an object, *a* being. Sound, as the emanation of the highest form of being, is given its value through the replication of Heidegger's sense of being's modalities, a sense he sees as bound to the very essence of what it is to be European. So, for Heidegger, to be is to be, finally, and within the inevitable re-duction to a singularist, antiphenomenological mode, a thing, a definite thing, a *European* thing, perhaps even, at the end of this declension, European Man. And, for Baraka, caught within the framing power of Heideggerian language, a power that transcends the desire of and for the opposite, to be is (ultimately, and as Paolo Freire might say) to be like. Nevertheless, in Baraka and in Heidegger, there is a remainder, one to be formalized through and beyond the optic of *différance*.

Here we come upon the crucial question concerning designation and representation of and in the music. It must be asked in view of the overwhelming and radical *present* of the performance, its existence within a deictic mark that shapes its otherness in space and time with regard to critico-ontological reflection such that "the beautiful sound," the mark of black spirit and phenomenality, is ultimately reduced to European antispirit and objecthood, by the fact that it *has gone* on and on. The music is in the past—as designation, representation, artwork, thing—though what it would designate and represent, for Baraka, is the progressive acting and essencing of black art working and (black—which is to say true) "being." Still there is that in the music that transcends the bounds of deixis and the ineluctably reductive systematicity of the opposition of phenomenon and object. It is that which gives the present of the music duration in Baraka's work. These are questions of time—in the language and in the music. These are questions of rhythm that are to be heard and improvised in the percussive aspiration of the very word "being" that animates the music of Baraka and Greene like a buried but radioactive and radiophonic chant.

Imagine that the buried, repressed cantor is Cecil Taylor, who will have emerged as the central—if practically absent—presence of "The Burton Greene Affair" and an indispensable figure in the massively erotic, re-en-gendered and re-en-gendering blackness of the 1960's New York avant-garde. His name briefly appears in Baraka's essay as that which Greene either hopes to or actually does arrive at.[80] Indeed, Baraka's ambivalence toward Taylor is much of what "The Burton Greene Affair" is about and that ambivalence is not just about whether Taylor, and, for that matter, any European-influenced black artist like, say, Baraka is black enough, a black enough man, a manly enough black man. This is to say that this sexual, racial, national ambivalence is also a political ambivalence, one in which ensemble and its experience continually emerge, in which the sense of the whole comes out precisely in the representation and transmission of a certain transportation. That transportation disrupts the exclusionary totalizations, the murders, that Baraka's poetic intends. Carrying on, here, is bound up with being carried off, with being carried away by something fundamentally unassimilable. Baraka would represent this transport as a kind of failure. Elsewhere, for instance in the figure of Lady Day, the willingness to fail was held by him as an object of praise. Here, that willingness, in its very dismissal, becomes the vehicle whose animative force allows a descent at once self-induced and involuntary. So that "The Burton Greene Affair"—which is to say both Baraka's essay and the event from which that essay claims its name—is an occasion for experimental, if not elemental, volition, for the generative expression of the black outside in all of its dissonant and fantastical sight and sound.

'Round the Five Spot

The flipside of fetishistic white hipsterism's recourse to black authenticity is a white avant-gardism whose seriousness requires either an active forgetting of black performances or a relegation of them to mere source material. So the hipsterism that Andrew Ross both critiques and enacts, especially but not exclusively in "Hip, and the Long Front of Color," is best understood in its relation to a kind of vanguardist counterpoint exemplified by Sally Banes in her *Greenwich Village, 1963: Avant-Garde Performance and the Effervescent Body.*[81] Interest in the history and theory of the avant-garde in black performance demands that one be more concerned with the b-side than the a-side of this now standard recording. This is to say that I'm willing to deal with, to observe, and even to participate in a little hipsterism in the interest of a more accurate account.

This account will emerge not only out of experiences of black performances; but even if it did, it would be something way more than an "earthy corrective" either of the idea of the avant-garde or of some consumptive, bohemian rapture. The opposition between earthiness and rapture is authored by Ross. The ones who stand in for these qualities are Amiri Baraka and Frank O'Hara, respectively. Ross invokes Baraka, then LeRoi Jones, in the interest of correcting what he sees as the anomalously clichéd descent into hipsterism that characterizes O'Hara's most well-known poem "The Day Lady Died."[82] The "earthy corrective" to the clichéd fetishization of blackness is, necessarily, black. This is to say that Baraka's black earthiness is invoked by Ross to counter O'Hara's necessarily inauthentic recourse to authenticity. The authentic recourse to authenticity, here, belongs to Ross. But I'm not here to dismiss what seems to me nothing if not a "new" kind of critical hipsterism. Rather, I'm willing to abide with such hipsterism in the interest of what it affords beyond such regressiveness. However, I do want to mark the distinction between O'Hara's and Ross's hipsterism in the interest of invoking both as correctives of the rather less hip Banes, to whom we'll return. This invocation must question the opposition of earthiness and rapture. That opposition contains the traces of some others: most obviously, black and white; authenticity and commodification is another, perhaps somewhat less obvious; the least obvious, though I guess it's not all that hidden either, is straight and gay.

Earthiness is given, for Ross, in this line from Baraka's poem "Jitterbugs": "though yr mind is somewhere else, your ass ain't." Ross claims that

> Baraka is addressing himself more to the contradictions of ghetto life than to those of the white bohemian in ritual thrall to the spectacle of jazz performance, but his tone here might serve as an earthy corrective to the rapt mood of O'Hara's last stanza.[83]

So earthiness resides here in Baraka's tone, though not exclusively so. Earthiness or some kind of authentic groundedness—a both literal and figural soiledness—is aligned with "ghetto life" rather than a necessarily antighetto lunch hour happily spending a little money up and down Sixth Avenue before being transported by a headline to some earlier transportation in or from a basement some blocks east, some months before, by Lady Day. Earthiness is what readers encounter in the voice and tone of Baraka's militant lyric subjectivity. By 1965, this militancy is more fully aligned with a heightened masculinity Baraka refers to as an "American Sexual Reference: Black Male."[84] It is opposed to an aestheticized Euro-cultural effeteness that is alienated, commodified, artifactualized, necessarily homosexual, and therefore fatally subject to the dangers of the very ecstatic syncopation that Ross deploys Baraka to correct. Meanwhile, the white (gay, male aesthete's) encounter with the figure of the black that induces such enrapture, is, according to Ross, given multiply in "The Day Lady Died": first, in O'Hara's "meeting" with what Ross describes as "the probably black shoeshine boy, who may be worried about how he is going to be fed in a way that is different from the poet's anxiety about his unknown hosts in Easthampton";[85] second in the poet's ecumenical consumption of "the poet's in Ghana"; third, and most importantly, in the encounter with Billie Holiday that punctuates the poem and brings to an end the ambulatory poet's frenzied consumption of blackness, among other things. Note that such aestheticism places blackness or black performance in an economy wherein ecstasy is the end of a perverse, interracial consumption, wherein the heterosexual and the homosexual cut and augment one another. It is the job of earthiness, on the other hand, in its authentically black authenticity, to correct such placement by deploying a purely and necessarily heterosexual, socially realistic (if not naturalistic), lyric masculinity.

So I'm differentiating between two hipsterisms here. And if I come out on the side of O'Hara's it's not because I want to dispense with Ross's. As I said, both lend themselves to another project of correction in which I'm interested. Nevertheless, I want to linger with O'Hara precisely at a point where Ross withdraws, leaving behind only this trace in the form of a footnote: "That it is a Lady Day and not a Charlie Parker being commemorated in this way is, of course, O'Hara's own personal touch. As a gay poet, and one of the most spontaneous of all camp writers, it is no surprise to find that it is a woman singer who shares the billing along with the goddesses of the screen which he celebrates in other of his poems."[86] This trace demands a further investigation of O'Hara's rapture and its sexual content. And this requires just two more brief introductory formulations.

The first is that it turns out that Baraka is a student of rapture as well. More specifically, he also investigates the very specific mode of rapture that Holiday induces or produces in "The Dark Lady of the Sonnets" and that essay's prose moves, by way of the sonnet's protocols of caesura or seizure, along a path that is punctuated by that aesthetic fascination whose intensity is all bound up with the fact that it is also *sexual*. That Baraka and O'Hara were friends, that O'Hara records his encounters with Baraka in his poetic recordings of his midday walk-abouts, that various lines of gossip and auto/biographical revelation suggest the possibility of a sexual relationship between the two and/or the possibility of Baraka's sexual ambivalence only adds a little bit to the mix.[87] And if there is in Baraka's approach to Holiday that which Ross might call earthiness, it operates wholly within that mix, wholly within the context of a lyrical analysis, at once formal as well as social, of the structures and effects—consumption and loss, eroticism and rapture, sight and sound, fascination and aversion, estrangement and desire—of the *event* that we call Billie Holiday and of the relation between that event, blackness as black performance, and the idea and enactment of advance.

The second formulation concerns the excessively simple opposition between Parker and Holiday that Ross invokes as if the alto horn emits only a heterosexual call, as if that sound is separable from the same engendering force that produces Lady and that she reproduces in all of its re-en-gendering power. The point, however, is that black performance, in improvising through the opposition of earthiness and rapture, immanence and transcendence, enacts a sexual differentiation—a sexual cut in Mackey's words, an invagination in Derrida's—of sexual difference. Indeed, one of the things that is most important and worthy of attention in the moment I'm trying to touch on here, the period between 1955 and 1965 when the avant-garde in black performance (figured in and by the likes of Holiday, Baraka, Thelonius Monk, Cecil Taylor, Audre Lorde, Archie Shepp, Adrian Piper, Adrienne Kennedy, Samuel R. Delany, and a host of others) irrupts into and restructures the downtown New York scene, is precisely this sexual differentiation of sexual difference that occurs at the convergence of fetishized, com-modified, racialized consumption and aesthetic rapture, that occurs as militant political and aesthetic objection. Whether in the virile homo-sexual friendship of the improvising ensemble (which could denote a group of jazz musicians or a group of adolescent boys engaged in high forms of violent verbal/racial/sexual play—I'm thinking here of Baraka's play *The Toilet*, to which I'll return) or in the eroticized field of public homosexual acts, downtown Manhattan was a fertile ground for this movement. It is, finally, an arrhythmia that I'm describing, a highly localized movement of syncopation, a Village disruption of the space-time continuum whose internal sexual difference marks the assertion, rather than negation, of radical blackness on the one hand, and totality on the other.

So the object is the trace or memory of a certain "libidinal saturation," as Delany puts it, the erotic circuit that embeds aesthesis and consumption in "the black radical tradition." This is about that trace and its eclipse or burial, the surplus and excess, the simultaneously out and rooted sexuality, sentimentality, and spatial politics of the black avant-garde. With fear and desire, Baraka ambivalently moves in such saturation. His recording of Lady's performance is one graph of an ensemble of events Baraka's staging, participation, and observation helped to determine that occurred between 1955 and 1965 in downtown Manhattan, right around the corner of St. Mark's Place and the Bowery. At that corner was located a club called the Five Spot. The music that was played there—most famously that played by Holiday, Monk, and Taylor—is structured by this temporal-affective disorder, displacement, and disjunction that I'll attempt to isolate and transmit. This irregular beat is like a general erotic economy that encompasses some live and musical performances and their phonographic and literary reproduction.

I'm especially interested in thinking the *syncope* that this new music of black performances instantiates in relation to the arresting visions of proto-postmodernist performance in "a secret location on the lower east side" and public sex at the St. Mark's Bathhouse that are both recorded by Samuel R. Delany in his memoir, *The Motion of Light in Water*. I also want to address the conflation of the sexually and aesthetically adventuresome that is contained in the dramatic rendering of a violent public oscillation between approach, reproach, and reapproach of homosexuality in *The Toilet*, which premiered at the St. Mark's Playhouse (located about thirty yards down the street from the club and right across the street from the bathhouse) on 16 December 1964. These events and their recordings circulate around the Five Spot, forming the ongoing production of a performance that offers some clues concerning the deconstruction and reconstruction of publicity and privacy, objectivity and subjectivity, liveness and reproduction. To be interested in the arresting effect or arrest of affect that the music produced and produces in the light of whatever recourse to authenticity, sentiment, or experience such recordings enact or parody is to ask what happens when the critical finger that points disapprovingly at an invocation of authenticity seems itself to devolve into an accusation of inauthenticity. Another way to put this would be: What will authenticity be after its rehabilitation? What will blackness be when it enters and receives the radical biological indeterminism, the ineradicable historicality, the inveterate transformationality that blackness as it is demands and makes possible?

Here, then, are some passages from Delany's text that will provide some protocols for reading 'round the Five Spot:

> When walking somewhere along Eighth Street, on the side of an army-green mail collection box I'd noticed a black-and-white mimeographed poster, stuck up with masking tape, announcing: "Eighteen Happenings in Six Parts, by Allan Kaprow." ...[88]

> There was general silence, general attention: there was much concentration on what was occurring in our own sequestered "part"; and there was much palpable and uneasy curiosity about what was happening in the other spaces, walled off by translucent sheets with only a bit of sound, a bit of light or shadow, coming through to speak of the work's unseen totality.[89]

> After a while, a leotarded young woman with a big smile came in and said, "That's it." For a moment, we were unsure if that were part of the work or the signal that it was over. But then Kaprow walked by the door and said, "Okay, it's over now." ...[90]

> And of course, there still remained the question for me over the next few days: how, in our heightened state of attention, could we distinguish what

a single happening was? What constituted the singularity that allowed the eighteen to be enumerable?[91]

It was lit only in blue, the distant bulbs appearing to have red centers.

In the gym-sized room were sixteen rows of beds, four to a rank, or sixty-four altogether, I couldn't see any of the beds themselves, though, because there were three times that many people (maybe a hundred twenty-five) in the room. Perhaps a dozen of them were standing. The rest were an undulating mass of naked, male bodies, spread wall to wall.

My first response was a kind of heart-thudding astonishment, very close to fear.

I have written of a space at certain libidinal saturation before. That was not what frightened me. It was rather that the saturation was not only kinesthetic but visible.[92]

Cecil Taylor and Amiri Baraka make music that looks and sounds like that, and we need to think about what it is they have to learn and repress in order to do so. I mean that their music looks and sounds like both of these performances and both sets of theoretical formulations they imply regarding totality and singularity, visibility and invisibility, event and trajectory, ungendering and re(en)gendering; and I mean to point out that we already know this little area 'round the Five Spot to be the place where the impossible event of the Dark Lady, in blue audio-visuality, improvises through the distinction between rupture and rapture. In her name, Delany improvises through the gap between the unseen totality of Kaprow's fragmented, singularized, modularized performance and the visible undulation of ungendered bodies re-cognized, by way of a prefigurative Spillers operation, enfleshed, *en masse*, the iconic dynamism of a seen totality. Number and mass—and the ontology, epistemology, and ethics they carry—are slain here; singularity and totality are both improvised, yet the arresting, fascinating, abjectively affective experience of the sublime (that which is experienced as a kind of temporal distancing and the out interinanimation of disconnection as it manifests itself in the St. Mark's bathhouse and in an apartment/performance space on Second Avenue) marks the infusion of a deep sexual energy, brings the experience to a felt and theorized stop, or, more precisely, reveals the internal complication of seen and seeing aspects that is never not to be seen in its formal similarity with the musical ensemble. Cecil's music is an acting out disconnected neither from Kaprow's performance (sharp and weird as in unexpected; way out, even, from the outside of the house, though still bound up within a certain set of inside exclusionary protocols that continue/d to animate the Euro-American avant-garde and mark its determinate relationship with that tradition from which it would break) nor from the performance at St. Mark's (an acting out as the performance of out—as openness and [homo]erotic publicity and the concomitant undermining of the complex that revolves around the juncture of perversion and solitude—though this performance of out is a proscribed revelation, an unconcealment with concealment at its heart and as its frame, hidden and held, a publicity both real and virtual), though both remain, finally, inside, which is to say never fully emergent in or as the public sphere that would reassert the *commons* of experience by enacting the out rationalization of a certain desire for the experience of (an) ensemble. Nevertheless, these performances and their transmission give us a clue that is both manifest (with all its critical and sexual energy intact) as and a refinement of Delany's framing of them. This is variation of not on, not but of, a theme and The Music is an improvisation of the clue. This is held as a possibility of the encounter, of descent and the ascension of dissent, of an action out from the outside of any earthy, bridgelike nostalgia, gratitude, and hope that won't hear what some rapt, airy, dying fall—through the cut, castration, invagination—makes possible.

Delany understands the theoretical force such an experience of performance has in this way:

> In the fifties—and it was a fifties model of homosexuality that controlled all that was done, by both we ourselves and the law that persecuted us—homosexuality was a solitary perversion. Before and above all, it isolated you.[93]

But what this experience said was that there was a population—not of individual homosexuals, some of whom now and then encountered, or that those encounters could be human and fulfilling in their way—not of hundreds, not of thousands, but rather of millions of gay men, and that history had actively and already created for us whole galleries of institutions, good and bad, to accommodate our sex.

Institutions such as subway johns or the trucks, while they accommodated sex, cut it, visibly, up into tiny portions. It was like *Eighteen Happenings in Six Parts*. No one ever got to see its whole. These institutions cut it up and made it invisible—certainly much less visible to the bourgeois world that claimed the phenomenon deviant and dangerous. But, by the same token, they cut it up and thus made any apprehension of its totality all but impossible to us who pursued it. And any suggestion of that totality, even in such a form as Saturday night at the baths, was frightening to those of us who'd had no suggestion of it before.[94]

See, it's not the fact but the vision (and its attendant sound, its content, that I want to bring out now) of male homoeroticism, of the homoerotic body as totality or the totality of the sexual—the writhing mass that seems to operate beyond any notion of singularity—that is liberatory for Delany. And this is connected to a certain understanding of speculative fiction (the refined, expanded denotation of science fiction that Delany employs and deploys) as a mark of the totality of the discursive, the total range of the possible, the implicit deconstruction of any singularist and set-theoretic conceptions of the total: a wider range of sentence and incident. The future metaphysics of the out, of the "to come," of the speculative is, instead, what's already given in the descriptive and prescriptive totality present in Delany's work as anarchic institution: the experience of critical enrapture marks the space-time, the externalizing gap and caesura, of an old-new institution: (the jazz) ensemble.

Joan Scott argues against any simple experience of totality, any simple visualization or perception, any unthought rendering of the real or whole; but the moment of Delany's affirmation of totality is also the moment of his critique of a no less problematic valorization of modularity, the imposed experience of fragmentation that he sees as a framework and opening of the postmodern.[95] Delany experiences the orgy retrospectively in its oppositional relation to an earlier, no less visualized or experienced sexual tableau that is formally aligned with Kaprow's happening. His is not a simple critique of modularity, no simple or naive desire for a hypersexual plenitude and openness—indeed, elsewhere in his work Delany engages modularity in an encounter governed by something other than the spirit of an absolute, if impossible, negation. Delany attempts, instead, a double distinction between the impossibility of a calculus of the world, the event, art, the happening, subjectivity, objectivity, and their reality and between experience and calculation. This cut, which is the field within which the relation between one and many is improvised, is also the site, or can be the site, of a certain nonexclusionarity, if we let Taylor reemerge in his submergence; it doesn't take much to imagine that he might have been playing too that night, not far from Kaprow's happening, somewhere 'round the Five Spot, his music the heretofore unheard and unheard of sound animating even scenes in and for which it is absent. As we shall see, the (sound of the) said exists. As we shall hear, the seen remains. This is the Cecil Taylor Unit.

Cecil Taylor is out in many respects. He is out of the outside/s that the music constitutes—of narrow and superficial understandings of (the) tradition, of certain harmonic constraints, of certain assumptions regarding tonality, of prior notions of totality and its relation or opposition to singularity, of the solo and the dominant theorization of its emergence from and disappearance within the group, of, therefore, a theorization of disappearance-in-performance that in some ways anticipates dominant contemporary understandings of performance. He is out of the outside/s only in the context of the group, or so it would appear, like that fold or invagination made visible by and in what Derrida calls "the law of genre," the one that extends and deepens the totality it ensures by way of violation, an extending and deepening violation that is never an erasure or disappearance or is only a disappearance in the partial way that erasure performs, a "foreshadowing description" of the outside that Set—the interinanimation of one and many that is our fate, "this is not prophecy but [foreshadowing] description," that divine Egyptian trace of fixity to which Baraka sometimes negatively and warily refers—takes in. He is out of the unit/s of performance, the song form, the song and its collection, the tune and the normal lineup of tunes, the "standards" (of performance); out of the set, which is to say the party, the jam, the get-together, the gathering, *logos*, outside of the imaginary disappearance of the *logos* in another kind of writing, another composition, another movement through composition and its other, another improvisation of improvisation. But only questions follow here, ones that ought to make you go back and try to cut the sharpness of a chain or run of assertions about the out of the music.

Like: (1) What is the Cecil Taylor Unit? First of all, The unit is present in Taylor's "solo" performances as surely as he "leads" (structures or feeds) the performance of the unit; the subject of ensemble is embodied in the piano, playing as Ellington played, orchestra held in the instrument, instrument become orchestra, each extensions of a single, divided, and abounding body-become-flesh. So is it him alone, a set continually invaded or complicated, divided or abounded, by a dominant singularity around which it is structured and which is violent to or excessive of that structure? Is the unit that which erases singularity in the name of a unity in which the singular reappears undifferentiated? Does Taylor participate without belonging and is that participation encoded in the name "The Cecil Taylor Unit," a unit of which Taylor is (not) a member, a unit dis/allowed by his non/membership? Is Taylor the living principle of invagination or the improvisation of that principle, an anarchization of that principle that would place the whole within the field that emerges between deconstruction and reconstruction? Embedded in these questions is the possibility of an invagination of invagination, the sense of what is out from the outside, the outside that is never brought back in.

And: (2) What is it to be out in The Music? What is the sound of this "out" and where is the sexuality of Taylor's music-poetry-dance-performance? Wherein lies the cut that exists within and for a single sex, a sex that is one or, at least, perhaps, the same? How's that sound and how's that sound performed or acted? How does out, the outness of the sexual cut within the same sex, sound? This is to ask: What's it sound like? But it is also to ask: How would it sound if it sounded? Does it sound? Is the out of The Music, The New Black Music, The New Thing, Taylor's music, the music of the Cecil Taylor Unit, the out of a sexuality that, while out, is not always as overtly referenced as the other elements of his identity or identities? What would an out performance—an acting out—be and what would the (homo)sexuality of Taylor's music, if there is a (homo)sexuality of this music, sound like? What would it look like?

And: (3) What is the relationship between the music of an outside sexuality, a music in which that sexuality is out, overt, visible as identity, and the music of blackness as another outside identity? What is the sound of a certain misogynistically and hyper-heterosexually politicized black manhood and how is it related to, diluted, changed, silenced, disappeared by, Taylor's sexuality? Here we can think Taylor as the site of an ambivalence regarding not only the complexities of individual sexuality or the sexuality or procreativity of an aesthetics, but regarding the question concerning the revolutionary potency or impotency of a highly, if impossibly, gendered and heterosexualized black politics and the multiple status and conflicted terrain of the outside as well.

For Baraka, back when people called him Roi, the music is the site of this "American Sexual Reference: Black Male," an out and visible sexual mark, an out, black heterosexuality indexed immediately to shadowed act, haunted and deferred action, motivated and concealed acting of a black revolutionary politics of which Taylor is outside because of an outside sexuality and what Jones saw/heard/read as the pale cast of a correspondent aesthetics sicklied over with a debilitating—which is to say alienating, feminizing, homosexualizing, whitening—bohemian intellectualism. That which is read as intelligence without feeling is thought to dilute the native black/straight/male hue of resolution, subjecting the act to the displacements of nomination. But Taylor is a fundamental figure in and prophet of the black musical outside. As such he is the member who disrupts and allows the Black political unit and unity, displacing the "home" Jones would hear in The Music. Out-from-the-outside, Taylor is located at the center of Baraka's ambivalence. It is apparent in his writing on Taylor, writing filled with so many veiled and submerged distancings, critiques, outings. These writings are the site of a dis/appearance or other appearance or complication of appearance of the outside, an oscillation of im/purity tied to an equally ambivalent rejection of and immersion in the (myth of the) European that also, ironically, characterizes Taylor's work, whose conceptualization is even today still bound to the notion of a critique of a Euro-aesthetic absence of emotion and the concomitant hegemony of an inauthentic intellectualism disconnected from its home or origin, which is to say from the feeling that would predict—prophesy, determine, foreshadowingly describe—it.

Is jazz a kind of closet, a withdrawal of (homo)sexuality negatively echoed in real and mythical carnal origins in explicit and illicit (hetero)-sexuality? But what of the inevitable, always already out and out from the outside, (primarily male homo)erotics of ensemble or of the femi-nized romanticism of a pianism of the body that is never not racialized, never not coded as the non-European, as the non-European within the European, even as it is coded as effeminate, overemotional, lustful, uncontrolled, animalistic or, at least, infused with too much *anima*, pos-sessed, transportive, out, ecstatic, gay? What about Taylor's approach to the piano, stabbing at sounds in the form of a seduction, the piano's body occupied from outside by way of incremental penetrations, ges-tures emitting light, light, sound in the course of out, out movements? What about the structures of a certain interplay, in the performance of the solo and in the "solo performance," where ghosts or living spirits return like Jimmy Lyons, saxophonist and longtime member—impro-viser in and out—of the unit, the love never not sexual that they out-wardly express and that is always put in (their) play and in their position in the improvising ritual of the cut as if acting out in groups were another name for the unit, another name for (the) ensemble?

Is Taylor out? Is there something on the order of an affirmation of his multiple identity (an out Blackness [or, negatively but more precisely, an out non-Europeanness] or an out Queerness) or is there an acting out or performance of it that becomes a kind of disappearance, a free and out negation of identity—lingering emergences in and from the fissure between and outside as well as in groups: the unit, blacks, queers, or whatever other identities operative at this point, here, in the silence of unmade declarations or of unasked questions? Would this redoubled or undoubled outness be the locus not of universals of performance but the performative improvisation of universality and the space or sphere, never not public (for the space of performance, the site of the creation of new models of reality, the rearrangement of the relations and the particularities of representation/resistance/identity is that proletarian, motley reconstitution of the public sphere, the site or precondition of politics, of a politics that improvises resistance) where performance or improvisation or (the) ensemble, the Cecil Taylor Unit, occur as one another's other selves?

Gayatri Chakravorty Spivak writes that

> we must connect with the subaltern presupposition where heterosexual reproduction is a moment in the general normativity of a homosexuality for which the sexual encounter itself is a case of the caress. And this difference between homo- and heterosexuality is as unrecognized as it is underived in that theatre.[96]

This is to say that that difference is in that it is performed, disappeared, or not apparent given the understanding of performance within which or without which we've been operating. Taylor is out in his performance to the extent that he enacts the disappearance of any differentiated identity in the reenactment of the caress, the dis/appearance of the sexual encounter that the musical performance always is. And that encounter is never not fecund, always produces or is generative, is generative through and in spite of and in the disappearance of whatever commodity might have been produced in or by its enactment such that the record is undone in a certain way by the precise difference, apparent and disappeared, between itself and the performance that it records, even if that recording is marked "live!" thereby signifying the erstwhile capture of a genuine and actual publicity, the transformative, dis/appearing, dis/apparent effects of audition.

The "mechanical reproduction of performance" can also be a rationalization (precisely of the social). And what might be thrown out from this out is not the general normativity of homosexuality but a variation of that theme. The encounter reproduces but its generativity or fecundity, the sexuality and procreativity of the music, the generativity of variation or improvisation, is not a function of difference but of its performance, which is to say its dis/appearance. The outness of blackness is similarly performed and dis/appeared, taken way outside, like the marks and logics of the old-new world order, critiqued in their dis/appearance and resisted in their re-citation, in re-citations that provide for us a transcendental clue about the direction of our own encounters and organizations. This is that out performance of the outness of subalternity, improvising blackness and its others, capitalism and its other, homosexuality and its others, in a subalternity without origin and possible everywhere, a subalternity of universality, a subalternity of ensemble.

Taylor at the Five Spot and the ritual (symposium, gathering, set) Delany records at the St. Mark's Bathhouse are each conditions of the other's possibility. This is the fantasy Baraka engages and cannot abide, distorts and records in *The Toilet*, letting us know, in spite of himself, that the space of the black avant-garde is a sexual underground. Therein he attempts to redraw the distinctions between eros and the sexual act, homosociality and homosexuality. The homoerotic and its radicalness, its performance in the music, are located in these interstices wherein the primary activity is to catch one's breath, to have one's breath caught, to think the syncope in its audiovisual origins also as an effect of performance, to think the performer catching her breath, Lady or Cecil pausing, pausing in performance and at the sight of what? Now we have to think the pauses of Delany and of O'Hara 'round the Five Spot and the sexual and aesthetic logic of interruption.

Suddenly, time falters.

First, the head spins, overcome with a slight vertigo. It is nothing; but then the spinning goes wild, the ears start to ring, the earth gives way and disappears, one sinks back, goes away.... Where does one go?

The subject, says the doctor, is inert, pale, without consciousness. Sensitivity is obliterated. There is no respiration, no pulse can be felt.... after a necessarily short time, the pulse reappears, so does the respiration; the skin regains color; the sick person regains consciousness. Otherwise, the ending is fatal; syncope leads to death.

Syncope: an absence of the self. A "cerebral eclipse," so similar to death that it is also called "apparent death"; it resembles its model so closely that there is a risk of never recovering from it. The romantic and clinical scenario has usually, in our society, been allotted to woman: it is she who sinks down, dress spreading out like a flower, fainting, before a public that hurries forward; arms reach out, carry the unresisting body.... People slap her, make her sniff salts. When she comes to, her first words will be, "Where am I?" And because she has come to, "come back," no one thinks to ask where she has been The real question would be, rather, "Where was I?" But no, when one returns from syncope it is the real world that suddenly looks strange.[97]

"Syncope" is a strange word. It pivots from the clinic to the art of dance, tilts toward poetry, finally ends up in music. In each of these fields, syncope takes on a definition. At first there is a shock, a suppression: something gets lost, but no one says what is won.

Suddenly, time falters.

The couple seems to walk rather than dance, briskly, entwined. Who could separate them? But the man takes the woman's waist, and—so quickly that the movement can hardly be seen—bends her at midbody to touch the floor, and there they are, the two of them, overturned, suspended, as if he had stabbed her, maybe, or kissed her. They stop there, as if frozen for an instant. . . . He raises her, whirls, starts again. Tango. She is called his partner, his "rider" (cavalière); in its day the Church prohibited the tango as indecent. Syncope—here syncopation—is evident in the backward dip, inherent in the step itself: three steady steps, at a trot, then nothing. Suspense. It is in the missing beat that one can falter. Obscenity.[98]

This is the anaesthetic of the syncope that Catherine Clément offers. It is anaesthetic by way of synaesthesia, the senses, now theoreticians in their practice, fully emergent in and as their communism. Meanwhile, O'Hara's been shopping; meanwhile, Baraka's hanging with O'Hara, a recurrent character in the consumptive, licentious, lunchtime bohemianism he now disavows. Lady makes people stop breathing at the Five Spot—by her sound and, as Taylor writes, by way of the visible: "As gesture jazz became: Billie's right arm bent at breast moving as light touch." The remembrance of her syncoptic power produces fear, terminates lines. Everybody stopped breathing. One emerges from the syncope with a memory, as if one had been on a trip. One comes back from somewhere and it seems to rupture or arrest all previous itineraries.

And there is a racialization as well as a sexualization of syncope. The syncope has an effect of further whitening the white, a loss of color signifying the always already given whiteness of the woman who falters. And it is the woman who falters rather than produces in others the syncope. But we know, between Frederick Douglass and Frank O'Hara, that the syncope is produced by black women, the extremest possibility of their impossibility, a trace effect of scream and whisper, "snikker and whine." Here a certain relation between syncope and orgasm, the little death that is marked for us already in the gesture and dance of shopping, syncope, and jazz. And there the syncope is a homosexual affair. But the dark lady of the sonnets is a writing of and out of syncope and its earthiness is, in this respect, the airy, disconnected earthiness of consumption, of that which Ross would invoke Baraka's earthiness to correct.

And when one thinks of the orgasm (by way of Baldwin at the end of *Just above My Head*, then Kristeva at the opening of *Powers of Horror*) as an impossible ingestion, one can think the relation between syncope and abjection as well, its effects and direction, who produces it, its relation to fascination, its aurality or vocality, the response to its call. All this is indispensable and it is indispensable, finally, to any possible understanding, say, of Douglass's Aunt Hester, or Bessie Smith, or Lady, producers or enactors of syncope, syncopation, sexual cuts, jazz, a certain black avant-guardedness.

This is, for instance, Monk's gestures and the sounds they produce, his movements circling away from and back to the piano in the ecstatic pause of somebody else's solo. Meanwhile, much of what is called postmodern dance, much of what is valorized as the essence of the iconoclastic downtown avant-garde by Banes, will have become the choreography of mass conformity, the Cold War's absence of affect, the postural articulation of the authoritarian personality, its outward forms and inner desolation. Paul Taylor in the gray flannel suit. Perhaps they would critique or break away from mass conformity by way of the movements and gestures of mass conformity. But you could have found some new movements at the Five Spot, where Monk, way beyond simply achieving, reorganizes and reaestheticizes the natural. Where maladjustment converges with the unassimilable, where communism converges with sexual nonconformity, where outward presence—as visual-gestural-aural-locomotive pathology—is given as the extension of just that kind of criminal insanity we call the ongoing resistance to slavery: that's what's at work at the Five Spot. 'Round the Five Spot lies the out internal differentiation of the metropole, an internal imperial maladjustment if not decay, the germ or trace, yet to be more fully disseminated—always in danger of appropriation or commodification since what we're talking here is the ongoing intervention of the commodity, the object—though here we're waiting for it to come around again. It comes around again as memory, memoir, recording. The ongoing refusal of adjustment or assimilation at the same time as a movement emerges, one that seems as if it's all about the desire to adjust and assimilate, the paradoxical inexorableness of what we now know to have been an impossible inclusion. The avant-garde is always subject to inclusion's injunction to pass. This is what Paul Taylor, businessman, teaches us. (This is a lesson also taught and retaught at various drag balls, as if in contrast to such a scene's other interventions, as if to signify Harlem's ongoing prefigurative recapitulation of the whole downtown scene.) This is the political limit of realness. Yet the movement was not given in the desire for realness but in the desire for the outside, always driven by a happy inability to include it. The critique of inclusion was ongoing 'round the Five Spot: the radical outness of certain movements through subjectivity by objects, by the objections of the ones who have been objects, is what responds to the impossibility of inclusion as desire or philosophy as a function of law or custom but also as the function of a quite particular refusal to adjust. The out gestures of this refusal or objection remain before whatever origin we imagine, passing through each and animating them all. It animates the inclusionary movement and makes it impossible.

The main character in *The Toilet* is named Ray but called Foots. It's not impossible to imagine that this has to do with a certain facility in running, running at the mouth as well as by the foots, the combination of which is the condition of possibility of a leadership that is always potentially undermined by the leader's unwillingness to fight. Foots is always moving in and with and as the shadow of a manhood problem; and the thing about Foots is a recurrent refusal that takes place at the entrance into the scene, a refusal to descend, or maybe ascend, into the ecstasy or rapture of his own initial emotional response. (This is a manhood problem too.) The play is, therefore, replete with a series of highly controlled syncopations that experimentally structure, destructure, and restructure Foots and, in so doing, mark a revealing, if unrevealed, lack of control. Foots exists most fully as this problematic combination of (narrated) gesture and movement. He's a main character given to us primarily in the words, gestures, and movements of others or by way of the stage directions that narrate his gestures and movements. The stage directions time and again show him suspending the suspension that emotion demands of him within the context of a play whose main action (Foots's fighting the boy, Karolis, who has sent him a letter "telling him he thought he was 'beautiful . . . and that he wanted to blow him'") will never really happen:

> FOOTS: Yeh, somebody told him Knowles said he was gonna kick Karolis' ass. *[Seeing KAROLIS [who has already been beaten by Foots's boys] in the corner for the first time. His first reaction is horror and disgust . . . but he keeps it controlled as is his style, and merely half-whistles.]* Goddamn! What the fuck happened to him? *[He goes over to KAROLIS and kneels near him, threatening to stay too long. He controls the impulse and gets up and walks back to where he was. He is talking throughout his action.]* Damn! What's you guys do, kill the cat?[99]

> KAROLIS: *[has brought his head up during the preceeding scuffle, and has been staring at FOOTS. As FOOTS and the others look over toward him, he speaks very softly, but firmly]* No. Nobody has to leave. I'll fight you, Ray. *[He begins to pull himself up. He is unsteady on his feet, but determined to get up . . . and to fight.]* I want to fight you.
>
> FOOTS *is startled and his eyes widen momentarily, but he suppresses it.*[100]

> KAROLIS: Yes, Ray, I want to fight you, now. I want to kill you.
> *His voice is soft and terrible. The word "kill" is almost spit out. FOOTS does not move. He turns his head slightly to look KAROLIS in the eye, but he is motionless otherwise.*[101]

But to say that the play's main action never really happens is imprecise. The fight does occur, it's just that it's most fully itself as dance, as embrace, as a movement of and in rapture that corresponds to nothing so much as what Du Bois terms frenzy, nothing so much as the intense erotics—sometimes hushed, sometimes violent—that prefaces and is the entrance into another scene. The combination of refusal and resolve that marks Foots's fight-as-flight is the aggregate of these halting entrances into the homosexual, interracial seizure Lady Day induces. Baraka's work, over the course of the early 1960s is, in large part, the struggle to embrace such seizure, to think and renew its political content and force. That embrace is literally and doubly enacted at the end of *The Toilet* when Ray, defeated, as it were, by Karolis's murderous hug, crawls alone back into the scene to cradle the boy's battered head in his arms. Baraka's work is also, at the same time, a massive disavowal of any such embrace, a disavowal continually given in his desire for a purified racial and sexual self-referentiality. This is to say that the condition of possibility of such embrace will become an ever more violent purification of frenzy or rapture, one that always threatens to erase what it is that makes rapture possible in the first place. The imaginary return to an originarily earthy blackness or black heterosexual maleness is the path that Baraka must always take toward this purification and so one must always beware any such invocations of the soil. Nevertheless, by way of a certain illegitimate return of Barakan earthiness, one is given access to that dialectical relation to those complexities of rapture that are, in fact, always the invaginating, propelling force of blackness, which is to say, of black avant-garde.[102]

In the meantime, Banes says that "there were no black underground filmmakers . . . there were no downtown black dancers . . . there were no black Happenings-makers; no black pop-artists. . . . That is, many black artists may not have had a taste for the kind of iconoclastic activity—the product of some measure of educational privilege—in which the white artists reveled."[103] I guess, in the end, it's not even that crucial to open an argument against her position by saying that she must not have been looking 'round the Five Spot. The downtown scene would have never come together as simply as she seems to imagine, and if it ever did there will have been no place for *anyone* to enter it. Instead, we can draw a broken circle 'round the Five Spot in the way that Mingus plays a broken circle 'round the Music's rhythmic center. This matrical, pulsive stoptime, this ruptural and enraptured disclosure of the commons, is the black avant-garde, where blackness is given as black performance in that improvisation of authenticity and totality that is the sexual cut of sexual difference.

CHAPTER 3

Visible Music

Baldwin's *Baraka*, His Mirror Stage, the Sound of His Gaze

> "Look," he said. Jimmy's eyes had already followed Beauford [Delaney]'s anyway, but he just saw water. "Look again," Beauford said. Then he noticed the oil on the surface of the water and the way it transformed the buildings it reflected. . . . it had to do with the fact that what one can and cannot see "says something about you."[1]

Look.

The first take like a start before the just rhythm; the second and the oil on water is music. The florescent music of St. Mark's Place, the music 'round the Five Spot, is a lover's complaint. Move in some more second looks.

Here's a passage from Lee Edelman's essay "The Part for the (W)hole":

> Yet as black men already burdened by the "double-consciousness" that reflects their historical determination by the demand *be* the part, the "tool," that white men alone can *have*, Arthur and Crunch [characters in James Baldwin's *Just above My Head*], at the moment of their erotic and emotional involvement with one another, risk psychic annihilation through the double dismemberment of synecdochic logic; violently

171

reduced by the racist synecdoche that takes genital part for the whole, they are subject as well to the distinctively homophobic rewriting of synecdoche that polices "masculinity" by decreeing that the (male) "part" can *only* properly "stand" for the (female) "hole." Given its ominous doubling of the "double-consciousness" that splits black identity, it is appropriate that this moment of sexual discovery—mixing as it does both terror and liberation—should take place while Arthur and Crunch are performing in a gospel quartet on a tour of the South. This juxtaposition of a repressive political geography against "the vast and unmapped geography of himself" that Arthur first dares to negotiate in his sexual relation with Crunch reinforces the novel's analysis of racism as congruent with homophobia rather than homosexuality, and it links the "racial" paranoia instilled in the gospel quartet by their consciousness in the South of "the eyes which endlessly watch them" with the homographic anxiety that Arthur will feel when, after his intimacy with Crunch, he starts to wonder "if his change was visible." Crunch will go mad and Arthur die young as a consequence of internalizing the abjectifying judgments, both racist and homophobic, of the culture around them: internalized judgments that condemned them for engaging in other acts of "internalization"—acts in which their bodies open up to take in the phallic signifier to which they will thereby be viewed as having ceded any legitimate claim.[2]

Edelman gets us to a couple of problems that Baldwin helps us with, if we ask for his blessing.

First: If the sensual dominant of a performance is visual (if you're there, live, at the club), then the aural emerges as that which is given in its fullest possibility by the visual: you hear Blackwell most clearly in seeing him—the small kit, the softness and slow grace of his movement; or Cecil most clearly in the blur of his hands. Similarly, if the sensual dominant of the performance is aural (if you're at home, in your room, with the recording), then the visual emerges as that which is given in its fullest possibility by the aural: you see Blackwell most clearly in hearing the space and silence, the density and sound, that indicate and are generated by his movement; or Cecil most clearly in sound's anticipation of dance at, to, and away from the instrument. These are questions of memory, descent, and projection. The visual and the aural are before one another. Blackwell gone, Cecil up ahead.

Second: Repression and amplification. The repression of the knowledge of the hole in the signifier is shadowed by another, not so easily sensed repression of the knowledge of the *w*hole in the signifier.[3] This is a repression of amplification, of sound and, most especially, of *abounding*, in the sense that Derrida employs, where the whole expands beyond itself in the manner of an ensemble that pushes conventional ontological formulation over the edge. The hole speaks of lack, division, incompleteness; the whole speaks of an extremity, an incommensurability of excess, the going past of the signifier, neither its falling short, nor some simple equivalence. This understanding of the whole is not formed in relation to an impenetrable and exclusionary integrity but is, as Derrida puts it, "a principle of contamination, a law of impurity, a parasitical economy" that raises the most severe and difficult concerns regarding the question of its own representation.[4] We'll return to the question of the relations between the part and the whole, the hole and the whole. For now it's enough to try to think the whole—as it has been formulated and identified, in a certain kind of poststructuralist thought, as a necessarily fictive, problematically restrictive, completeness—in its relation to and difference from the *w*hole whose incompleteness is always also a *more than completeness*.

These problems lie at the intersection of totality and the *materiality* of sound, where Guattari's "a-signifying economy of language"[5] encounters Derrida's "parasitical economy" of "the law of the law of genre." Baldwin is The Economist.

> Let us hold him in our hearts and minds. Let us make him part of our invincible black souls, the intelligence of our transcendence. Let our black hearts grow big world absorbing eyes like his, never closed. Let us one day be able to celebrate him like he must be celebrated if we are ever to be truly self determining. For Jimmy was God's black revolutionary

mouth. If there is a God, and revolution his righteous natural expression. And elegant song the deepest and most fundamental commonplace of being alive.[6]

In the eulogy he read at Baldwin's funeral, Amiri Baraka speaks of Baldwin's "world absorbing eyes." This text is supposed to be something like a preface to an engagement with those eyes, with Baldwin's gaze and the sound of that gaze as it is manifest in and as his very substance. That gaze's sound and content, which carries with it all of the negative weight of our history, also holds a blessing, a *baraka*, something all bound up with Baldwin's being what Baraka called "God's black revolutionary mouth" *and more*, and something all bound up with Baldwin being what Lee Edelman might call a homographer *and more*.[7] This chapter begins with an appreciation of the *and more* in Baldwin, an extra substance or content held in the generative, appositional, copresent nonconvergence of the ensemble of the senses and the ensemble of the social. This meeting is manifest, in one way, as a critique of what in Baraka all too easily becomes homophobic phonocentrism and of what in Edelman's text "The Part for the (W)hole" (in part a reading of Baldwin's *Just above My Head*) threatens to become an ocularcentric textualism that is not but nothing other than Eurocentric. This section's title would reflect such meeting and resound the echo of two compositions and of two directions: their (non-)hybridity or, again, their generative (non-)convergence. That's what happens, for instance, in Anthony Braxton's recent quartet music or in a duet he recorded with David Rosenboom called "Transference," which I was trying to listen to when I first started to work on this: (the sound of [the]) ensemble in and as (the) ensemble's internal space.

This is after what Guattari would call a "graft of transference"[8] (and it's important here to recall that transference is a kind of resistance; it's that mode of being of the psychoanalytic encounter that is determined by a syncopative interruption of interpretation):[9] of the music in black literature, of the black aesthetic and philosophical tradition in the discourse of psychoanalysis, of all of these in the text of western philosophy. These grafts are neither purely oppositional and impossible nor some more or less possible hybridity or intersection. I also want to think about sound and its occlusion and, therefore, to think about how certain earlier versions of these grafts, both unconscious and conscious, operate with regard to sound, voice, their occlusion and exclusion and in light of attempts to remedy that occlusion or at least to mark it. In the end I want to talk about music, not as that which cannot be talked about but as that which is transferred and reproduced in literature as a function of the enabling disability of the literary representation of aurality. I want to linger in the cut between word and sound, between meaning and content, build me a willow cabin, so to speak, improvise, in a way that Lacan sounds but then talks, which is to say interprets his way out of via what he calls "reducing the non-meaning."[10] Again, I would move with Baldwin in an attempt to reverse what Guattari calls that "grave error on the part of the structuralist school to try to put everything connected with the psyche under the control of the linguistic signifier."[11] I would do much. I've got to augment in the ways of an appositional encounter, of what Nathaniel Mackey might call a "discrepant engagement."

Recall Mackey's formulations of "wounded kinship" and "sexual cut" and, along with the following passages from Lacan, let them stand in for the terms and/or subjects of this encounter:

> [A] certain dehiscence at the heart of the organism, a primordial discord betrayed by the signs of uneasiness and motor unco-ordination of the neo-natal months. The objective notion of the anatomical incompleteness of the pyramidal system and likewise the presence of certain humoral residues of the maternal organism confirm the view that I have formulated as the fact of a real *specific prematurity of birth* in man.[12]

> This development is experienced as a temporal dialectic that decisively projects the formation of the individual into history. The *mirror stage* is a drama whose internal thrust is precipitated from insufficiency to

anticipation—and which manufactures for the subject, caught up in the lure of spatial identification, the succession of phantasies that extends from a fragmented body-image to a form of its totality that I shall call orthopaedic—and, lastly, to the assumption of the armour of an alienating identity, which will mark with its rigid structure the subject's entire mental development. Thus to break out of the circle of the *Innenwelt* into the *Umwelt* generates the inexhaustible quadrature of the ego's verifications.[13]

I'm interested in what appears to be a kind of black anticipatory doubling of some of the fundamental conceptual apparatuses of psychoanalysis: of the primal scene and of the mirror stage that might—via Baldwin—be seen to operate at the level of a *racial* as well as sexual determination that is marked in the black tradition though largely unmarked or occluded in psychoanalysis. One other thing that becomes clear is that black mirror stages and/or primal scenes operate on different registers, at the level of what might be called an extended infantilism despite the fact that in another way there are no children here. A question of childhood, then—more vexed than ever when, in a black context, it is filtered through a conceptual apparatus constructed out of terms like "primitivity," "prehistory," and "phylogenetic heritage"—is what I would address. One of the things I'd like to think about is how these terms operate within a sort of love/hate relationship with childishness and with the childlike. What I'm talking about, though, is not some valorization of what might be called an arrested or deferred development but a radically critical previousness vis-à-vis natality, a sexual cut that disrupts the familiar constellation of formulations constructed around primitivity and infantilism as racial and sexual attributes.

This question of natality and of a catastrophic break that could not but be disruptive and augmentative of (dominant understandings or formulations of) identity and that would certainly be played out upon a field shaped, if not determined, by the scopic leads us to the issue of castration and its doubling. That question could be thought in terms of wounded kinships or phantom limbs and it would, therefore, seem to lend itself to the kind of interpretation that either a Freudian hermeneutic or a feminist, post-Freudian anti-hermeneutic might pro-vide.[14] But this black castration is, in a fundamental sense, *ante*-hermeneutic, which is to say before (in every sense of the word) the psychoanalytic, not only in the sense of a kind of anticipation of its insights but before the natal occasion, namely castration, out of which the psychoanalytic understandings of identification and desire emerge. It is important to note in this regard that black castration is not just to be seen as *prospective* figure and *symbolic* inability, since for the black tra-dition, castration is not just phantasmic possibility or introjection based on a fleeting glance at that which is read as sexual difference, but is also the proper name of an oft-repeated literal, historical, material event. Similarly the question of castration, in a way that is not only to be indexed to the psychoanalytic chain of disavowal and fetishization, leads back to the question of the blessing, the *baraka* as Lacan terms it, a pos-sibility of augmentation, abounding, or of a dynamic whole that oper-ates in a complex relation with loss or lack or incompletion or static hole. Here, the *baraka* is an aurally infused gaze that manifests a bene-ficence improvised through the opposition of prophylaxis and evil. It is also a transfer of substance that *jazz* implies and performs. It is not the prematurity (of ejaculation) that Adorno critiques—though there is nothing here if not ejaculation (and here one thinks of Hall Montana's slow awakening from a dream in *Just above My Head*, about which more later). And it is not quite that "dehiscence at the heart of the organism, a primal discord" that marks for Lacan the "fact of a real *specific pre-maturity of birth* in man," though in the end there is nothing here if not the individual's projection into the augmentative atonality of a history in and of resistance/transference, nothing if not the individual's bearing some "residues of the maternal."

I want, though, not to deny (the mark of) castration—as a consti-tutive and fundamental theoretical element of psychoanalysis and of the psyche—but to think castration as the condition of possibility of an en-gagement that calls castration radically and, I think, irrevocably into an abounding or improvisational question. I want to listen to what sound does to interpretation and note how insurgent, anti- and ante-interpretive song, correspondent to "neither time nor tune" bears the repressed, resistant, transferred content of the piercing sound—"the heart-rending shriek"—of the black improvisation of the primal scene. Our passage(s) raise the question of castration's relation to the problematics of reading and of meaning and the possibility of significance at the level of what abounds or augments meaning, the way in which nonmeaning renders meaning more significant and the way this demands a critique of (psychoanalytic) interpretation. The way such a critique is embedded in the black radical aesthetic tradition, in the way it anticipates both a Freudian-phallic as well as a post-Freudian-anti-phallic reading and outstrips them both—to the extent that he is shaped by the complexity of his identifications as much as it is determined by the force of its representations and to the extent that it knows (or, at least, shows) how sound both shapes and cuts interpretive circles or communities—is crucial here and is what is implied in this notion of the ante-, the before, another interinanimation of "insufficiency and anticipation" that not only cuts mirror stages and primal scenes, but destabilizes the very idea of—need or desire for—suture.

And all of this is tied to those problematics of meaning in relation to the originary separation from the object that are themselves called into question vis-à-vis this doubling such that the entry into language, that entry into the symbolic order that takes away what it gives and is the condition of possibility and impossibility of the subject's relation to the object, is doubled by an entry into *another's* language, and the concomitant theft and loss—in Amiri Baraka's words—of one's "ooom boom ba boom"[15] that, just as it is seen as a cut or break that is easily reconfigured as a loss, is also reconfigured as an augmentation—something brought to the language one enters, by way of the language one has lost—that bears the lineaments not only of the most abhorrent and horrific deprivations and violations but also of the most glorious modes of freedom and justice, like the anarchic and anarchronic modes of expression and organization that are played, which is to say played out, in The Music (wherein, Ellison says, if we linger, we might commit an action).

And this, in turn, leads to the question of the relation between castration and alienation, between castration, on the one hand, and disavowal and fetishization, on the other hand, in the Freudian and Marxian registers. Here we can begin to examine how a particular line of psychoanalytically influenced inquiry—say, from Adorno to Silverman—operates against the backdrop of these racial-historical determinations of language and the background of a reduction of the phonic substance of language that bends their analytics of aurality in the direction of an overwhelming ocularcentrism. For Adorno, black aural culture is defined by its fetish character in a way similar to the definition of female body/voice that Silverman sees in classic cinema. After all, according to Adorno, "[p]sychologically, the primal structure of jazz may most closely suggest the spontaneous singing of servant girls . . . [,] the domesticated body in bondage."[16] But I'm interested, here, in the insight Adorno's deafness carries: for what is borne in work of the black radical aesthetic tradition—and not only at the site of its recitations of terror and violation but also in the critical and metacritical discourse it produces on its own productions—is nothing other than the cries of a servant girl, the material-phonic substance that is transferable but not interpretable from either inside or outside the circle, the aural content that infuses and transforms (our dominant understandings of) primality, extremity, or extension out from inside or outside. Here I want to establish black aurality as the site of an improvisation through the structures both Silverman and Adorno talk about. Ultimately, I want to show how Baldwin's *baraka*, his blessing, moves in the tradition of the servant girl and in the encounter with psychoanalysis and in light not just of castration but of augmentation, of a beneficent and song-producing prosthesis—the augmentation of vision with the sound that it has excluded, the augmentation of reason with the ecstasy it has dismissed—that improvises through the determinations of lack and alienation, not via some direct adequation between word and object, but through the object's transferential reproduction in and as the (re)production of sound and of an ensemblic, dynamic totality. What I'm trying to talk about is another address of Lacan's "question of a horn," about which more in a minute. That address takes into account those transferences of the servant girl's scream in the black musical and literary traditions, the "afro-horn[s]," say, of Henry Dumas or of Albert Ayler, phallic instruments infused and reconfigured by the materiality (content-substance-objectivity) of the maternal and by the knowledge of freedom the experience of bondage affords.[17]

So that I want to trace a movement from the reduction of the phonic substance (of whose workings in texts from Descartes to Saussure Derrida writes in *Of Grammatology* and whose critical effects Edelman assumes in his essay on Baldwin) to the denial of the mark/inscription of castration on the maternal body to the absenting or exclusion of the maternal, the body and the mark[18] to "the inscription of 'the homosexual' within a tropology that produces him in a determining relation to inscription itself" (that tropology being what Edelman refers to as "homographesis").[19] I want to think about the way that writing's description of sound (the literary representation of aurality) is also a de-scription of sound, a writing *out* of sound, that corresponds both with the "unconscious denial that the maternal body is inscribed with the mark of castration [that] is . . . the precondition, at the level of the subject, for the philosophical exclusion or suppression of the maternal, the body, and the signifying mark"[20] and with a denial, both conscious and unconscious, of the very idea of the whole. This requires that I establish an equivalence between the denial of writing or inscription— which is also a denial of castration—and the denial of the aural in writing—an aurality that augments and redoubles castration, destabilizing its determinations: of meaning, disavowal, fetishization, alienation. Note, again, that this would be not a denial of castraton but an invaginative cut, a "sexual cut" of castration by way of aurality, one that carries with it the transferential mark of the anoriginal but insistently previous materiality and maternity of otherwise occluded sensuality, otherwise occluded sound, otherwise occluded *content*, in logocentric traditions and in their grammatological supplements.

Some of you may recall that this conception originated in a feature of human behavior illuminated by a fact of comparative psychology. The child, at an age when he is for a time, however short, outdone by the chimpanzee in instrumental intelligence, can nevertheless already recognize as such his own image in a mirror. This recognition is indicated in the illuminative mimicry of the *Aha-Erlebnis*, which Köhler sees as the expression of situational apperception, an essential stage of the act of intelligence.

This act, far from exhausting itself, as in the case of the monkey, once the image has been mastered and found empty, immediately rebounds in the case of the child in a series of gestures in which he experiences in play the relation between movements assumed in the image and the reflected environment, and between this virtual complex and the reality it reduplicates—the child's own body, and the persons and things, around him.

This event can take place, as we have known since Baldwin, from the age of six months, and its repetition has often made me reflect upon the startling spectacle of the infant in front of the mirror. Unable as yet to walk, or even to stand up, and held tightly as he is by some support, human or artificial (what in France we call a *'trotte-bébé'*), he nevertheless overcomes, in a flutter of jubilant activity, the obstructions of his support and, fixing his attitude in a slightly leaning-forward position, in order to hold it in his gaze, brings back an instantaneous aspect of the image[21]

Since every stick and stone was white and since you have not yet seen a mirror you assume you are too until around the age of 5 or 6 or 7 . . .[22]

I was determined to be served or die; I wanted to kill her but wasn't close enough so I threw a glass into the mirror, and when it shattered, when the glass hit the mirror, I woke up.[23]

TORT: *No, I wanted you to say more about that temporality to which you already referred once, and which presupposes, it seems to me, references that you have made elsewhere to logical time.*

LACAN: Look, what I noticed there was the suture, the pseudo-identification, that exists between what I called the terminal time of the arrest of the gesture and what, in another dialectic that I called the dialectic of identificatory haste, I put as the first time, namely, the moment of seeing. The two overlap, but they are certainly not identical, since one is initial and the other is terminal.

I would like to say more about something which I was not able, for lack of time, to give you the necessary indications.

This terminal time of the gaze, which completes the gesture, I place strictly in relation to what I later say about the evil eye. The gaze in itself not only terminates the movement, it freezes it. Take those dances I mentioned—they are not always punctuated by a series of times of arrest in which the actors pause in a frozen attitude. What is that thrust, that time of arrest of the movement? Is it simply the fascinatory effect, in that it is a question of dispossessing the evil eye of the gaze in order to ward it off? The evil eye is the *fascinum*, it is that which has the effect of arresting movement and, literally, of killing life. At the moment the subject stops, suspending his gesture, he is mortified. The anti-life, anti-movement function of this terminal point is the *fascinum*, and it is precisely one of the dimensions in which the power of the gaze is exercised directly. The moment of seeing can intervene here only as a suture, a conjunction of the imaginary and the symbolic, and it is taken up again in a dialectic, that sort of temporal progress that is called haste, thrust, forward movement, which is concluded in the fascinum.

What I wish to emphasize is the total distinction between the scopic register and the invocatory, vocatory, vocational field. In the scopic field, the subject is not essentially indeterminate. The subject is strictly speaking determined by the very separation that determines the break of the *a*, that is to say, the fascinatory element introduced by the gaze.[24]

F. WAHL: *You have left to one side a phenomenon that is situated, like the evil eye, in the Mediterranean civilizations, and which is the prophylactic eye. It has a protective function that lasts for the duration of a journey, and which is linked, not to an arrest, but to a movement.*

LACAN: What is prophylactic about such things is, one might say, allopathic, whether it is a question of a horn, whether or not made of coral, or innumerable other things whose appearance is clearer, like the *turpicula res*, described by Varro, I think, which is quite simply a phallus. For it is in so far as all human desire is based on the castration that the eye assumes its virulent, aggressive function, and not simply its luring function as in nature. One can find among these amulets forms in which a counter-eye emerges—this is homeopathic. Thus, obliquely, the so-called prophylactic function is introduced.

I was thinking that in the Bible, for example, there must be passages in which the eye confers the *baraka* or blessing. There are a few small places where I hesitated—but no. The eye may be prophylactic but it cannot be beneficent—it is maleficent. In the Bible and even in the New Testament, there is no good eye, but there are evil eyes all over the place.[25]

I'm after a way of rethinking the relation between the mirror stage and the *fascinum/baraka* of the gaze, to think the gaze as something other than necessarily maleficent, but not by way of a simple reversal or inclusion within the agencies of looking; rather within another formulation of the sensual, within a holoesthetic nonexclusionarity that improvises the gaze by way of sound, the horn, that accompanies the blessing, that has effects Lacan cannot anticipate[26] in part because of his ocularcentrism, because of the way his attention to language is always through an implicit and powerful *visualization* of the sign, a visualization never not connected to the hegemony or law of the signifier that Guattari decries and would break. So I'm talking about something like the possibility or trace of aurality in Baldwin's gaze, conferred upon himself and others, the nonexclusion of the gaze's aurality as the condition of possibility of its blessing. But what's the relationship between these representations of the mirror stage? How is the process of identification constituted in black culture? Is there a black mirror stage? Is the plenitude of Lacan's mirror stage always already an illusion, one that always already demands compensation for or an impossible reconstitution of that which it would constitute? Is this not all part of a process of deconstruction of the absolute singularity or alterity, the unitary trait, of the individual or group? Is Lacan's mirror stage simply the constitution of a phantom or phantasmatic singularity, an illusory plenitude or fullness? Doesn't Baldwin's mirror stage divest us even of the possibility of that illusion by bringing into the mix, precisely at the moment of its constitution, *race* such that the moment of the constitution of an originary differentiation or singularization is interminably deferred?

Listening to Lacan and interlocutor on the gaze, at the occlusion of sound, when the horn is dismissed or bracketed within the oscillational economy of phallus/castration (the virtual or symbolic economy of a reified sexual difference and a reified relation of subject and object), one hears that what that bracketing forecloses remains foreclosed only until the before of Baldwin removes or redoubles or returns to open sound's opening back up again. All this happens in the Mediterranean, as if—in the name of the Sheik and the Trojan—prophylaxis (or something uncontrollable that requires it) had this site as its natural home; deeper still, as if that which would be prophylactic or protective is merely phallic and aggressive, an aggression that is assured in and by a prior interpretive racialization of human desire's basis in castration. The horn is dismissed as phallic, thought only in its immaterial, if forceful, absence. Yet a kind of gap occurs due to the improvisational orality and aurality of the seminar, the unequal exchange of question and answer. This gap occurs when Lacan refers to those forms, those amulets,[27] as potentially in excess of an understood or assumed economy of visually and spatially determined meaning and difference. If the horn—by way of the specter of an organized sound, a music—brings to bear on the sign's visual/spatial regime a system of differences that does not signify, as Kristeva would say (though here, that this system would not signify does not mean that it would not communicate or effect, produce or induce affect, protect or ensure, endanger in the interest of some saving power), then we can understand why Lacan would attempt to bracket it just as his readers, either for the sake of his readability or his unreadability, bracket the noise he must have made, a noise connected not only to aurality but to aurality in improvisation. This bracketing allows the requisite conclusion: there can be no beneficent eye, that no eye can convey a blessing, that the horn, reduced to a sign, a substitute for the lost object, can only reveal the anxiety and aggression of a desire born in castration. But the horn is what conveys the *baraka*, and this blessing, bound up in the nonexclusion of sound from the holoesthetic field, is what allows the possibility of a more than prophylactic gaze, that beneficent and world-encompassing gaze, the *baraka* of which Baraka speaks and sings. What is held and carried in that gaze is the eruptive content of a transferred history; the material substance of a music that is more than aural: anticipatory, premature, insistently previous, jazz.[28] We have known this since Baldwin, since the man referred to in the index of the English translation of *Écrits* as "Baldwin, J." Since him. J. Baldwin knew something about the way sound works, something about the work of sound. Between or outside of or improvising through protection and arrest, what did Baldwin confer upon us when he looked at us and what did he confer upon himself when he first looked into his own eyes?

Edelman operates within an occlusion of sound similar to that of Lacan's, an occlusion that occurs sometimes in the name of a deconstruction of phonocentrism and always within a tradition of logocentrism, which has at its heart a paradoxically phonocentric deafness. And so, in spite of the value of his work, we're still left with the question, how will we receive (a term of great importance to Edelman and to his valorization of a kind of ethics of mutual penetrability) or celebrate (as Baraka would have it) Baldwin? Now I am not advocating a reading that would be a simple return or (re)capitulation to a metaphysics of meaningful voice, one that would parallel the rendering of homosexuality and blackness as secondary/sterile/parasitic that Edelman describes. Nevertheless, the primal scene must be heard; one must be attuned to its sound and perhaps, then, even to a real reformulation of, rather than dismissal of, spirit. Hear, for instance, recorded, if you will, in Leeming's biography, the devastating aurality of a Baldwinian primal scene that one would invoke in order to justify the search for a homographic aurality in the text, one that augments Edelman's critique with sonic interruptions.

> Baldwin remembered as one of the "most tragically absurd" moments
> of his life lying in bed with a lover in Saint-Paul-de-Vence ... both of
> them crying as they listened to the sounds of Lucien [Happersberger,
> the man Baldwin described as the love of his life] making love with the
> lover's supposed girlfriend in the room above.[29]

Now I'm not trying to say that Edelman is wholly unattuned to sound;
indeed part of what I want to pay special, though brief, attention to here
is his reading of sound and music in *Just above My Head*. I am trying
to say that Baldwin, at least with regard to the question of politics
and also with regard to the importance of sound, in light of a desire to
move beyond the oscillation between resistance and domination, would
have at least been wary about anything like a kind of homographesis
or negrographesis that didn't give the *phonê* its due. At any rate, what I
want to argue is that the nonexclusion of sound, the nonreduction of
nonmeaning, is tied to another understanding of literary resistance, one
that moves within and without the black tradition, activating the sound
in a way that opens the possibility of a nonexclusion of sexual difference
whose exclusion has otherwise marked that tradition and that has been
an inescapable part of that tradition's own scopophilia. His writing is
pierced with screams and songs and prayers and cries and groans, their
materiality, their maternity, and that's important.

More importantly, these elements are not to be read, are not to
be thought in relation to a formalism that reduces (phonic) substance
in the construction of a sound-image that is itself integrated into the
semiotic ground of the science of grammatology. As Derrida writes,
"[W]ithout this reduction of phonic matter, the distinction between
language and speech, decisive for Saussure, would have no rigor."[30]
And it is this particular mode of rigor that is decisive for Edelman to
the extent that his homographesis is an extension, via Derrida, of Saussure's scientific project. And shortly we'll note in Edelman's reading
how the reduction of the phonic matter to a sound-image that is read-
able, meaningful, and therefore held within the very visual economy
he attempts to disturb marks the reinscription of a phonocentrism—a

central remergence of the metaphysics of voice into the homographesis Edelman performs and sees Baldwin performing—that paradoxically renders the text silent. Or, more precisely, substanceless, both with regard to the text's materiality and its (immaterial, semantic) content. The reduction of the phonic substance that determines Edelman's reading of Baldwinian aurality in its relation to the homographic disturbance of "manhood" and the "ego" is important not simply because it might serve to suppress what Houston Baker would call the text's "racial poetry,"[31] a poetry he all too quickly aligns with an understanding of the "meaning" and "identity" of blackness that never escapes the very scopic determinations that, as Edelman rightly points out, connect Baker's work to homophobic *and* racist regimes he would surely have intended to resist. *Rather, the reduction of phonic substance must be thought precisely because it iconically represents the exclusion of materiality in general wherein the liberatory force of an invaginative racial poetry lies.* In *Of Grammatology* Derrida quotes Hjelmslev's interpellation and extension of Saussure: "[s]ince language is a form and not a substance (Saussure), the glossemes are by definition independent of substance, immaterial (semantic, psychological and logical) and material (phonic, graphic, etc.)."[32] If Edelman's mode of reading is a further variation on Saussure's formalism, and I think it is, how can it be adequate to Baldwin if Baldwin is, and I think he is, substantial? Please note that this question is meant to initiate an augmentation, not a rejection, of the homographic project—a substantial augmentation that will, in turn, make possible another kind of encounter with Baldwin's substance, with his im/materiality—both sensual and social. And note, too, that it would be wrong to suggest that Edelman is unaware of the substance of Baldwin's text that escapes the visual-aural binary. Check the holosensual field that is created in the following passage from *Just above My Head*:

> Curious, the taste, as it came, leaping, to the surface: of Crunch's prick, of Arthur's tongue, into Arthur's mouth and throat. He was frightened, but triumphant. He wanted to sing. The taste was volcanic. This taste, the aftertaste, this anguish, and this joy had changed all tastes forever.

The bottom of his throat was sore, his lips were weary. Every time he swallowed, from here on, he would think of Crunch, and this thought made him smile as, slowly, now, and in a peculiar joy and panic, he allowed Crunch to pull him up, upward, into his arms.

He dared to look into Crunch's eyes. Crunch's eyes were wet and deep *deep like a river*, and Arthur found that he was smiling *peace like a river*.[33]

That field is remarked by Edelman. We must remark the insistent inter-articulation of "reading" and "seeing" in Edelman's remarks.

Fittingly, in light of this last remark, Arthur and Crunch confirm their new understanding of "identity" by performing gospel songs and hymns identical to those they sang before they began their erotic involvement. Now, however, what is patently the same is also, and at the same time, different; as Arthur and Crunch contain each other, so, too, do the various "meanings" of their apparently identical songs. Like the homographic sameness of two signifiers, visually indistinguishable from one another—signifiers that are actually products of different histories and etymologies—the "same" text now exhibits discontinuous, potentially contradictory meanings that reflect its determination through contiguity to different parts of the context that contains it. Thus the spiritual devotion implicit in "*So high, you can't get over him*" cohabits with the homoerotic specific-ity of the song's performance by Arthur and Crunch. And just as Arthur, contemplating the aftertaste of Crunch's ejaculation into his mouth, is "frightened, but triumphant" and wants, as Baldwin declares, "to sing," so the experience of singing in the novel comes to figure the erotic exchange of inside and outside, the taking in and giving back of a language seen as the prototype of the "foreign" substance that penetrates, and constitutes, identity.

To the extent, then, that Arthur and Crunch reinterpret "manhood" and thus, in Western terms, subjectivity in its paradigmatic form, as the ability to incorporate what is "foreign" without experiencing a loss of integrity, and without being constrained (hetero)sexist either/or logic of active and passive, they point to the partial understanding of "manhood" that passes in dominant culture for the whole, and they disarticulate the coercive "wholeness" of an identity based on fantasmic identification with a part. They thus make visible to the novel's reader the invisible operation of *différance* that destabilizes every signifier, offering a glimpse of the process through which a signifier like "manhood" can communicate the singularity of a fixed identity only where a community of "readers" has learned how *not* to see the differences within that identity and its signifier both. "Perhaps history," as Baldwin suggests, "is not to be found in our mirrors, but in our repudiations: perhaps the other is ourselves"; and as if generalizing from the mutual containment of Arthur in Crunch and Crunch in Arthur, Baldwin expands on this supposition by declaring: "Our history is each other. That is our only guide. One thing is absolutely certain: one can repudiate, or despise, no one's history without repudiating and despising one's own. Perhaps that is what the gospel singer is singing."[34]

An initial reading reveals that Edelman subordinates taste and touch to aurality. More precisely, Edelman submits the tactile materiality that infuses Baldwin's passage to a *reading*—which is to say, for Edelman, a seeing or visualization—of aurality that is already stripped of its particular materiality precisely because the holism of the sensual ensemble is broken. That holism is collateral damage incurred in the assault on the illusory totality of a synecdochically derived identity. What is herein visualized—that which displaces both the phonic and semantic substance of language with a semiotic formalization and is, for Edelman, the making visible of the workings of *différance*—is described succinctly by Derrida:

> *Différance* is therefore the formation of form. But it is *on the other hand* the being-imprinted of the imprint. It is well-known that Saussure distinguishes between the "sound-image" and the objective sound. He thus gives himself the right to "reduce," in the phenomenological sense, the sciences of acoustics and physiology at the moment that he institutes the

science of language. The sound-image is the structure of the appearing
of the sound which is anything but the sound appearing. It is the sound-
image that he calls *signifier*, reserving the name *signified* not for the thing,
to be sure (it is reduced by the act and the very ideality of language), but
for the "concept ..." The sound-image is what is *heard*; not the *sound*
heard but the being-heard of the sound. Being-heard is structurally phenomenal and belongs to an order radically dissimilar to that of the real
sound in the world.[35]

Derrida's description is telling because it allows us to understand what
is a fundamental contradiction in Edelman's work, namely, *the valorization of language as prototypical substance from within a tradition of linguistic
analysis that thinks language as pure form. The attunement to sound is here
revealed as the literary experience of a psychic imprint;* the substance of language is metaphorical and the substance of Baldwin only apparent. This
is also to say that Edelman's critique of an identity whose "coercive
'wholeness' ... [is] based on fantasmic identification with a part" is itself
based on the phantasmic identification of the wholeness of the material
substance of Baldwin's text with a part of that substance, namely the
representation of song. This identification is operative in the reading—
which is to say visualization—of that singing and that reading's necessary reduction of that singing's phonic substance.

There is that in the phonic substance of Baldwin's text that does
much more than "make visible to the novel's reader the invisible operation of *différance*." Indeed, Edelman's text carries, or more precisely
transfers, something whose substance is not merely formal. In order to
get to that something it's helpful to follow a certain clue embedded in
Guattari's move toward the indetermination of the "necessary" relation
between the psyche and the signifier and in his attention to those sonic
extremities that infuse the signifier, disturbing the reader's visualization of it—disturbing the sound-image—with a reemergent *substance*
that marks not only its own irruptive penetration but that of other
modes of sensuality and desire as well.[36] "Deep River" in the sound of
Arthur's gaze, in the wetness and depth of Crunch's eyes, in the taste

of Crunch's prick and cum, is tactile. Attention to the sound—and not merely to the sound-image—of the gaze he represents gives us access to the *whole substance* of Baldwin's materiality; so we start, but do not finish, there, where before us it remains to recall in our experience of him the shock of a blessing, a substantive transfer, from which homographesis bars us unless it is augmented. What this requires is neither a reduced emphasis on writing nor some new or more elaborately justified inattention to sound. Rather, an augmentation of reading's attention to the sound-image as Saussure thinks it, which would in turn lead to an augmentation of the experience of the audio-visual in its substantive im/materiality, which would in turn allow a fuller experience of the ensemble of the senses as it is experienced in Baldwin's writing. Improvising through the space between Baldwin's texts and his audio-visual projection in/on film, one is held within the very distillate of aesthetic experience: an erotics of distant receptivity where, in this particular case, phonic materiality opens to us its own invagination, a libidinal drive toward ever greater unities of the sensual where materiality in its most general—which is to say substantive—sense is transmitted in the interstice between text and all it represents and can't represent and the audio-visual and all that it bears and cannot bear. When in this space a *mater*ial tactility is transferred, the affective encounter of the ensemble of the senses and the ensemble of the social is given as a possibility of this erotic drive that now can be theorized in its most intense relation to the drive for, and the knowledge of, freedom.

At one point in Karen Thorsen's film *James Baldwin: The Price of the Ticket*, Baldwin says, "I really do believe in the New Jerusalem." This faith—the substance of things hoped for, the evidence of things unseen but heard (things therefore operating in the interruption of an occular-centric order, a visual code or overdetermined politics of looking that locks in a certain oppositional encounter that Baldwin sang against)—is manifest as an ongoing concern with how you sound, where the critique of sound's occlusion is all bound up with being, as Baraka says, in the tradition, the tradition where the development of society is the focus of art, the tradition where The Music disrupts and reorganizes the forms of sensual expression in the interest of that development. But it is also the evidence of things unheard, something transferred not only in the sound but in the ensemblic materiality of that world-encompassing gaze that sound only indicates. This something is not in the audio-visual experience of Baldwin or in the literary experience of his texts but in . something that is really even before and in improvisation of Baldwin and of these formal projections of Baldwin, something upon which he improvises, something transferred to him from the way back and way before wounded kinship, forced and stolen labor, forced and stolen sexuality. At the risk of being misleading, I would think the more acute attention to what is transferred, to sound + more (not lyric but song + more) in writing and/or film *and what it opens up in them*, as another and more intense encounter with the music, where music is understood as content that irrupts into generic form, enacting a radical disorganization of that form.[37] To sustain the music would be to hold on to another understanding of organization, to improvise another form in extension and in the interest of augmentative musical content. Sustenance, encountering. As Baldwin knows, as Edelman knows both because and in spite of the analytic he employs and to which he is given, to receive the blessing of this substance—to see and hear and touch and smell and taste it; to receive the gift that does not cohere but exists in its abounding of its own internal space; to receive and in so doing to acknowledge the fact of the *w*hole as a kind of distance: this is what it is to linger in the music.

Black Mo'nin' in the Sound of the Photograph

In her essay, "'Can you be BLACK and look at this': Reading the Rodney King Video(s)," Elizabeth Alexander recites a narrative:

> Here is the story in summary: In August 1955, in Money, Mississippi, a fourteen-year-old Chicago black boy named Emmett Till, nicknamed "Bobo," was visiting relatives and was shot in the head and thrown in the river with a mammoth cotton gin fan tied around his neck, for allegedly whistling at a white woman. In some versions of the story, he was found

with his cut-off penis stuffed in his mouth. His body was shipped to Chicago, and his mother [Mamie Till Bradley] decided he should have an open casket funeral; the whole world would see what had been done to her son. According to the Chicago-based, black newsweekly *Jet*, hundreds of thousands of mourners "in an unending procession, later viewed the body" at the funeral home. A photograph of Till in the casket—his head mottled and swollen to many times its normal size—ran in *Jet*, and largely through that medium, both the picture and Till's story became legendary. The caption of the close-up photograph of Till's face read: "Mutilated face of victim was left unretouched by the mortician at the mother's request. She said she wanted 'all the world' to witness the atrocity."[38]

And here are two passages from Mackey's *Bedouin Hornbook* that invoke a sound correspondent to the massive implications of the image Alexander has brought again into view and into question:

> I'm especially impressed by its long overdue disinterment of the occult, heretofore inchoate arcana intuitively buried within the reaches—the wordless reaches—of the black singer's voice. Would it be going too far to say that in your essay the black falsetto has in fact found its voice? (Forgive me if I embarrass you.) In any case, the uncanny coincidence is that the draft of your essay arrived just as I'd put on a record by Al Green. I've long marveled at how all this going on about love succeeds in alchemizing a legacy of lynchings—as though singing were a rope he comes eternally close to being strangled by.
>
> . . . One point I think could bear more insistent mention: What you term "the dislocated African's pursuit of a meta-voice" bears the weight of a gnostic, transformative desire to be done with the world. By this I mean the deliberately forced, deliberately "false" voice we get from someone like Al Green creatively hallucinates a "new world," indicts the more insidious falseness of the world as we know it. (Listen, for example, to "Love and Happiness.") What is it in the falsetto that thins and threatens to abolish the voice but the wear of so much reaching for heaven? At some point you'll have to follow up this excellent essay of yours with a

treatment of the familial ties between the falsetto, the moan and the shout. There's a book by a fellow named Heilbut called *The Gospel Sound* you might look into. At one point, for example, he writes: "The essence of the gospel style is a wordless moan. Always these sounds render the indescribable, implying, "Words can't begin to tell you, but maybe moaning will." If you let "word" take the place of "world" in what I said above the bearing this has on your essay should become pretty apparent. (During his concert a few weeks back Lambert quoted an ex-slave in Louisiana as having said, "The Lawd done said you gotta shout if you want to be saved. You gotta shout and you gotta moan if you wants to be saved." Take particular note of the end of "Love and Happiness," where Green keeps repeating, "Moan for love.") Like the moan or the shout, I'm suggesting, the falsetto explores a redemptive, unworded realm—a meta-word, if you will—where the implied critique of the momentary eclipse of the word curiously rescues, restores and renews it: new word, new world.[39]

Flaunted Fifth heard the noise of a helicopter overhead. He noticed the cops in the police car looking this way. The emotional figure he absentmindedly toyed with was given an abruptly ominous edge by the setting sun, the helicopter overhead and the police car circling the block, all of which put an inverse halo around it. A panicky rush ran thru him as the cops continued to look his way. He couldn't help remembering that several black men had been killed by the L.A. police in recent months, victims of a chokehold whose use there were now efforts to outlaw. The V-shaped warmth in the crook of his right arm seemed to detach itself, rise up and, like an ironic boomerang, press itself against the front of his neck. He imagined himself held in the sweaty crook of a cop's arm.

It was hard not to be overwhelmed by the lethal irony which invaded everything. Flaunted Fifth was suddenly haunted by once having written that the use of the falsetto in black music, the choked-up ascent into a problematic upper register, had a way, as he'd put it, of "alchemizing a legacy of lynchings." He'd planned to make use of this idea again in his lecture/demonstration, but the prospect of a cop's arm around his neck reminded him that every concept, no matter how figural or sublime, had its literal, dead-letter aspect as well. It now seemed too easy to speak of "alchemy," too easy not to remember how inescapably real every lynching had been. He'd always thought of himself as an advocate of spirit. He should have known the letter might someday do him in.

The ominous edge he picked up on was also, he realized, an attribute of spirit. Overtones and resonances inhabited the letter, causing it to creak like the floorboards and doors in a haunted house. That the emotional triad he absentmindedly toyed with, the triangulation he'd made a note of to himself, should creak with overtones of strangulation came as no surprise. That Namesake Epigraph #4 should be haunted by patriarchal patrol cars and helicopters, that it should creak with patriarchal prohibitions against public speech, equally came as no surprise. It all confirmed a "creaking of the spirit" he'd heard referred to in a song from the Bahamas many years before. That the creaking might kill was the price one occasionally paid. "No blues without dues," he reminded himself, making another mental note for his pilot radio show.[40]

Some attribute to Emmett Till—which is to say to his death, which is to say to the famous picturing and display, staging and performance, of his death or of him in death—the agency that set in motion this nation's profoundest political insurrection and resurrection, the resurrection of reconstruction, a second reconstruction like a second coming of the Lord.[41] If this is true, how is it true? On this question Alexander subscribes to James Baldwin's formulation, in *The Evidence of Things Not Seen*, that Till's murder—which in its particularity is not unlike a vast chain of such events that stretches across a long history of brutal violence—can stand out, resonate, or be said to produce effects, only because of the moment of its occurrence, a moment possible only after the beginning of the insurrection and resurrection it is claimed to have sparked. As Alexander remarks, Baldwin's claims regarding this matter are astute: Till's death bears the trace of a particular moment of panic when there was massive reaction to the movement against segregation. (That particular moment of panic is a point on an extended trajectory, where that panic seems almost always to have been—among other things though this is not just one thing among others—sexual. So that the movement against segregation is seen as a movement for miscegenation and, at that point, whistling or the "crippled speech" of Till's "Bye, baby" cannot go unheard.[42] This means we'll have to listen to it along with various other sounds that will prove to be nonneutralizable and irreducible.) The fact that whatever force Till's death exerted was not originary does not mean, however, that that force wasn't real. For even if his death marks panic and even if that panic had already led to the deaths of so many so that that death was already haunted, its force only the animating spirit of a train of horrors, something happened. Something real—in that it might have been otherwise—happened. So that you need to be interested in the complex, dissonant, polyphonic affectivity of the ghost, the agency of the fixed but multiply apparent shade, an improvisation of spectrality, another development of the negative. All these have to do with another understanding of the photograph and of a deferral of some inevitable return to the ontological that would operate in the name of a utopian vision and in the sharpest critique of those authoritarian modes of (false) differentiation and (false) universalization (ultimately, the same thing) that seem to have ontology or the ontological impulse as their condition of possibility and seem to indicate that that impulse or activity could never have ended up in any other way. So I'm interested in what a photograph—what *this* photograph—does to ontology, to the politics of ontology, and to the possibility and project of a utopian politics outside of ontology.

How can this photograph challenge ontological questioning? *By way of a sound* and by way of what's already there in the decision to display the body, to publish the photograph, to restage death and rehearse mo(ur)nin(g). This includes a political imperative that is never disconnected from an aesthetic one, from a necessary reconstruction of the very aesthetics of photography, of documentary and, therefore, of truth, revelation, enlightenment, as well as of judgment, taste and, therefore, of the aesthetic itself. Mackey moves toward this and yet what is made in such sounding, or, rather the theory and theorist of such making, is haunted by a destruction she or it can never assimilate or exhaust. And this is not just about some justification, as if the blues were worth it. Rather you have to think about the fact that an aesthetic appropriation could be said to desacrilize the legacy of lynchings, precisely by way of an "alchemizing" that seems to fetishize or figure on the literal, on the absolute fact and reality of so many deaths while, at the same time, continually opening the possibility of redemption in out sensuality. Which is to say that the blues are not worth the dues pai(n: trace of something something made me type; I had to leave it in: Payne: it'll come back later)d in order to produce them, but they are part of the condition of possibility of the end of such extortion. So this is about the cut music enacts on the image and after the fact of a set of connections between death and the visual, between looking and retribution—as arrest, abduction, and abjection. What did the hegemony of the visual have to do with the death of Emmett Till? What effect did the photograph of his body have on death? What affect did it send? How did the photograph and its reproduction and dissemination break the hegemony of the visual? "Cousins remembered him as 'the center of attention' who 'liked to be seen. He liked the spotlight,'" but he'll be heard, too, broken speech and talking wind by a cry from outside, interior exteriority of the photograph.[43]

In positing that this photo and photographs in general bear a phonic substance, I want to challenge not only the ocularcentrism that generally—perhaps necessarily—shapes theories of the nature of photography and our experience of photography but that mode of semiotic objectification and inquiry that privileges the analytic-interpretative reduction of phonic materiality and/or nonmeaning over something like a mimetic improvisation of and with that materiality that moves in excess of meaning.[44] This second challenge assumes that the critical-mimetic experience of the photograph takes place most properly within a field structured by theories of (black) spectatorship, audition, and performance. These challenges are also something of a preface to such theory and attempt to work out a couple of that theory's most crucial elements: the anti-interpretive nonreduction of nonmeaning and the breakdown of the opposition between live performance and mechanical reproduction. All this by way of an investigation of the augmentation of mourning by the sound of moaning, by a religious and political formulation of morning that animates the photograph with a powerfully *material* resistance. We've got to try to understand the connection between that resistance and political movement, locating that movement's direction toward new universalities held within the difference/s of phonic substance, in the difference of the accent that cuts and augments mourning and morning, a difference semiotics has heretofore thought either to be fatal to its desire for universality or proof of the foolishness and political and epistemological danger of that desire.

There is the trace of what remains to be discovered, a topic, a path I'm trying to take that moves through a shudder I can never escape when gazing, or even after the fact of an arrested and arresting glance, at the broken face of Emmett Till. Looking at Emmett Till is arrested by overtonal reverberations; looking demurs when looking opens onto an unheard sound that the picture cannot secure but discovers and onto all of what it might be said to mean that I can look at this face, this photograph.[45] This is to say not only look at it but look at it in the context of an aesthetics, look at it as if it were to be looked at, as if it were to be thought, therefore, in terms of a kind of beauty, a kind of detachment, independence, autonomy, that holds open the question of what looking might mean in general, what the aesthetics of the photograph might mean for politics and what those aesthetics might have meant for Mamie Bradley in the context of her demand that her son's face be seen, be shown, that his death and her mourning be performed.

Emmett Till's face is seen, was shown, shone. His face was destroyed (by way of, among other things, its being shown: the memory of his face is thwarted, made a distant before-as-after effect of its destruction, what we would never have otherwise seen). It was turned inside out, ruptured, exploded, but deeper than that it was opened. As if his face were the truth's condition of possibility, it was opened and revealed. As if revealing his face would open the revelation of a fundamental truth, his casket was opened, as if revealing the destroyed face would in turn reveal, and therefore cut, the active deferral or ongoing death or unapproachable futurity of justice. As if his face would deconstruct justice or deconstruct deconstruction or deconstruct death, though this infinite and circular chain seems too muddled, too crazy, too twisted or clotted, as if it, too, were in need of another cut, it was shown. As if that face revealed "the beginning of death in cut time" as if this was a death unlike other deaths, a death that prompts a mourning whose rehearsal is also a refusal, a death to end all deaths or all other deaths but one, his face was destroyed by its display.[46] His casket was opened, his face was shown, is seen—now in the photograph—and allowed to open a revelation that first is manifest in the shudder the shutter continues to produce, the trembling, a general disruption of the ways in which we gaze at the face and at the dead, a disruption of the oppressive ethics and coercive law of reckless eyeballing, reckless whistling, which contains within it a call, the disruption of the disruption that would have captured, an arrest of the spirit that arrests, a repetitive close.[47] Memory—bound to the way the photograph holds up what it proposes, stops, keeps—is given pause because what we thought we could look at for the last time and hold holds us, captures us, and doesn't let us go. And why is the memory of this mutilated face, reconfiguration of what was embedded in some furtive and partial glance's refusal, so much more horrible, the distortion magnified even more than the already incalculable devastation of the actual body? Does the blindness held in the aversion of the eye create an insight that is manifest as a kind of magnification or intensification of the object—as if memory as affect and the affect that forges distorted or intensified memory cascade off one another, each multiplying the other's force? I think this kind of blindness makes music.

The fear of another castration is all bound up in this aversion of the eye. Emmett Till's death marks a double time, rhythm-a-ning, redoubled nothing-ing, dead and castrated. But his mother, absent, present, reopens or leaves open the wound that is redoubled, the nothing that is redoubled in her son's murder. Ms. Bradley opens, leaves open, reopens, the violent, ritual, sexual cutting of his death by the leaving open of the casket, by the unretouching of the body, by the body's photo-graph, by the photograph's transformation in memory and nightmare of which many speak (for instance Roland Barthes, about whom more later). That leaving open is a performance. It is the disappearance of the disappearance of Emmett Till that emerges by way of exhibiting kin-ship's wounds (themselves always refigured and refinished in and as and by exogamous collision). It is the ongoing destruction of the ongoing production of (a) (black) performance, which is what I am, which is what you are or could be if you can listen while you look. If he seems to keep disappearing as you look at him it's because you look away, which is what makes possible and impossible representation, reproduction, dream. And there is a sound that is seemingly not there in this per-formance that this performance is about; but not just a sound since we are also concerned with what that sound would invoke—immortal or utopian longings, though not the utopianism of a past made present, not the recovery of a loss, and not just a negation of the present either, in the form of an ongoing displacement of the concrete. Rather, here is an abundance—in abundance—of the present, an abundance of affirma-tion in abundance of the negative, in abundance of disappearance.

Such is the aesthetic cut, invasive evasion, shock of the shock, adding form and color to a verbal discourse, adding extensional cry and sound to the word's visualization. An image from which one turns is immediately caught in the production of its memorialized, re-membered reproduction. You lean into it but you can't; the aesthetic and philo-sophical arrangements of the photograph—some organizations of and for light—anticipate a looking that cannot be sustained as unalloyed looking but must be accompanied by listening and this, even though what is listened to—echo of a whistle or a phrase, moaning, mourning, desperate testimony and flight—is also unbearable. These are the com-plex musics of the photograph. This is the sound before the photograph:

Scream inside and out, out from outside, of the image. Bye, baby. Whistling. Lord, take my soul. Redoubled and reanimating passion, the passion of a seeing that is involuntary and uncontrollable, a seeing that redoubles itself as sound, a passion that is the redoubling of Emmett

Till's passion, of whatever passion would redeem, crucifixion, lynching, middle passion, passage. So that looking implies that one desires something for this photograph. So that mourning turns. So that the looker is in danger of slipping, not away, but into something less comfortable than horror—aesthetic judgment, denial, laughter, some out and unprecedented reflection, movement, murder, song. So that there is an inappropriable ecstatics that goes along with this aesthetics—one is taken out, like in screams, fainting, tongues, dreams. So perhaps she was counting on the aesthetic.

This aural aesthetic is not the simple reemergence of the voice of presence, the visible and graphic word. The logos that voice implies and requires has been complicated by the echo of transgressive whistle, abortive seduction, stuttered leave-taking, and by reconstructive overtones of mo'nin'. Something is remembered and repeated in such complications. Transferred. To move or work through that something, to improvise, requires thinking about morning and how mourning sounds, how moaning sounds. What's made and destroyed. We'll have to do this while keeping in mind all that remains urgent and needful and open in the critique of phonologocentrism Derrida initiates. Nevertheless, we've got to cut the ongoing "reduction of the phonic substance" whose origin is untraceable, but that is at least as old as philosophy, at least as old as its paradoxically interinanimate other, phonocentrism, and predates any call for its being set into motion, either in Descartes or Saussure or in Derrida's critical echo of them. The refusal to neutralize the phonic substance of the photograph rewrites the time of the photograph, the time of the photograph of the dead. The time of the sound of the photograph of the dead is no longer irreversible, no longer vulgar, and, moreover, not only indexed to rhythmic complication but to the extreme and subtle harmonics of various shrieks, hums, hollers, shouts, and moans. What these sounds and their times indicate is the way into another question concerning universality, a reopening of the issue of a universal language by way of this new music so that now it's possible to accommodate a differentiation of the universal, of its ongoing reconstruction in sound as the differential mark, divided and abundant, dividing and abounding. But how many people have really listened to this photograph? Hieroglyphics, phonetic writing, phonography—where is the photograph placed in all this?

Black mo'nin' is the phonographic content of this photograph. And the whistle is just as crucial as the moan; train whistle, maybe; his whistle carrying the echo of the train that took his particular origins north, the train that brought him home and took him home and brought him home. There's a massive itinerancy here, a fugitivity that breaking only left more broke, broken and unbroken circle of escape and return.[48] And the gap between them, between their modes of audibility vis-à-vis the photograph, is the difference within invagination between what cuts and what surrounds, invagination being that principle of impurity that, for Derrida, marks the law of the law of genre where the set or ensemble or totality is constantly improvised by the rupturing and augmentative power of an always already multiply and disruptively present singularity. So that speech is broken and expanded by writing; so that hieroglyphics is affected by phonetic script; so that a photograph exerts itself on the alphabet; so that phonographic content infuses the photo. And this movement doesn't mark some orbital decay in which signification inevitably returns to some simple vocal presence; rather it's the itinerary of the force and movement of signification's outside. The implications of this aural aesthetic—this phonographic rewriting of/in the photograph—are crucial and powerful then, because they mark something general about the nature of a photograph and a performance—the ongoing universality of their absolute singularity—that is itself, at least for me, most clearly and generously given in black photography and black performance. (This is, for instance, what Ma/ckey always brings, always knows.)

Blackness and maternity play huge roles in the analytic of photography Roland Barthes lays down in *Camera Lucida*, Barthes's extended and elegiac meditation on the essence of photography that revolves around an unreproducible, unobservable photograph of his mother as a young child (the "Winter Garden Photograph"), a woman remarkable to Barthes in part because, he says, she made no observations.[49] Blackness is the site or mark of the ideal object, the ideal spectator (and these are everything for Barthes's analytic since the doing or operation of photography is bracketed and set aside early on in *Camera Lucida*). Blackness is the embodiment of a naïveté that would move Barthes, the self-styled essential phenomenologist, back before culture to some pure and unalloyed looking.[50] The paradox, here, is that the reduction phenomenology desires seems to require a regression to a prescientific state characterized by what Husserl, after Hegel, would call the incapability of science. Those who are incapable of science are those who are outside history, but that exteriority is precisely the desired starting point for phenomenology, which would move not through philosophical tradition but directly toward and in the things themselves. And indeed, this is how empire makes phenomenology possible, figuring a simplicity structured by regression, return, and reduction refigured as refinement. Empire's mother fixation is phenomenology's obsession with blackness. Blackness is situated precisely at the site of the condition of possibility and impossibility of phenomenology and, for Barthes, that's cool because the object and the spectator of photography reside there as well. This interstitial no-space is where photography lives, this point of embarkation for the europhallic journey to the interior, to the place of the other, the dark continent, the motherland that is always coded as an imperial descent into self. This regressive return to "that-has-been" and/or to where-you-been is the staging area for the performance of that violent and ruptural collision that is both the dramatic life of blackness and the opening of what is called modernity.[51] The lynching and photographing of Emmett Till, the reproductive display of his photographed body by his mother, the Barthesian theory of photography that is founded in part on a silencing invocation of that mother and of his, are all part of the ongoing production of that performance. It ought not be surprising, then, that Barthes's analysis in *Camera Lucida* is structured by a set of problematic moves: a disavowal of the historical in photography that reduces it to a field of merely "human interest"; a figuring of photographic historicality as overwhelmed by that univocal intentionality of the photographer that can only ever result in "a kind of general enthusiastic commitment . . . without special acuity"; an ontological differentiation between photography and the photograph; and a semiotic neutralization of the unorderable or nonmeaningful phonic substance of photography.[52] It is especially the first and last of these elements that emerge here:

> The photograph is unary when it emphatically transforms "reality" without doubling it, without making it vacillate (emphasis is a power of cohesion): no duality, no indirection, no disturbance. The unary Photograph has every reason to be banal, "unity" of composition being the first rule of vulgar (and notably, of academic) rhetoric: "The subject," says one handbook for amateur photographers, "must be simple, free of useless accessories; this is called the Search for Unity."
>
> News photographs are very often unary (the unary photograph is not necessarily tranquil). In these images, no punctum: a certain shock but no disturbance; the photograph can "shout," not wound. These journalistic photographs are received (all at once), perceived. I glance through them, I don't recall them; no detail (in some corner) ever interrupts my reading: I am interested in them (as I am interested in the world), I do not love them.[53]

Barthes's turn from the vulgar, unary photography of the shout and toward the refined photography of the prick or wound is tied to an ontological questioning that is founded on the unreproducibility of a photograph and the theological veiling of the original in the interest of a theory of photographic signification.[54] Against the backdrop of Emmett Till, the silencing of a photograph in the name of that interstitial space between The Photograph and Photography is also the silencing dismissal of a performance in the name of that interstitial space between Performance and Performativity. And, again, paradoxes are here produced seemingly without end, so that Barthes's critique of the unary photograph is based on the assumption of the unary sensuality of photography. And this is a prescriptive assumption—photography ought to be sensually unary, ought not shout so that it can prick. Wounding photography is absolutely visual; that's the only way you can love it.

So what's the relationship between the necessary presence of the interinanimation of naïve blackness and pre-observational motherhood in Barthes's theory and the necessary absence of sound? Perhaps it is this: that the necessary repression—rather than some naturalized absence—of phonic substance in a general semiotics applies to the semiotics of photography as well; that the semiotic desire for universality, which excludes the difference of accent by excluding sound in the search for a universal language and a universal science of language, is manifest in Barthes as the exclusion of the sound/shout of the photograph; and, in the fundamental methodological move of what-has-been-called-enlightenment, we see the invocation of a silenced difference, a silent black *mater*iality, in order to justify a suppression of difference in the name of (a false) universality.

In the end, though, neither language nor photography nor performance can tolerate silence. Which is to say that the universalities these names would mark exist only in the singularities of a language, a photograph, a performance, singularities that cannot live in the absence of sound. Repressed accent returns precisely in the doubling that these things require, that the theory of these things demand; so that sound and recording are fundamentally connected in their disruptive necessity to language, photography, and performance. This aural aesthesis is what she counts on to intensify the politics of the performance whose production she extends. The meaning of a photograph is cut and augmented by a sound or noise that surrounds it and pierces its frame. And if, as Barthes suggests, that meaning or essence or *noeme* is death, the "*that-has-been* of the photographic object," then sound disturbs it in the interest of a resurrection. The content of the music of this photograph, like that of black music in general according to Amiri Baraka, is life, is freedom. The music and theater of a black photograph is erotic: the drama of life in the photograph of the dead.

So what's the difference between the son's inability to reproduce the photograph of his dead mother and the mother's insistence on the reproduction of the photograph of her dead son? The difference has to do with distinguishable stances toward universality, with what the discovery of a performance or a photograph has to do with universality, with the meaningful and illusory difference and relation between Performance and Performativity, the Photograph and Photography. If "the Winter Garden Photograph was indeed essential, it achieved for [Barthes], utopically, *the impossible science of the unique being.*"[55] This impossible science, the unique and universal word or logos, is achieved only in a kind of solipsism, only in the memory that activates the unique photograph's capacity to wound. Meanwhile, Ms. Bradley sidesteps (by way of an insistent publicity wherein is carried the echo of whistling and mo'nin'; in the interest of getting to some other—which is to say real—place) the utopic intersection of hermeneutics, phenomenology, and ontology that mark the origin and limit of Barthes's desire. For Barthes the inability and/or unwillingness to discover a photograph is driven by the positing of a universality and singularity that can only be mourned; for Ms. Bradley the discovery of a photograph in the fullness of its multiple sensuality moves in the drive for a universality to come, one called by what is in and around the photograph—black mo'nin'.

About twenty-five years before *Camera Lucida,* in an essay called "The Great Family of Man," Barthes made some assumptions in the form of a question regarding what "the parents of Emmet [sic] Till, the young Negro assassinated by the Whites" would have thought about the Great Family of Man and the celebrated traveling photographic exhibit called *The Great Family of Man.*[56] He uses those assumptions to argue for the necessity for progressive humanism of an ongoing historicization of nature rather than an uncritical photo-affirmation of certain universal facts like birth and death. After all, he writes, "to reproduce death or birth tells us, literally, nothing. For these natural facts to gain access to a true language, they must be inserted into a category of knowledge which means postulating that one can transform them, and precisely subject their naturalness to our human criticism."[57] Indeed, for Barthes, the failure of such photography lies in its inability to show

> whether or not the child is born with ease or difficulty, whether or not his birth causes suffering to his mother, whether or not he is threatened with a high mortality rate, whether or not such and such a future is open to him: this is what your exhibition should be telling people, instead of an eternal lyricism of birth. The same goes for death: must we really celebrate its essence once more, and thus risk forgetting that there is still so much we can do to fight it? It is this very young, far too young power that we must exalt, and not the sterile identity of "natural" death.[58]

At the end of his career, however, Barthes produced a text that requires that we ask how a critique of the suppression of the determining weight of history is left behind for a stance that is nothing if not ahistorical. Where history and that singularity that exists as a function of depth/ interiority, a certain incursion into the interior of the photograph and of identity, merge in "The Great Family of Man," history and singularity are reconfigured each in relation to the other in *Camera Lucida*. There, history exists only in relation to the sovereign ego that is given and represented by the wounding, arresting force of the photographic *punctum*, the placement of the interiority of a subject on endless trial.[59] Where difference was once tied to the historical injustices it both structures and is structured by, now it marks only the uniqueness of an ego, is "that time when we were not born," or, more particularly, "the time when my mother was alive *before me*."[60] And, indeed, the representation of injustice, of historical alienation, is now configured only as banality. This configuration marks the return, paradoxically, of an empty humanism of death (and birth) that elsewhere and earlier Barthes had critiqued. *The photograph as such* is now just the universal visual fact of death, of pastness, of that-has-been, of the essence or *noeme* of photography that, again, is the object of Barthe's analytic desire. On the other hand, a *photograph* will remain, for him, not invisible but simply unreproducible. The fundamental absence of depth, held now in the very form of the print, allows only the sad gesture of turning the photograph over. The appeal to the possibility of a particular identity's historical materiality is transformed into the flat memorialization of the photograph's train. This analytic is shaped by the recrudescence of that humanism that marks what Louis Althusser called "the international of decent feelings";[61] though here feeling is numbed by a violent egocentrism. An intensely melancholic phenomenology of photography emerges from that egocentrism, one in which what might be called the loss of historical particularity or of the particularity of *a* photograph is displaced by the loss of the desire for these objects and for the object as such.

But there is already something amiss in "The Great Family of Man"; an opposition between the modes of production of the human and human essence that is precisely what Ms. Bradley cuts. It is the split in which totality is a/voided in the interest of historical particularity and it is displaced, in *Camera Lucida*, by a reified ontological concern with *studium* and *punctum*, a phenomenological privileging of essence that reveals history to be fundamentally personal, fundamentally deictic, and thus still forecloses not only the totality Barthes already disavows in the earlier text but the singularity he desires in the later one. In other words, historical particularity becomes what Bertrand Russell would have called egocentric particularity. So that this is about how listening carefully to the muted sound of the photograph as it resonates in Barthes's texts on photography, through his repression and denigration of it, gives you some clues about the inevitability of a certain development in which egocentrism and ontologism, perhaps each to the other's regret, are each tied to the other in theory, which is to say, in epistemologies of unalloyed looking. And perhaps whatever speech and writing that comes after or over a photograph or a performance should deal with this epistemological and methodological problem: how to listen to (and touch, taste, and smell) a photograph, or a performance, how to attune oneself to a moan or shout that animates the photograph with an intentionality of the outside. Barthes is interested in, but, by implication, does not love the world. The shout that structures and ruptures the photograph of Emmett Till with a piercing historicality, that resingularizes and reconstructs his broken body, emerges from love, from a love of the world, from a specific political intention. When Barthes invokes Ms. Bradley in a critique of the naturalistic and universalizing photography of the bare fact of death but fails to recognize her own meta-photographic contribution to that critique, he reveals a quite specific inability that will be fully activated years later in another discourse on photography that is equally dependent on black images.

Of course, Emmett Till's death (which word wrongs him and her) was not natural and the photograph shows this. It shows this and the *death's* difficulty, the suffering of the mother, the threat of a high mortality rate and the seemingly absolute closure of his future. But it does so not by way of an erasure of lyricism or even of "the natural," for these reemerge, by way of an unbearable and vicious dialectic, in the photograph's music. Barthes's question was only rhetorical, though. He didn't really ask Ms. Bradley what she thought. She told us anyway. And so this photograph—or, more precisely, the natural and unnatural fact that is photographed and displayed—cannot simply be used as an inarticulate denial of an always and necessarily false universality. Because it is in the name, too, of a dynamic universality (which critically moves in, among other things, grief, anger, hatred, the desire to expose and eradicate savagery) whose organization would suspend the condition of possibility of deaths like Emmett Till's, that the photo was shown, is seen. It is in the interest of a certain defeat or at least deconstruction of death, a resurrective or (second) reconstructive improvisation through death's pride and through a culture that, as Baraka points out in a recent poem, "believe[s] everything is better/Dead. And that everything alive/is [its] enemy[,]" that Till's body was shown, was seen and that the photograph of Till's body is shown, is seen. But Barthes wasn't trying to hear the sound of that display, the sound of the photograph's *illumination* of facticity that holds an affirmation not of, but *out of* death. Black Art, which is to say Black Life, which is to say Black (Life Against) Death, which is to say Black Eros, is the ongoing production of a performance, the ongoing production of a performance: rupture and collision, augmented toward singularity, motherless child, childless mother, heartrending shriek, levee camp moan, grieving lean and head turn, fall, *Stabat mater*, turn a step, loose booty funk brush stroke down my cheek, yellow dog, blue train, black drive. The ways black mo'nin' improvises through the opposition of mourning and melancholia, disrupts the temporal framework that buttresses that opposition such that an extended, lingering look at—aesthetic response to—the photograph manifests itself as political action. Is the display of the picture melancholic? No, but it's certainly no simple release or mourning either. Mo'nin' improvises through that difference. You have to keep looking at this so you can listen to it.

So in the name of this bright section of winds, some variations on Alexander's question: Can you look at this, which is to say, can you look at this again (such repetition being a constitutive element of what it means and is to be BLACK)? Can you be BLACK and not look at this (again)? Can you look at this (again) and be BLACK? There is a responsibility to look every time, again, but sometimes it looks like that looking comes before, holds, replicates, reproduces what is looked at. Nevertheless, looking keeps open the possibility of closing precisely what it is that prompts and makes necessary that opening. But such an opening is only held in looking that is attentive to the sound—and movement, feel, taste, smell (as well as sight): the sensual ensemble—of what is looked at. The sound works and moves not just through but before another movement, a movement that is before even that affirmation that Barthes didn't hear. A photograph was seen, was shown, in a complex path, a dissonant and polyphonic drive. In the death of Emmett Till, insurrection and resurrection are each insistently *before* the other waiting for a beginning that is only possible after the experience of all of what is held in the photograph. What is held in a photograph is not exclusive to the photograph, but this photograph moves and works, is shown, was seen, shone, says, is animated, resounds, broken, breaking song of, song for, something before, like The Music that is, as Mingus says, not just beautiful, but *terribly beautiful.*

So here is the performance I discovered by way of this "legacy of lynchings": At my Aunt Mary's funeral (she was my favorite aunt but I was scared to look at her face in the photograph I couldn't help but look at that they made of her at the funeral home), Ms. Rosie Lee Seals rose up in church, out from the program, and said, "Sister Mary Payne told me that if she died she wanted me to give a *deep moan* at her funeral." And, at that moment, in her Las Vegas-from-Louisiana accent, condition of impossibility of a universal language, condition of possibility of a universal language, burying my auntie with music at morning time, where moaning renders mourning wordless (the augmentation and reduction of or to our to oa releasing more than what is bound up in the presence of the word) and voice is dissonanced and multiplied by metavoice, Sister Rosie Lee Seals mo'ned. New word, new world.[62]

Tonality of Totality

Three Material Lectures. Three Maternal Lectures.[63]

Step to the League of Revolutionary Black Workers, a dissident group of autoworkers formed in Detroit in the late 1960s, and through the film the League produced, *Finally Got the News.*[64] Approach the film, and the specific aesthetic and theoretical interventions the League makes in the film, by thinking the inscriptive force of the lecture as a form. Move after the phonography of a kind of performance—the writing of the lecture, the reading of speech—the marked and marking *mater*iality of an event. The tradition from which the League and its film emerges is one that requires a (specifically phonic) re*mater*ialization, one driven by a mode of kinship that could be said to be both wounded and irrational, that provides the open foundation for the production of black political sound, in particular, and black political sensuality, in general.

Say something whose phonic substance will be impossible to reduce, whose cuts and augmentations have to be recorded. Speak and break speech like a madrig, like a matrix (material, maternal). Read aloud about the out, loud reading of a set of inscriptions, inscriptions of and against cruelty and terror, amputation and administration, the disciplinary subordination to the instruments of production. Operate on and not simply in Marxist tracks. Cut those tracks with the force of that phonic materiality and impossible maternity that they relinquish, perhaps necessarily, almost at their scientific outset in the analytic of the commodity. In her *Critique of Postcolonial Reason* Spivak moves to rediscover that force that is, for her, manifest in the "perspective of the 'native informant' [that, she suggests,] has been foreclosed in the tradition of Marxism and continues to be excluded":[65]

> The commodity-form is the locus of the sustained homeopathic monitoring of the chronic difference between socialism and capitalism—because, with things, it generates "more" (*Mehrwert* = surplus-value), and with people, it permits abstraction and thus separation from individual intention. . . . Let us unfix the binary opposition between "labor-power [as] *only* a commodity" and the heterogeneous hierarchies of race-gender-migrancy . . . and see a shuttle where the rational calculus of commodification protects from the dangers of a merely fragmented identity politics—and not in the economic sphere alone. [Étienne] Balibar describes "the term 'proletariat' [as] only connot[ing] the 'transitional' nature of the working class, . . . accentuat[ing] the difficulty in holding together, without aporia or contradiction, historical materialism and the critical theory of *Capital*." . . . Balibar sees this transitionality as an inability "to formulate the concept of *proletarian ideology* as the ideology *of proletarians*." . . . We must read it as the moment where the Marxian text transgresses its own protocols—so far Balibar is our guide—so that it can be turned around and let the subaltern (who is not coterminous with the proletarian) enter in the colonial phase, and today make room for the globe-girdling nationalist-under-erasure Southern (rather than only the Eurocentric migrant) subject who would dislocate Economic Citizenship by constant interruption, "permanent parabasis."[66]

Such rediscovery resides in (the call for) what is made possible by the Marxian text's cutting and augmentation of itself, though this internal disruption is always activated by a cry from outside, a cry that text can only figure subjunctively. Spivak's call is itself a recording of that cry—a subaltern sound, a lecture written through and past and in some impossible speech. The de Manian imperative of "permanent parabasis" animates her text as well, as anima, an animality that moves with the interruptive-connective force of polyrhythmic organization. It's a disciplinary rhythm, a rhythm of the line, but that discipline responds to something that was there before it, something located where disruption and creation meet as irregularity, the condition of im/possibility of the standard. When Spivak writes in this book of the book she cannot write, she moves toward a difficulty less absolute and more particular: "If I were writing this section today, I would smell out here a foreclosure of the woman who will be the agent of Marxism today in the inevitable docketing of European as 'international' and organized internationality as 'men's.'"[67] Her nonstandard phonography is meant to forestall such disclosure and such docketing. These lectures are the amplification of what is before such foreclosure in the text of Marx. There's something there, parallel to the perspective Spivak seeks to valorize, that these lectures bring. They bring it by way of the unfixing of a binary opposition that even Spivak leaves alone: the opposition between things and people. Indeed, thinking labor-power as a commodity requires brushing against, if not necessarily fully confronting, the trace of a breakdown between the person and the thing that is, on the one hand, before the absolute differentiation of these terms each from the other, and on the other hand, reestablished always and everywhere in the fact of slavery. These lectures are recordings of the sound of that which Marx figures, in the discourse on the fetish-character of the commodity and its secret, as impossible: the speech of the commodity. If the commodity could speak it would say that its value is not inherent; it would say, ultimately, that it cannot speak. But commodities speak and scream, opening tonal and grammatical fissures that mark the space of the very globe-girdling, nationalist-under-erasure political agency and theoretical intervention (this is to say that ideology of the proletarian that is not one) (that is at least touching that space) for which and from which Spivak calls. The League and the audiovisual lectures that move through it work that way too. These lectures are delivered by the trace of the commodity.

The trace of the commodity is inseparable from its fetish-character. Spivak says, "In [Marx's] mature theoretical texts, he is not centrally concerned with ideology but rather with the positive task of acquiring the rational x-ray vision that would cut through the fetish-character of the commodity."[68] So challenge such seeing or cutting through, such violently imposed transparency, while at the same time thinking the immeasurable value of the fetish-character of the commodity as lens, as condition of possibility of another vision, another rationality, even another enlightenment. Spivak continues, by way of a telling moment in Marx:

> The worker would understand and set to work the circuit of commodity capital. Consider the role of rendering transparent assigned to rationality in the following passage [from volume 2 of *Capital*]: "The commodity capital, as the direct product of the capitalist production process, recalls its origin and is therefore more rational in its form, less lacking in conceptual differentiation, than the money capital, in which every trace of this process has been effaced.... The expression $M \ldots M'(M = m)$ is irrational, in that, within it, part of a sum of money appears as the mother of another part of the same sum of money. But here this irrationality disappears.[69]

It's a strange passage to consider and a difficult one. The commodity is more rational, according to Marx, in that it recalls its origins and is, seemingly, less lacking in conceptual differentiation. This relatively greater rationality is aligned with a certain transparency; we are able to see through the commodity to its origins. And this seeing through to origins is set over against the opaque—even delusional—maternal appearance of money, when one part of money seems to have given birth to another part of the same sum. When Marx aligns what we will come to think as finance capital with the irrational kinship of a merely apparent maternity, we are called upon to think, along with him, of some originary authenticity that is outside or before maternity. The anti-maternal, ante-maternal commodity would emerge from an origin that reduces difference. The reduction of difference and the reduction of the maternal coincide with a certain reduction of the material that animates the sciences of value from Marx's revolutionizing of them to Saussure's equally far-reaching application of that revolutionary move. This is to say, of course, that the reduction of phonic substance, phonic materiality, that Saussure requires in order to form a universal science of language is anticipated by Marx in *Capital*. Again, this reduction of (phonic) materiality moves along the trajectory of a reduction of (a certain phonic) maternity as well. In a way that Spivak anticipatingly, echoically turns away from and toward, try to bring back all of that noise. The force of that return is a function of such reduction. The richly differentiated commodity screams poetically, musically, politically, theoretically; the commodity screams and sings in labor. The spirit of the *mater*ial.

None of this will have been meant to deny that the model of blackness as black performance as black radicalism I've been trying to think about is extreme in its masculinism. Indeed, this model is marked by the ongoing projection of a specific notion of masculinity that emerges as the response to and repudiation and repetition of the violation of black maternity. This model of masculinist radicalism is so old that we can't really locate its origin, no matter how tantalizing certain dates or events. It is, again, the radicalism of filial severance, the aesthetic and political assertion of motherless children and impossible motherhood, and it can neither be dismissed nor denied. We can see its contours in and trace its trajectory from Douglass's participant observation to R. Kelly's wish. And this is to say that this black masculinist radicalism is manifest as a particular rhetorical tradition, a line of lectures, if you will, that is itself in need of the reassertion of the materiality and maternity that lies at its core. To attempt such reassertion is to be marked by a kind of absorption and transfer of matrical experience that is, at the very least, once removed from the intense repression of that experience that drives the phantasmatically uncut rhetoric of masculinist black radicalism. In the meantime this other materialism has to be read and it must occur at and as a matrix of voices, dubbed or overdubbed like a palimpsest. It's in the way one reads a lecture that theoretical interventions about, say, value, or postmodern global space reside. This is to say that they reside in the lecture's internal space and organization and in the internal space and organization of the lecture's medium.

The interinanimation of the maternal and the material that is iconically manifest in the female voice, particularly in the way that the scream or cry of the female voice is irreducible to meaning, is part of what I'm interested in here. This is, of course, terrain that Kaja Silverman has famously and rigorously explored, but I have to think about it differently than she because I have a different sense of the value of sounds that are irreducible to meaning. That value is bound up with the reconstruction of value and of the sciences of value. This different sense of the scream's value stems from a tradition whose massive aesthetic, and political resources emerge precisely through, if not from, such screams where those screams are always so much more than primal. The condition of possibility of such emergence is the ability critically to think the scream, to offer what the scream demands that is before— which is to say both prior to and past—both interpretation and reading. Following Silverman, but a little bit off her track, I want to suggest that a quite specific asynchronicity between sound and image marks the spot of a radical intervention. This off-set or off-rhythm animates the audiovisuality (the arrhythmia of its multiple tracks) of the commodity, in general. In this tradition, in spite of whatever powerful voices of disavowal, the man's voice is a woman's voice and the high-pitched truth of the falsetto is revolutionary tone and content.

Two encounters seem to occur but don't, I think, in Fredric Jameson's essay "Cognitive Mapping": the encounter with the aesthetic (and, by extension, between the aesthetic and the political) and the encounter between Jameson's theoretical resources and aspirations and those of the League. These are resources and aspirations having to do with possible understandings, both prescriptive and descriptive, of the aesthetic and of representation, categories Jameson privileges in his essay. These resources and aspirations are thoroughly and richly documented in the League's journalism and are manifest in the aesthetic, organizational works and forms they created, especially in *Finally Got the News*. In "Cognitive Mapping" Jameson mentions the film—even calls it a "fine and exciting" one—only in order to dismiss it as the very icon of the League's ultimate "failure" and of the reasons for that "failure" and as a kind of slippage, by way of the ineluctable contradiction embedded in the opposition of the global and the local (what Jameson calls "spatial discontinuity" or "the inability to map socially"), into mere "spectacle," the imaged disappearance of its referent, the League and its movement. More to the point, Jameson sees the film and the League as an example of failed representation that can then be framed within a more "successful spatial representation"—a "narrative of defeat which sometimes, even more effectively, causes the whole architectonic of postmodern global space to rise up in ghostly profile behind itself as if some ultimate dialectical barrier or limit." Such a narrative is where the terms and conditions of such failure are most clearly shown. And so he engages not with the League and with its mediated self-representations but rather with the indisputably valuable volume on the League, *Detroit, I Do Mind Dying*, by Dan Georgakas and Marvin Surkin.[70] The object Jameson engages, then, is not the film the League produces, not its own representation of itself, but rather the representation of the League's failure, which is, ultimately, understood by Jameson to be a failure adequately to represent itself (in relation to postmodern, post-Fordist, postindustrial global capital and global space). But if that other aesthetic, the aesthetic of cognitive mapping as Jameson understands it, is possible; if, as a matter of fact, it is given as a kind of magnificent chance or opening in the very encounter between Marxist theory and the theoretical resources and political-economic aspirations held within (the work of) the black aesthetic that Jameson marks in a framing that is also an erasure; then the problem of an inability to confront those resources can't be overlooked. Jameson's essay provides not only the opportunity to deal with this problem, it also provides for us the occasion to look at a model—the film itself—of such an encounter, for it is at the non/intersection of an emergent aesthetic of cognitive mapping, on the one hand, and a critical extension of the black aesthetic in its broadest historical sense, on the other, that *Finally Got the News* is situated.

Here is the opening of "Cognitive Mapping":

> I am addressing a subject about which I know nothing whatsoever, except for the fact that it does not exist. The description of a new aesthetic, or the call for it, or its prediction—these things are generally done by practicing artists whose manifestoes articulate the originality they hope for in their own work, or by critics who think they already have before their eyes the stirrings and emergences of the radically new. Unfortunately, I can claim neither of these positions, and since I am not even sure how to imagine the kind of art I want to propose here, let alone affirm its possibility, it may well be wondered what kind of operation this will be, to produce the concept of something we cannot imagine.[71]

Jameson says that we are in need, but incapable, of those forms of representation—political and aesthetic—that would allow for both a description of postmodern global space and a prescriptive vision of that space transformed, resocialized. And note that this spatial problematic is immediately bound to a temporal/historical problem concerning the relation between prescription, or prophecy, and description while remembering Ellison's formulation, from the epilogue of *Invisible Man*, as a particularly elegant and succinct articulation of this complex. Whether it be the restricted frames of various forms of aesthetic or even journalistic realisms or the violent and absurd inadequacies of representative democracy and their corollary problematics of leadership, these problems of representation emerge with a special intensity in the age of multinational capital, the particular spatial form (of contradiction) that corresponds to it, and the temporal and historical frames within which that space is cognized, successfully or not.

So Jameson describes or calls for or predicts another aesthetic in the interest of another politics. And this interest, he acknowledges, immediately raises the possibility that the aesthetic or theoretical attention to the aesthetic is just "a kind of blind,"[72] just a pretext for debating the-oretical and political issues that become dominant after the fact of the emergence of something called "post-Marxism." In particular, Jameson wants to rehabilitate the concept of social totality, without which there can be neither a description of capital/ism nor a prescription for social-ism. To do so he would employ particular and traditional uses of the aesthetic, namely, those bound up with teaching, moving, and delight-ing. He employs Darko Suvin's notion of the cognitive as a term that binds together and describes these uses, though importantly he abstracts the key word "increment" from Suvin's formulation, thereby losing the potential force of a possible disruptively augmentative kind of energy that could be held within and be itself disruptive of Suvin's additive notion of aesthetic cognition. I want to get back to this—the weight of a kind of augmentative or invaginative musicality and the aesthetic—a bit later. But now it's important to point out that Jameson's recovery of these uses of the aesthetic are bound up with a necessary attempt to rehabilitate the notion of representation, a notion that he equates with figuration as such and not with, as I indicated earlier, restrictive notions of more or less impossible forms of verisimilitude. The call for a new aesthetic is the call for a new mode of representation. And what is to be represented or figured is social totality, itself neither characterized by nor iconic of anything other than capital itself.

Jameson goes on to trace his particular periodization of capital. He charts the correspondence between its three stages—market, impe-rialist, multinational—and their particular spatial forms—the Cartesian grid of infinite extension and an equally infinite imagined ability to picture or model the entirety of the grid and the relations situated within it; the unencompassable world space of imperialism in which the appearance of the local only marks the absence of a distant, space-time separated "essence"; the spatio-temporal compression of that modernist/imperialist space-time separated distance, a compression characterized by the massive accelerations, foreshortenings and foreshadowings made possible by cybernetics and manifest in what amounts to a debilitating and overwhelming immediacy wherein subjects, themselves fragmented by the force of this compression, are thrust into a set of multiple realities where this double fragmentation exceeds even the aesthetic apparatus of a modernism that had learned how at least partially to reconstruct some ruins. It is at this point that Jameson gives his account of the book about—rather than the film about *and* by—the League of Revolutionary Black Workers, hipping his audience to the fact that he thinks we're all "sophisticated" enough to be able to theorize the aesthetic, to think the concept of what we cannot imagine, via Georgakis's and Surkin's work of nonfiction. This sophistication allows the League and the film they produced to be relegated to the status of an example that is, in itself, essentially unworthy of any attention but is important in that it allows certain other phenomena, more general phenomena, totality or at least the need for and absence of its conceptualization, to show up. Only in this limited but enabling way, by precisely having nothing whatever to say about totality, does the League have anything to do with any possible understanding of totality.

But in a crucial moment in the film, League spokesman Kenneth Cockrel's lectural voice emerges and holds forth precisely on totality, on the nature of the world order and the League's position within it. His voice emerges from an off-screen source in and as that mode of being that Michel Chion, in *The Voice in Cinema*, calls the *acousmêtre*. The lecture's content marks it as of the worker though the images on screen are now of the bodies of administration and the milieu of circulation and consumption of the automobiles that the workers make. The fact that Cockrel is a lawyer completes the chain of known and unknown discrepancies that structure the film and our experience of it. If we think these discrepancies as disruptions of audiovisual, ideological, and theoretical synchronies, then the question of a reading of the film might be said to enter terrain laid out by Chion and by Kaja Silverman's critique of Chion in *The Acoustic Mirror*.[73] An improvisation of the lecture demands other protocols that bear a trace of Silverman and Chion acquired in the movement through the space between them.

So I want to begin to tie a preliminary investigation into the possibility of a Marxian analytic of acousmatrical sound (or, more precisely, of the *musical* non/conjuncture of the aural and the visual) in film to a reading of Jameson's description/call/prediction (the ambivalence with which he names his project is important) of and for an "aesthetics of cognitive mapping." Jameson's otherwise forceful argument for the necessity of totalizing thinking to not only the accurate description and representation of "postmodern global space" but also to the vision of that space reborn is undermined precisely by an *unaugmented* appeal to what elsewhere he calls "figures of the visible." Chion makes us aware of the uncomfortable proximity of the *acousmêtre* to "the paranoid and often obsessional *panoptic fantasy*, which is the total mastery of space by vision" that is given in the very fantasy of the maternal voice that Silverman catches him reproducing.[74] This constellation is, of course, disturbingly close to the very imaginative faculty Jameson desires. But tone and sound in *Finally Got the News* transform representation into a synaesthetic substitute for vision—wherein a narrative of defeat turns into a projection of victory—which is borne in the film as a kind of potential energy and is the trace of the particular and powerful force of aurality in the Afro-diasporic political and aesthetic tradition that the film, and the movement it portrays, extends. The irruption of sound into Jameson's argument for the necessity of a picture of the social ensemble for any utopian sense of how the world should be, makes an understanding of that ensemble possible precisely by way of a disruptive augmentation of the very idea of a purely visual picture. Meanwhile the operations of certain sonic elements in *Finally Got the News* move within the project of representing and transforming postmodern global space while keeping in mind the fact that such operations—part of the historical tendency of the aesthetic to reconstruct the sensual/cognitive ensemble—are partial and preliminary. The *acousmêtre* is revolutionary here precisely in that it is not all-seeing, thereby going against the grain of Chion's analytical description. Ultimately, the irruption of sound into Jameson's picture, which reorganizes filmic space (the space of and between various registers of film's sensual ensemble), reconfigures the aesthetic as a mode of inhabiting and improvising that space that iconically represents a corollary mode of inhabiting and improvising social/global space. So that the justness of Jameson's claims regarding the necessity of a sense of the utopian and the necessary link of such a sense to a representation of the social ensemble depends upon the connection between such representation and the ensemble of the senses.

Sound, not speech (meaning); sound in speech: a teaching tone, a tone calibrated to one of what Jameson calls "the traditional formulations of the uses of the work of art" that will still be operative for this new aesthetics of cognitive mapping. The lecture moves in joint directions: toward something that will have been described at the convergence of a generative phonology of the language of totality/utopia and a Marxian analytic of accent. This is about what sound and tone do to counteract the "perceptual barrage of immediacy"; how to be both in and outside the city (both one and many). These are things all bound up with what sound can open up for you here. So the narrative of defeat as condition of possibility of victory is all bound up with a corrective to the ocularcentric discourse of image and spectacle that is fundamental to Jameson's analytic of postmodern space and to the understanding of that space that he derives from film when film's aurality, its phonic substance, is forgotten. What can sound do to overcome spatial discontinuities? (This is not but nothing other than an attempt at a slight variation on and injection of rigor into a set of clichés about music as universal, which is to say totalizing/utopianizing, language). It's all about the crucial importance of sound to *Finally Got the News* that remains nameless in its spare mention in Jameson's piece though even the sound the nameless object bears comes back in the name of the object substituted for it, since the book's title comes from a blues—a local and inverted variation on an old Delta theme—that at one point animates the film. And the film's title comes from a slogan, from the tone of a voice (how this tone breaks voice as well as gaze is for another time): "finally got the news on how are [union] dues are being used." It is left to us to think these relations: prescription/organization, description/ representation, in order to investigate the emphasis placed on description and representation in Jameson's project. When prescription comes up it comes out as vision. How can we make that sound? This is about the importance, which is to say the politics, of how you sound. This is all about an analytic/organization of ensemble: the ensemble of the social and of the senses. The cognitive increment is given only in the encounter, in the space-time of the encounter that is between encountering. In such space-time (separation), in such a cut, lies certain chances. The encounter is in the cut that tone instantiates and rhythm holds. If we linger in that cut, that music, that spatio-temporal organization, we might commit an action. *Finally Got the News* predicts, describes calls for such a cut. If the film is image and spectacle it is also sound and music. This means that it is not merely, ultimately, "an example that may serve to illustrate." It is also the counter-example (counter even to the very logic of exemplarity) that serves to sing where the musicality of film form is the material imaging of victory.

This is all to say that something that will have been encountered as a product of a black aesthetic ongoingly stages the piercing insistence of the excluded. Such insistence is not only of excluded identity but also of excluded sense. And this is not only in the interest of a dissident particularity but in the interest of ensembles that are manifest in such particularity: the ensembles of the senses, of labor, of human identity. Such an encounter would have indexed a kind of parallel—between sound in the sensual space of film and blackness in the political space of labor and of postmodern global economic space more generally. And this conflation of blackness and sound will have already been cut and augmented—invaginated (to index a chain of analysis and suggestion that moves from Silverman to Spivak to Derrida and beyond)—by a sexual economy Silverman diagnoses and disavows. It is at this point, where nonconvergent audiovisuality instantiates the interarticulation of race as phantasmic sexuality and sex as phantasmic raciality (to use and abuse a phrase of Balibar's), that the black radical tradition and the aesthetics of cognitive mapping emerge in and as a kind of encounter. See, what the League did is important because of what their doing opened, which was precisely the possibility of that universality and/or totality, which some might say they suspended in practice and in theory. This opening works precisely in the sound/tone of their descriptions of totality, in their eloquent vulgarity (which is to be read doubly: doctrinaire and vernacular) and musicality. The point is that what is held in the *description* is the clue—namely, the sound—of a *prescription* materially embodied in the sensual space of the film itself. Cockrel seems to have a pretty good grasp of the problematics of postmodern global space. It is conveyed to us in what Georgakas and Surkin would later call a "high-pitched voice," a voice pitched high and over against a visual montage that turns from assembly line to management office. And it's not that the content that he screams is a misrepresentation; it's just that it's better to be hip also to the form through which that content is conveyed because it gives an opening to a more glorious content, the "foreshadowing description" of how the world would be that cuts and augments the form of the description of how fucked up the world was then and is now. This cut and augmented form and content is a function of the radical force of the fantasy of the maternal voice in black politics and black art. Here are two such fantasies, musical lectures driven by an impossibility (and I should mention Spillers here again as she is the most invaluable analyst of this impossibility—this broken, wounded, irrational, doubly invaginated, invaginative maternity that is multiply one, that is not one, that is more than one, that is of the whole that is multiply and is not and is more than one) that is at once psychic, political, economic, legal, and geographic.

We've seen that Mackey understands the falsetto to be the strained, maternal, and material residue of "a legacy of lynchings" that illuminates and amplifies that legacy's ongoing sexual cut of sexual difference. Cockrell and Marvin Gaye, in the dissonance of dissidence and seduction, converge at this apocalyptic break, the falsetto setting the conditions and need of another cryptonomy, one that might acknowledge and amplify the out harmonics of maternal fantasy that drive such lectural phonography.

Therefore, this is about the erotics of Marvin Gaye, mechanical (re)production and the space-time of black vocal performance. It works from two initial premises: (1) Marvin Gaye's phrasing reveals something to us about the erotics of time; (2) Marvin Gaye's erotics are always also a politics. These premises require a space internal to the performance that is given only electronically, only in the recording, only in the performance that is recording, the engineering of musical ~~re~~production. This building of musical space is accomplished with overdubbing, with a certain contrapuntality of soul that Gaye pioneers and perfects in his 1971 masterpiece *What's Going On*.[75] This creation of internal musical space is paralleled by the sense of a new and other cognitive mapping, a whole other thing emerging from Detroit that Berry Gordy had to be brought kicking and screaming into, on the one hand, but that had already been at the bottom—*as* the bottom but also high and winding above and through—of the Sound of Young America. This political aesthetic was never separate from Gaye's massive and ongoing commitment to and immersion in the erotic. The same technical innovations used to offer up new prescriptive and descriptive social visions are deployed in the no less important work of seduction. Gaye's masterpiece "Since I Had You"[76] exemplifies this, disturbing or disrupting the lectured narrative of love abandoned and retrieved with the ecstatics of unadorned, irreducible and highly aestheticized phonic substance, the eruption of what Austin would have called the "merely phonetic," itself always carrying the trace of what Althusser would have called the "merely gestural," cut and augmented always by the flavor of what Adorno might have dismissed as the "merely culinary." The recording is the only possible site of this refusal to reduce the phonic substance and this reordering of aesthetic space. It marks and makes possible that resistance of the object—to dis/appearance or interpretation—that constitutes the essence of performance. In the production of the recording, Gaye produces that new space whose essence is the ongoing call for the production of New Space, of a new world, by holding—which is to say suspending, embracing—time.

My initial interest, therefore, is rhythmic, though the harmonic complexities of a technically facilitated counterpoint—in the very pressure that it puts on rhythm—is also at issue here. I want to show how the imposition of certain specific and repressive temporal regimes of labor—which Adorno characterized as "the rhythm of the iron system"—are both echoed and disrupted in "Since I Had You." This double movement enacts not only that labor of negation that Adorno argued was beyond the reach of popular music in general and black popular music in particular, but moves beyond such enactment and toward something like the affirmative musical imaging of unprecedented space and unanticipated time, something like what José Gil + Samuel R. Delany might call a theoretical image of the city. This affirmation is, however, not to be reduced to that affirmative movement or action of culture that Marcuse describes as the hallmark of appropriative aesthetics. This reduction is resisted in spite of the best efforts of producers, record company executives, music journalists, and so on, who move ever more quickly toward the domestication of radical sound, and it is this resistance that demands analysis.

In *Rethinking Working Class History*, Dipesh Chakrabarty, after Marx, reminds us that "the everyday functioning of the capitalist factory ... produced documents, hence knowledge, about working-class conditions."[77] This knowledge is an effect of disciplinary surveillance. But there is also that disciplinary modality that is embedded in the technical subordination of worker to machine. Here one must raise the question concerning the knowledge of—which is the ground of that technical subordination to—the instruments of labor as well as that knowledge that is essential to the disciplining (and standardization of the products) of the worker. The Marxian tradition that Chakrabarty extends teaches that such knowledge is also the condition of possibility of a revolutionary consciousness that threatens surveillance, the domination of the machine and the uniformity of the product. This knowledge is both a condition and a condition of possibility of another knowledge; it is the product and producer of other documents. In the case of much of the popular music of Detroit, this other knowledge of the worker is the knowledge of freedom itself encoded in a particular knowledge of music, a prefigurative inscription counter to industrial-phonographic power. This isn't just about what Baraka called "the changing same," though it is bound to that; nor is this another variation on the thematics of the hidden transcript, especially since organization and technical knowledge are unquestioned here. This is about a certain adisciplinary counter-inscription before the fact, if you will, of discipline; this is a counter-inscription that is situated precisely in the gap Marx locates between "(the knowledge of) human *nature* and its life-situation," though that knowledge or gap is located in sites Marx didn't fully anticipate and Adorno couldn't find. This is to say that it is not only located after the point or moment of a postemancipatory, postmigratory emergence into wage-labor, in which a specific form of alienation associated with such labor is manifest; it's before that. And so the document or music, similarly, is not just the hidden transcript of repressed knowledge of alienation but is the reservoir of a certain knowledge of freedom, a counter-inscription anticipatory of the power/discipline that it overwrites and the life-situation against which it prescribes, out from the outside of the regime of signs we now inhabit. This is the knowledge of freedom that is not only before wage-labor but before slavery as well, though the forms it takes are possible only by way of the crucible of the experience of slavery (as forced and stolen labor and sexuality, as wounded kinship and imposed exile). Gaye ought to be situated in an ongoing thematic investigation of the relation between the production of knowledge and the production of economic and aesthetic value, between production in the factory and production in the studio. "Since I Had You" is indelibly marked with this soundwriting against standardization by way of the most intimate knowledge of worker discipline, a knowledge that is, as it were, cut into the groove of the record just as surely as the groove cuts against the very grain of the uniformity of the line.

This is also not just about the circulation of social energy; this is about its conservation. And not just as matter or materiality (not just the mechanics of a certain process that is both social and physical), but as reserve. It demands thinking the form, content, and matter of the song as reservoir holding the theoretical image of the city beyond code and/or encoding. In Detroit, there is resistance of and to the object. The loss of a hand, for instance, bridges the gap between whipping and fines as modes of inscription, disciplinary texts. This is what the League fought in a certain rewriting of sound against the line—an echoed or, more precisely, overtonal disruption of the assembly line and the dangers of its oppressive demands by the bass line. In Gaye's work after *What's Going On*, the contrapuntal is constructed not only by way of such polyrhythmic and extraharmonic intervention (a kind of irregularity or nonstandardization of pulse-to-hummm-or-buzzzzzz to whose differentiating force Adorno was unattuned), but as the disruption of the disciplinary hegemony of another powerful technic, namely, the rhetoric of the love song, a generic technicality that produces its own large set of problems. Here subordination to the technical apparatus of the love song is again cut by manipulation of, by technical in/subordination to, the recording apparatus. The lyric subject of the love song is disrupted by Gaye's own other voices. The rhetoric of a most instrumental rationality is cut by the rhetorician's own rapture. Listen to the song and think about how the theoretical image of the city might be held in and might emerge from the interconnection of the knowledge/discipline of labor and sexuality that this particular aesthetic space-time contains.

Marvin Gaye hips us to the erotics of time. Marvin Gaye's erotics are always also a politics. The call to sing that is song, that whole so-called postmodern, metafictional, improvisational arrangement, the internalization of call and response in the form of a deconstruction and reconstruction of the song and of the song form itself: this is an integral part of 1960s black popular music but goes all the way back to the complex and unavailable origins of black performance. Again, something like this self-reflexive reanarrangement is often cited as a hallmark of so-called postmodern art, though its often more subtle and sophisticated parallel or antecedent is never thought within the context of investigations of postmodernism; and, finally, with good reason, or with reason in addition to the bad reasons of racist and exclusionary canon formation. For in Marvin Gaye, in the midst of a certain sounding of despair and desire, there is a renewal that is never tantamount to the kind of incredulity toward narratives of transcendence that is said by some to characterize canonical postmodernism, to accompany the fiction's ironic self-reflexiveness or self-*destruktive* inward turns. Rather, in Gaye we get a vicious critique, but never an abandonment, of these narratives and their destinations—freedom and, more to the point for "Since I Had You," pleasure. Thus the intersection of rhythms and the allegories they carry; thus the doubleness of Gaye iconized in the rhythmic arrest that is not an arrest. The cut he enacts is given as a juxtapositional drive from fast to slow, from joy to tragedy, from soul to gospel, from the devil to the Lord, from writing to improvisation: all of what is held in phrasing, particularly in that moment of suspension when he implores, "Don't make me wait!"

This expression of desire is where the aesthetics of cognitive mapping that Jameson imagines but can't describe is located. Remember, Jameson's desire for that aesthetic is prompted by a couple of so-called failures localized in Detroit. One is the supposed "failure" of the League of Revolutionary Black Workers to adequately position itself in the space of postmodern global capital. The other is what Kevin Lynch describes as a "failure" of arrangement and rearrangement of the Detroit space that leads to a general inability to form a cognitive map of the city. The thing is, all along such mapping and imaging is embedded in the music of the city, written in the rhythm of the beat and the technical mixing and remixing of voices. This writing or knowledge is distilled in a phrase that acts, more than anything, like a kind of landmark, a suspension of or after the bridge, the bridge of deferred—if not lost—matter and desire, the carving out of a new square or sphere. Another way to put it, way after Raymond Williams, is that this phrase gives one the feeling of a reconstruction. You move through a soundscape you get moved by and enter another scene.

This has been the mutation of a memory, a memory of a revolutionary tone recently muted in black discourse, a muting all bound up with relinquishing the promise of communism (or, perhaps better, the commons; and I'll say what I mean by this in more detail later—for now I'll just say that I mean the radical, invaginative universalization or proletarianization of the ensemble of the senses and the ensemble of the social) (or: the socialization of the ensemble of the senses, the sensualization of the ensemble of the social) in black politics and aesthetics. I wanted to amplify the memory of a politics of sound that I fell in love with or that one falls in love, or something kinda like love, to.

When I first heard Angela Davis's voice I got the news. Again, you might call it something about a revolutionary tone recently de-amplified—along with a certain revolutionary rhetoric—in black political discourse. Not that preacherly thing that persists, like a degraded aural shadow of King, like Wynton to Clifford or Miles, ultimately bearing nothing as much as the weaknesses of the clown show; rather something I first heard a long time ago in Angela Davis's voice, a hanging or lingering or dying fall of or at the end of consonants, open to but outside of a certain kind of chant and for a certain kind of affirmation, precisely + more that one Jameson prescriptively elegizes in "Cognitive Mapping," an affirmation of the sound of resistance in a narrative of defeat where sound and tone function as elements necessary to any (analytic of "successful") spatial representation. Such representation would be erotic, sensual, of a certain notion of ensemble, and these lectures are about the tonality of totality, the revolutionary tone and how it carries forth precisely that which Jameson says is lost. The ensemble cuts harmony; and "the rhythm of the iron system" is broken as the beat goes on by the tone of the DRUM.

Davis has rigorously seen through the fetishistic commodification of her own photographic image and would, I'm sure, have a stringent critique of the way I am fetishizing her voice.[78] At the same time, even as I cringe myself at my own fetishizing impulse, I would echo Spivak's call for a move beyond what she terms, by way of Balibar, "commodity pietism."[79] These lectures move always in the interest of those political uses of the erotic that exceed the lyric and readings of the lyric, even Davis's reading of the work of Ma Rainey, Bessie Smith, and Billie Holiday.[80] Davis's critique of commodification and the atrophy of political memory it induces is focused on the figure and ground of arrest, of her own image in an arrest perpetrated by the police and reproduced in and circulated as the photograph. Davis reads her own commodified, replicated image as an embodied soullessness, fixed, artifactualized, in a way that erases "the activist involvement of vast numbers of black women in movements that are now represented with even greater masculinist contours than they actually exhibited at the time."[81] After the sexual politics of movement(s) and of the movement(s) are examined in their processual actuality and in their fetishized arrest, Davis calls for a political animation of what has been arrested, a reanimation even of the photograph, and focuses on the shadowed women of past movements. Davis contests representations of the phallocentrism of (the) movement(s) of black arts and black power and her work is crucial precisely because she implies that that phallocentrism, while productive of real social facts, was invaginated all along, thereby instantiating the cut totality of movement(s) in such a way as to provide a clue for a historically grounded reanimation of black politics beyond anti-essentialist and anti-totalizing skepticisms. The necessary critique of the uses and abuses of fetishization and the romanticization and disavowal of maternity animates Davis's work as fully as it does that of Silverman. But sometimes that critique seems to mute the very sound that animates it, which is the sound of a lecture.

These lectures are the mutation of the memory of attending a lecture by Angela Davis in 1973 when I was ten, a lecture that my mother took me to, and of having everything seem to stop, or at least slow down enough for someone to begin moving by way of that insistently previous and unlocatable maternal and material motif of black radicalism. The opening to the new city and the new world is this: the crypt where his falsetto (interruptive-connective bridge of lost and found desire, lost and found matter) and her dying fall (the sounding, musical descent where action is made possible) glance and brush. Dance.

Resistance of the Object:
Adrian Piper's Theatricality

What if the beholder glances, glances away, driven by aversion as much as desire? This is to ask not only, what if beholding were glancing; it is also—or maybe even rather—to ask, what if glancing is the aversion of the gaze, a physical act of repression, the active forgetting of an object whose resistance is now not the avoidance but the extortion of the gaze?

In spite of a presence that could scarcely be called anything other than foundational, black artist/philosopher Adrian Piper barely shows up for certain critics who have taken on the task of defining and explaining modernism, postmodernism, and the avant-garde. (I'm thinking, here, of major critics like Rosalind Krauss, who once said something to the effect that there must not be any important black artists because, if there were, they would have brought themselves to her attention.[1] For Piper this avoidance would be cataloged alongside a host of other "ways of averting one's gaze."[2] Piper's insistence on what she calls the "indexical present," the deictic-confrontational field her art produces and within which it is to be beheld, emerges precisely as a kind of resistance to such aversion, an insistent bringing of herself to the in/attention of somebody like Krauss. That aversion marks the spot of both Michael Fried's famous theoretical dismissal of theatricality in contemporary art (in his seminal essay "Art and Objecthood")[3] and the objection, by a host of critics, including—most prominently—Krauss, to that dismissal. This is to say that Fried's aversion to this particular moment in the history of artistic theatricality and his critics' aversion of their critical attention from Piper converge at the point where a quite specific legacy of performance as the resistance of the object becomes clear. That clarity is given by the force of aurality in Piper's work. To avert one's gaze from Piper is to refuse to hear the sound in her work of that quite specific objecthood that joins blackness and black performance. And the critique of Fried's dismissal of objecthood and its complex, ambivalent grounding in Clement Greenberg's in/famous assertion of the necessary optical purity of authentic modernist art is possible only by way of the exploration of that specifically black objecthood that it has been Piper's project to investigate.[4] If, as Zora Neale Hurston suggests, the essence of the Negro is drama, theatricality, then perhaps this is how that theatricality works.[5]

Piper's concern with finding, elaborating, and enacting objections to the various ways of averting one's gaze has led her to deploy a mode of theatricality or objecthood Fried had not anticipated or taken into account. Piper's methods, much to her chagrin, are anything but surefire. And this doesn't even mean that this would rehabilitate her under the aesthetic limits laid down by Fried, who thinks that anything surefire is necessarily inartistic. Piper would only repudiate Fried's modernist aesthetics in the interest of a theatricality that reconstitutes and redoubles the realm of ethics. The essential theatricality of blackness, of the commodity who materially objects beyond any subjunctively posited speech, is evoked in the service of metaethics. The resistance of the object is the condition of possibility of a metaethics whose fullest enactment is in Piper's art, though it is informed very much by the project of a metaethics that is proper to her philosophy.

Piper traces the boundary between critical philosophy and racial performance and thereby allows us to think the place of the latter in the former, to dwell on what happens when racial performance is deployed in order to critique racial categories and to investigate what happens when the visual singularity of a performed, curated, or conceptualized image is deployed in order to move beyond what she calls the "visual pathology" of racist categorization.[6] Piper opens such questions by way of her intense engagement with Kant, by way of her belief in the liberatory value of an ongoing redefinition of necessarily incomplete categories and the therapeutic, self-transformational power her performances are intended to exert to that end. This belief raises further questions regarding the place or echo of racialized performance in the construction of Kant's formulations, not only at the level of the object or example, but also at the level of the iconic theorizing subject, Kant himself. Thinking Kant through Piper and vice versa allows us to ask: Is critical philosophy always already infected and structured by this visual pathology? Can we so easily separate visual singularity from visual pathology? Can singularity ever be singularly visual? Might it not be necessary to hear and sound the singularity of the visage? How do sound and its reproduction allow and disturb the frame or boundary of the visual? What's the relation between phonic materiality and anoriginal maternity? If we ask these questions we might become attuned to certain liberating operations sound performs at that intersection of racial performance and critical philosophy that had heretofore been the site of the occlusion of phonic substance or the (not just Kantian) pre-critical oscillation between the rejection and embrace of certain tones. *Sound gives us back the visuality that ocularcentrism had repressed.* Meanwhile, there is a cumulative effect of the impure and aggressively de-purifying soundtrack in Piper that marks that holosensual, invaginatively ensemblic internal differentiation of the object that the most influential art criticism of the last fifty years has heretofore seemed unable to reach. A major aspect of Piper's intervention is this phonic recovery of the artwork's visual materiality (or, as she would put it, singularity) that Fried's (somewhat idiosyncratic) Saussureanism requires him to reduce. A phonology is missing in Fried, one that would be attuned to visual art's phonography.

For Piper, to be for the beholder is to be able to mess up or mess with the beholder. It is the potential of being catalytic. Beholding is *always* the entrance into a scene, into the context of the other, of the object. This is a very different experience of beholding, a very different experience of the beholder, than that offered by Fried. The Friedian beholder, even in his fascination, never moves out of himself, never achieves or is submitted to a kind of ecstasy, the transportative force of the syncope. The beholder is never estranged, never lost or even dark to himself; rather he continually fulfills that self in the ascription of meaning to the beheld and, more fundamentally, in the ascription of greatness or not, authentic and autonomous aestheticity or not, to the artwork. The beholder arrives at that self-possessive sense or knowledge of self that is the essence of what Fried calls conviction. The beholder becomes a subject again in this profoundly antitheatrical moment. One isn't absorbed by the painting as in an entrance into its scene; instead, one is, in the instant of the frame, in the visual experience of flatness as an instantaneous moment of framing, absorbed into or by flatness reconceived as a mirror. The painting is a mirror. Absorption is self-absorption. Such self-absorption comes in moments of calmness, not under the disruptive and catalytic pressure of an object even if that object is there for you, the disruptive and catalytic pressure of an *other* even if that other is there for you. There's something too dangerous about this broke, brokedown, breaking energy of objection. So Fried is not into the fact that

> when you encountered minimalist work you characteristically entered an extraordinarily charged mise-en-scène.... It was as though their work, their *installations*, infallibly offered one a kind of "heightened" experience, and I wanted to understand the nature of this surefire, and therefore to my mind essentially *in*artistic, effect.[7]

Rather, Fried, after Diderot, is concerned with "the conditions that had to be fulfilled in order for the art of painting to successfully persuade its audience of the truthfulness of its representations."[8] But it is, finally, the complex double bind of subjection that is the condition Fried and Diderot are after. The painting moves, depending upon its historical moment, in and as the complexity of that possession and forfeiture of self that constitutes the establishment of the subject-in-subjection. Everything moves from, Fried writes from, the position of a subject who, in the very fullness of a presence that could never admit its own psycho-political ephemerality, is not there; the (self-)absorbed beholder is an absent beholder, an absented or subjected subject, located no place: the view(er) from nowhere. This viewer from nowhere, this nowhere of viewing, this instantaneous no time of viewing, of the viewer, is what he calls "presentness," as opposed to presence.[9]

For Fried, presence, as theater, is between (the arts, the beholder, and some passive-aggressive object) like a bridge. It is incumbent upon us, by way of Piper and the tradition she extends, to think the bridge as translation or transportation, where matter and desire are both lost and found. Meanwhile, what Fried opposes to theatricality is significa-tion and what separates the artwork from the mere object is precisely that difference that is the condition of possibility of signification. This difference that is internal to the artwork is what Fried calls the art-work's syntax. For Fried, the mere object is never differential, never syn-tactic. It is neither different from the rest of the world nor from itself, and that absence of difference produces an absence of conviction in the beholder—a quite specific inability to see the object as an artwork that takes its place in the history of artworks. This absence of conviction stems from the indifferent's necessary and ongoing production of non-meaning that will have devolved, always, into an infinitely expandable list of "merelys": the culinary, the theatrical, the phonetic, the decora-tive, the tasteful, the gestural, the literal, the cultural. It's important to remember that Fried denies the internal difference of the object even as he valorizes the internal difference of the artwork. This is to say that he denies the interiority of the object even as he valorizes the interior-ity of the artwork. But this internal difference of the artwork is nothing other than the mirror through which the beholder is absorbed into the dangerous maelstrom of his own internally different interiority, the place where he is lost in the very act of finding himself, the place where loss constitutes the foundation of self-possession. So that consciousness of art is nothing other than consciousness of self. The conflation of art-consciousness and self-consciousness is something to which we'll return by way of Piper's active objection to it.

Meanwhile, Fried says that the success and survival of the arts depend upon their ability to defeat theater; that art degenerates as it approaches the condition of theater; that the concepts of quality and value, central to art, exist only in the individual arts and not in their in-between, which is theater. The material of painting and sculpture—its material constraints, supports, elements—must be confronted *and, most importantly, reduced or dematerialized* so that meaning can be produced in and by the artwork, so that something beyond the object can be given. Here, in a sense, Fried extends a kind of antimaterialism that animates the work of Saussure. If, as Derrida argues, Saussure's quest for a universal science of language requires "the reduction of the phonic substance,"[10] then the search for a certain convergence of meaning and universality that we might call, after Derrida, "the truth in painting," requires a reduction of the visual substance. This is why Fried is critical of Greenberg's reduction of modern painting to visuality. He's moving under the aegis of a much more fundamental reduction, a reduction *of, not to*, visuality.

What Fried is after is fullness and inexhaustibility, but not the inexhaustibility of the bare object. This latter inexhaustibility is a function of the object's emptiness or hollowness and it produces the experience of the literalist, minimalist, or theatrical work as an experience of duration rather than that instantaneousness wherein one is given the unlimited fullness of the genuine, composed, and compound work *at a glance*. This is to say that the experience of the genuinely modernist work seems to have no duration because "*at every moment the work itself is wholly manifest.*"[11] The totality of the work is given momently and in the instant. This presentness defeats theater. It's the aversion of attention from the object that is given in and by a moment's attention to the compositionally enframed, rather than a lifetime's everyday attention precisely to the quotidian presence of things. But Piper is all about fighting what Fried refuses to recognize: the absolute ongoingness and continuity not of attention to objects but of the aversion of one's gaze from objects. So that the intensity and grace of presentness, of the experience of a work that at every moment is wholly manifest, is opposed not to some infinitely durative experience of the object but to the infinite avoidance of certain objects. Just because we are all literalists most of our lives does not mean that we actually ever pay attention to or experience objects in their intensity. What one is after, by way of a certain sustenance of attention, is the presentness of the object in all of its internal difference, in all of its interiority and internal space. The stakes of such disruption of the aversion of the gaze at objects are especially high when object, person, commodity, artist, and artwork converge. The glance, this averted gaze, is realigned by the force of a glancing, appositional blow; the internal dialogue is interrupted by a voice from outside; subjection as beholding is cut by a sharp objection.

In a eulogy for John Coltrane, Baraka echoes Trane's self-assessment: "He wanted to be the opposite."[12]

To act on the desire to be the opposite, the desire not to collaborate, is to object. How might such resistance suspend the process of subjection?
Here is one of what Piper calls her "metaperformances."

Untitled Performance for Max's Kansas City

Max's was an Art Environment, replete with Art Consciousness and Self-Consciousness about Art Consciousness. To even walk into Max's was to be absorbed into the collective Art Self-Consciousness, either as object or as collaborator. I didn't want to be absorbed as a collaborator, because that would mean having my own consciousness co-opted and modified by that of others: It would mean allowing my consciousness to be influenced by their perceptions of art, and exposing my perceptions of art to their consciousness, and I didn't want that. I have always had a very strong individualistic streak. My solution was to privatize my own consciousness as much as possible, by depriving it of sensory input from that environment; to isolate it from all tactile, aural, and visual feedback. In doing so I presented myself as a silent, secret, passive object, seemingly ready to be absorbed into their consciousness as an object. But I learned that complete absorption was impossible, because my voluntary objectlike passivity implied aggressive activity and choice, an independent presence confronting the Art-Conscious environment with its autonomy. My objecthood became my subjecthood.[13]

Till now, Daniel Paul Schreber's has been the prototypical body without organs, an exemplary becoming-objective or becoming-animal in the words of Derrida, on the one hand, Deleuze and Guattari, on the other.[14] Schreber's screams are always coupled with a being-entered, which he characterizes as an unmanning or feminization, a kind of tutelage self-imposed and self-overcome. This is important: the body without organs marks a certain psychotic enlightenment, the re-en-gendering disruption or overcoming of a self-imposed tutelage. One could think, therefore, psychotic enlightenment or becoming-object as a motive of desiring-production. But now, Piper is exemplary of the body-without-organs. The *Untitled Performance for Max's Kansas City* marks this becoming-objective of an object, ears shut, eyes pinched, a refusal of collaboration, a positive resistance to the "self-consciousness of art-consciousness," to self-consciousness as art-consciousness, in all of its oedipalization. To be absorbed into their consciousness like a depth charge. A passive aggression of the object, a recalibration of absorption, that Fried does not anticipate. And this by way of a dematerialization; in other words, the subject becomes an object by way of a sensory shutdown. This is, among other things, an enactment at the end of a long, dematerialized transmission of another performance that works by way of violently imposed sensory overload, rather than voluntary sensory deprivation, even though the screaming soundtrack animates the object body-in-performance with a force that exceeds either subjunctive or actual speech. Being materially tied to such immaterially transmitted scenes, there is, inevitably, the desire for the maintenance, in Piper, of a certain privacy. This would be the resistance to deformation, to being messed up or messed with by others, by the omnipresent and oppressive other. This is to say that she is moving in, has already recognized the riches and satisfactions of interiority, the blessed, invaluable side effect of repeatedly thwarted communication. Not for such as me the luxuries of repression, absent-mindedness, or inchoate thought sublimates into impulsive or irresponsible behavior.... So instead we *consider* what we see but are prevented from voicing. We take it into our selves, we muse on it and analyze it, we scrutinize it, extract its meaning and lesson, and record it for future reference. Our unspoken or unacknowledged contributions to discourse infuse our mental lives with conceptual subtlety. We become deep, perceptive, alert, and resourceful.

It seems to me now that the writings in these two volumes are best understood as evolving expressions of a coerced, reflective interiority that develops in response to my increasing grasp of the point: that I am not, after all, entitled simply to externalize my creative impulses in unreflective action or products, because, being merely a foreign guest in the private club in which I entertain, my self-confident attempts at objective communication with my audience would be permanently garbled, censored, ridiculed, or ignored, were it not for a critical and discursive matrix that I—with effort—eventually supply.[15]

And the recognition of this privilege-that-is-not-one of interiority is all bound up not only with what it has meant at times to take on precisely those perquisites that we associate with what Piper calls "the upper-middle-class heterosexual WASP male, the pampered only son of doting parents."[16] It is, more fundamentally, the extension of that experimental, performative, objectional, sensually theoretical, *public* privacy that animates the aesthetics of the black radical tradition.

This double-identification, with both Aunt Hester and the Master, the substitutive mother and never fully constituted father, links Piper to Douglass. This is to say that Piper's performance work moves at the intersection of a feminist, anti-slavery aesthetic and the emergence and convergence of conceptual and minimalist art. This black feminist, anti-slavery minimalism makes possible the reappearance of the art object after the fact of the disappearance of the object that conceptual art had instantiated. This reappearance or reassertion of the object (of the artist *as* art object in the case of Piper) moves along specific lines. Butler puts forward an extraordinarily rigorous model of subjectivity-as-subjection, a model that knows the subject by way of the severity of its (political and, especially, temporal) limits. Meanwhile, Hartman is thinking the way these limits of subjectivity/subjection are negotiated in the lived experience of and opposition to slavery and in the transition from slavery to "freedom." Piper's work seems to be tapping into some things that go on in the field Butler and Hartman explore. These things indicate a lived critique of the assumed equivalence of personhood and subjectivity and, by extension, a force of resistance or objection that is always already in excess of the limits of subjection/subjectivity. In the end, Piper's conceptualism allows her rich historical animation of the minimalist object. Ironically, this force of objection is best described in Fried's dismissal of it, his recoil from that force of the object that animates minimalism.

Here is Greenberg from his essay "Modernist Painting":

> I identify Modernism with the intensification, almost the exacerbation, of this self-critical tendency that began with the philosopher Kant. Because he was the first to criticize the means itself of criticism, I conceive of Kant as the first real Modernist.
>
> The essence of Modernism lies, as I see it, in the use of characteristic methods of a discipline to criticize the discipline itself, not in order to subvert it but in order to entrench it more firmly in its area of competence. Kant used logic to establish the limits of logic, and while he withdrew much from its old jurisdiction, logic was left all the more secure in what there remained to it.
>
> The self-criticism of Modernism grows out of, but is not the same thing as, the criticism of the Enlightenment. The Enlightenment criticized from the outside, the way criticism in its accepted sense does; Modernism criticizes from the inside, through the procedures themselves of that which is being criticized.[17]

If, as Greenberg suggests, Kant is the first modernist, Piper might be the last. And the question concerning the source of Piper's modernism is undetached from that concerning the source of Kant's. Piper's immanence, toward which she is ambivalent in the extreme, is out from the outside.

Something like a final approach to that immanence requires a few more questions. What is an object? What are the limits of the object? More specifically (and crucially, for Piper the philosopher and Fried the aesthetician, both working within complex Kantian genealogies), what is the relation between the (multiple: *Ding*, *Gegenstand*, *Objekt*) notion of the object offered by Kant and the rather more undifferentiated notions of the object offered by Fried and Piper?[18] Fried claims, after Stanley Cavell, that for Kant the artwork is not an object. What kind of object is specifically *not* the artwork for Kant? And what does the artwork's limit, boundary, frame, its *parergon*, have to do with such an object? Would the *parergon* count as differential in the work of art for Fried? This is to ask, is it syntactical? The answer appears to be yes. Does a Friedian object, precisely as nonartwork, "have" a *parergon*, a constitutive outside-on-the-inside? The answer appears to be no; only the artwork, and not the object, only the meaningful or meaning-producing representation "has" the *parergon*. One could also ask: Does the minimalist or literalist object/work (and the point, here, is the complex encountering of the object and the work) have a support, a frame, a boundary? Note that to have, here, is to confront or engage the support by way of figuration, as if dealing with the fact of the support by way of figuration actually makes the support, as *parergon*, a (possessory) fact. And does the minimalist work/object have a support/frame/boundary that sharply divides it from its milieu (as milieu is given in sharp distinction from the *parergon* by Derrida in *The Truth in Painting*)? Perhaps the real importance of the frame/support/boundary is that it divides the work from the milieu that defines and contains what Fried describes as our quotidian literalism. The *parergon* is, here, the condition of possibility of what Fried valorizes and hopes for: presentness as grace, presentness as opposed to presence. The literalist work/object is without or in denial of the *parergon*. The two relations to be thought, here, are lack and denial, *parergon* and milieu.

The relationship between object and objectivity in Piper is disjunctive. Think about objectivity as universality, as a set of faculties or attributes given in the set of human beings; objectivity is the quality of being universal, that which is true for everyone. When Piper speaks about wanting to eliminate subjective judgments (i.e., valuative or aesthetic judgments, the question of beauty and, even, pleasure—what might have been called the immanent aesthetic) from her experience of art, she moves within a certain desire for the objective (i.e., epistemological/ethical, the categorical and its imperatives, the transcendental aesthetic as the ideality of space-time) in art. Similarly, when Piper turns herself into an object of art she could be said to be moving in the desire for a detachment from certain subjective/invalid judgments. What she calls, in her description of the *Untitled Performance for Max's Kansas City*, the self-consciousness of art-consciousness, especially in that it is shaped by the visual pathology of racist categorization, is the field of such bad judgment.

But Piper seems to deny the implications of what is, for Kant, an enabling paradox: the objective-transcendental ground of humanity seems inseparable from a certain subjective condition of its possibility— the ideality of space-time is always conditioned, *made possible*, by a specific experience of space-time. And this experience or immanence is always susceptible, has always been susceptible, to bad judgment, to the irrationality that is, at once, constitutive of the rational and the rational's necessary extension when it reaches its limits. And in this last lies the rub since one must tap into the possibility of bad judgment— aesthetic judgment—in order precisely to work these necessary augmentations of (devolved or delimited) rationality. The repression or denial of the subjective conditions of objectivity in Piper's philosophy is overcome by an aggressive critique of the subject enacted in and by the rematerialization of the object. But this rematerialization of the object is always also the rematerialization of the artwork. So that the repression or denial of the subject/ive, which moves into a critique of the subject/ive, is enacted by way of a return or recovery of the subject/ive where the subject/ive is (the) reanimated, re*mater*ialized personhood as *objet d'art*.

If the categorical imperative were an art object, what would it look like? What does art or the immanent aesthetic do to the categorical imperative or to category as such? It deregulates it, cuts and augments it. It also founds it. This is what Piper philosophically represses and artistically enacts in both her philosophy and her art. Kant's philosophy, in its perhaps inadvertent openness to the irrational condition of possibility of rationality, is more radical than Piper's; but Piper's art is a radical improvisation of Kant's philosophical radicalism. This long passage from *The Truth in Painting* allows a fuller exposition of this:

> Is the palace I'm speaking about beautiful? All kinds of answers can miss the point of the question. If I say, I don't like things made for idle gawpers, or else, like the Iroquois sachem, I prefer the pubs, or else, in the manner of Rousseau, what we have here is a sign of the vanity of the great who exploit the people in order to produce frivolous things, or else if I were on a desert island and if I had the means to do so, I would still not go to the trouble of having it imported, etc., none of these answers constitutes an intrinsically aesthetic judgment. I have evaluated this palace in fact in terms of *extrinsic* motives, in terms of empirical psychology, of economic relations of production, of political structures, of technical causality, etc.
>
> Now you have to know what you're talking about, what *intrinsically* concerns the value "beauty" and what remains external to your immanent sense of beauty. This permanence—to distinguish between the internal or proper sense and the circumstance of the object being talked about—organizes all philosophical discourses on art, on the meaning of art and meaning as such, from Plato to Hegel, Husserl and Heidegger. This requirement presupposes a discourse on the limit between the inside and outside of the art object, here a *discourse on the frame*. Where is it to be found?
>
> What they want to know, according to Kant, when they ask me if I find this palace beautiful, is if I find that it *is beautiful*, in other words if the mere presentation of the object—in itself, within itself—pleases me,

if it produces in me a pleasure, however indifferent *[gleichgültig]* I may remain to the existence of that object. "It is quite plain that in order to say that the object *is beautiful*, and to show that I have taste, everything turns on the meaning which I can give to this representation, and not on any factor which makes me dependent on the real existence of the object. Every one must allow that a judgment on the beautiful which is tinged with the slightest interest, is very partial and not a pure judgment of taste. One must not be in the least prepossessed in favour of the real existence of the thing *[Existenz der Sache]*, but must preserve complete indifference in this respect, in order to play the part of judge in matters of taste.[19]

Remember that for Fried, working in a Kantian mode by way of Greenberg, the authentic experience of the authentic work of art is an experience of the work as representation, as that which is productive of meaning. It is an experience in which the beholder discerns that meaning, and discerns it momently, immediately, in its entirety, in the entirety of its internal differentiation, as if it were a sign. To the extent that this raises the question of the limit or frame of the artwork, one could understand that Fried, after Greenberg, thinks the specificity of modernist painting as the critical engagement with the limit in its limitations, limits here being flatness, the flatness, literally, of the support, of the bounded enframedness of the painting. For it is the frame that marks the limit of significance and the boundary between the real existence of the object and any possible aesthetic consideration. Inauthenticity occurs when the object aggressively foists itself upon the beholder, theatrically so, so that the beholder is forced to encounter its materiality, a materiality that has to be reduced in order to discern its meaning. But it's important to note that this inauthenticity is a violation not just of a contingent, presently needful formulation of the essence of painting, but of a more general and transhistorical formulation regarding the possibility of discerning beauty as such. More specifically, the proximity of the questions concerning the support or flatness in Fried and Greenberg to the questions concerning artwork and frame—*ergon* and *parergon*—in Kant is an immeasurable nearness.

Meanwhile, the *parergon* is as problematic for Piper as it is for Fried. It is, for her, the extraesthetic that can impinge upon a certain privatized interiority of the art work/er. For him, it's the charged atmosphere that surrounds the literalist object. For both, one might say, the *parergon* marks the interinanimation of (the question of the work's) totality and ideology. For both, the *parergon*, in a way, is inseparable from context, milieu. But both would, in various ways, deny this charge. Here again is Derrida:

> In the search for the cause or the knowledge of principles, *one must avoid* letting the *parerga* get the upper hand over the essentials. . . . Philosophical discourse will always have been *against* the *parergon*. But what about this *against*.
>
> A parergon comes against, beside, and in addition to the *ergon*, the work done *[fait]*, the fact *[le fait]*, the work, but it does not fall to one side, it touches and cooperates within the operation, from a certain outside. Neither simply outside nor simply inside. Like an accessory that one is obliged to welcome on the border, on board *[au bord, à bord]*. It is first of all the on (the) bo(a)rd(er) *[il est d'abord l'à-bord]*.
>
> . . . The *parergon*, this supplement outside the work, must, if it is to have the status of a philosophical quasi-concept, designate a formal and general predicative structure, which one can transport *intact* or deformed or reformed *according to certain rules*, into other fields, to submit new contents to it.[20]

There is nothing between the elements of the work and its content. There is the atmosphere, the context, that brushes up against the work, like an adornment, one could say, carrying an always possible deformation. The accessory or augmentation that cuts, an invaginative foreign guest one is obliged to welcome on the border, a boarder, the exteriority that interiority can't do without, the co-operator. Piper is disturbed by the *parergon*, even as she is both the *parergon* and that which, in Fried's eyes, continually, duratively reproduces or, at least, charges, the *parergon*. Meanwhile, for Fried, when the object, by way of a strange reversal, is made to stand in for the representation of the object, when presence stands in for presentness, when literalness stands in for or represents representation by way of a vulgarization of abstraction, then all you have is context, all you have is *parergon* in the absence of the artwork, in the oppressive and aggressive presence of the object. Derrida, here, in summarizing Kant, perfectly encompasses Fried's attitude toward the literalist object:

> What is bad, external to the pure object of taste, is thus what *seduces by an attraction:* and the example of what leads astray by its force of attraction is a color, the gilding, in as much as it is nonform, content, or sensory matter. The deterioration of the *parergon*, the perversion, the adornment, is the attraction of sensory matter. As design, organization of lines, forming of angles, the frame is not at all an adornment and one cannot do without it. But in its purity it ought to remain colorless, *deprived of all empirical sensory materiality.*[21]

Modern painting, for instance, is, finally, in a struggle not so much with the support that it cannot do without, or, more generally, with the outside that co-operates in its operation. It is, rather, struggling with the exteriority of what is internal to it—not the primordial convention that it is there to be beheld, but the primordial actuality of its sensory materiality. That brushing against of the *parergon* is itself a complex substitute for the more fundamental problem of the irreducible sensory materiality of the work/object itself, the disruptive exteriority of what is most central, most interior, to the work itself. The lack of meaning, the hollowness of the literalist object is, as Fried himself admits, virtual. The *parergon* corresponds, finally, not to a lack within the work (a hollowness in Fried's formulations) but to a certain material fullness of the work that presents itself as a lack of—or, more precisely, as an irreducible and irreducibly disruptive supplement to—meaning. As Derrida says, "What constitutes them as *parerga* is not simply their exteriority as a surplus, it is the internal structural link which rivets them to the lack in the interior of the *ergon*."[22] But when Derrida says that *parergon* intervenes, in Kant, between the material and the formal, we need to be aware that this intervention carries its own shadow. The material is a lack in that it is also a supplement to form (which is its supplement). It's as if the material is understood as a lack of the figural in form. But we know, again by way of and through Derrida, that the material—in/as the *parergon*, in/as the milieu—figures too. Derrida says that the *parergon* stands out not only from the *ergon* but from the milieu. It stands out like a figure from the ground, but it stands out from the figure as a ground. And it stands out, with respect to each of these, in some merger with the other of these. But I would argue that the milieu (the external world into which one would or must withdraw) is a ground, as well. So that the *parergon* could be said to be a figure that stands out from three grounds: milieu, object, first figure. And to the extent that the *parergon* has catalytic effects, it reproduces the milieu as figure. The material figures, re/con/figures, the milieu.

Meanwhile, what about the question of beauty, not only for Piper, but of Piper? What about the beauty of Piper and of Piper's work, the beauty of Piper as Piper's work? Piper is the *parergon*, the foreign guest, withdrawing from the artwork and the art world, into the exterior, into the external world, into that which makes the withdrawal possible, that which demands it, namely the fact that it is this exteriority—this convergence of materiality and milieu, this material reconfiguration of milieu, this understanding of materiality as milieu—that is most internal to the work, that is most proper to the work, that is the essence of the work. The *parergon* is beautiful. In this sense, Piper's work is not a suspension of the aesthetic but a kind of return to it, precisely by way of its materiality. You don't have to privilege the ethical over the aesthetic in art if the aesthetic remains the condition of possibility of the ethical in art.

But Piper would enact such privilege in part as a function of her denial of the pseudorational in Kant. This denial is a repression by way of problematic distinctions between the "minor" or lesser writings and the critical philosophy (though the Third Critique, in both the different senses of Piper and Deleuze[/Guattari] would be a minor writing too). We ought to look at the Third Critique not only to engage its racist foundations (which Spivak points out so well and which Robert Bernasconi also examines in some recent essays) but, deeper still, to see the whole complex interplay of accord and discord that not only disturbs the racist foundations of the Third Critique but their prior manifestation as a certain foundation for the transcendental aspirations of the First Critique.[23] And such an examination of those foundations would seem to be necessary to precisely that antiracist expansion of category that Piper's artwork seeks to enact. Is the body without organs, the ensemble of the senses, the limit of the faculties? This gets back to the link between Aunt Hester's Passion and the *Untitled Performance for Max's Kansas City*.[24] And what's the relation between the limits of the faculties (and the limits of the work of art) and the relations of the faculties each to the other? And the relations of these to the ensemble of the senses and their relations each to the other? Does the body without organs constitute the performance/recording of these relations? The critique of the hegemony of the visual (in art and life) and the recalibration of the faculties/senses and their ensembles: both have to do with the relation between these expansive, invaginative and invaginated ensembles and the expansive universality, the nonexclusionary universality of the categories. Meanwhile, it's not that racism, or xenophobia more generally, is a visual pathology as much as it is about the relation between the hegemony of the visual in art, life, racism, and their intersection. So part of what's at stake in Piper's work is not an eclipse of the visual but its rematerialization, which Fried would recognize and abdure. But not only this. It's a rematerialization or reinitialization of visual pleasure and visual desire, as well. As Derrida says on and after Kant, it was always about pleasure all the time. The question Piper raises for us (it's not a new question, just different, now), perhaps against herself, is this: can the object not only resist visual pleasure but resist by way of visual pleasure? Is the problem visuality or pleasure? Both. Neither.

Piper talks of partitioning herself in order to avoid accommodating people's needs for an oversimplified other. Such overt internal differentiation in the name of complexity—of syntax, if you will—would make Fried proud. It is, of course, part of the particular work Piper has done to make herself into an art object. Like funk music (in her understanding of it), Piper is modular, syntactical, internally differentiated, polyrhythmic, high fantastical. But compartmentalization is all bound up with privatization even if that privatization, that taking on of all tasks in the figure of one, is later to be resocialized by way of more humane forms of exchange. We could think all this as a conflict of the faculties, but if we did we'd also have to think a certain valorization of counterpoint, here, a kind of embrace of the interplay of accord and discord, along lines Deleuze opens up, lines to and out of the Third Critique—lines of deregulation. Such deregulation is all bound up with the limit, with that being that is neither inside nor outside, that Piper reproduces, as herself, as her artwork.[25]

In the transition from slave labor to free labor, the site or force or occasion of value is transferred from labor to labor power. This is to say that value is extracted from the ground of intrinsic worth (remember Marx's bemusement at the confusion that troubles the writings of English political economists who deploy "a Teutonic word for the actual thing, and a Romance word for its reflection") and becomes *the potential to produce value*.[26] This transference and transformation is also a dematerialization—again, a transition from the body, more fully the person, of the laborer to a potential that operates in excess of the body, in the body's eclipse, in the disappearance of a certain responsibility for the body. This will crystallize, later, in the impossible figure of the commodity that emerges as if from nowhere, the figure that is essential to that possessive and dispossessed modality of subjectivity that Marx calls alienation. Meanwhile, what Aunt Hester enacts, by way of the participant observation of Douglass and the master, by way of Douglass's recitation and its concomitant recitations in music and in the discourse on music, is a rematerialization of value. Now the commodity is rematerialized in the body of the worker just as the worker's body is rematerialized as the speaking, shrieking, sounding commodity, each emerging not from some originary moment but through the catalytic force of an

event before natality. This rematerialization is a music Marx's dematerialization demands. This is to say that the dematerialization that is
necessary to a universal revolution and the universal science of revolution is in anticipation of a rematerialization that Marx predicts without
working toward, or produces without discovering in Althusser's idiom,
in the *1844 Manuscripts*.[27] Aunt Hester's performance-in-objection is a
kind of *parergon*, an outwork, a prefigurative working out, or supplemental materialization before the fact, of Marxian science. Whereas the
1844 Manuscripts spookily prophesies the rematerialization of value in
communism, Aunt Hester actually enacts the senses as "theoreticians in
their immediate practice."[28] Here, communism is given as discovery
procedure and not just as discovery along lines Marx himself would
actually endorse: as he says, "Communism is the act of positing as the
negation of the negation, and is therefore a *real* phase, necessary for the
next period of historical development, in the emancipation and recovery of mankind. *Communism* is the necessary form and the dynamic
principle of the immediate future, but communism is not as such the
goal of human development—the form of human society."[29]

So Aunt Hester is, at this point, that which Piper reenacts and/or
calls for: the artist(-critic-dealer-collector-art historian-social theorist)-
as-art-object, the invaginated totality or gathering—the locus and
logos—of a division of labor, the (audiovisual) rematerialization of
value. And just as C. L. R. James could assert—by way of a kind of magic
that seems impossible but whose reality is something to which every
worker might surreptitiously attest—that socialism is already in place
on the shop floor, so can we assert, by way of Aunt Hester and the
theoretical catalysis she enacts, that communism-in-(the resistance to)
slavery is the discovery procedure for communism out from slavery's
outside. Meanwhile, Aunt Hester's performance-in-objection is recited
for us in Douglass, then transmitted or transferred, by way of a repressive dematerialization, into a discourse on music. Aunt Hester enacts
a rematerialization that is a necessary preface to, though it emerges
only after the fact of, dematerialization. It's a cutting augmentation
of Marx's own necessary materialist preface, in "Private Property and

Communism," to the dematerializing theoretical forces that are gathered and unleashed in *Capital* that Piper re-performs, forging new relations of production and reproduction in this socialization of objection and its surplus. This is what objection is, what performance is—an internal complication of the object that is, at the same time, her withdrawal into the external world. Such withdrawal makes possible communication between seemingly unbridgeable spaces, times, and persons.

In the end, what I'm trying to get to is this: there is a massive and dense discourse on the object, on what it will be in communism, on what it will bring about as communism, that Marx puts forward in 1844. Most simply put, communism is that "positive *supersession* of *private property as human self-estrangement*, and hence the true *appropriation* of the *human essence* through and for man" that is actually constituted in and by and as a new approach of and toward the object.[30] Marx adds, "To sum up: it is only when man's object becomes a *human* object or objective man that man does not lose himself in that object. This is only possible when it becomes a *social* object for him and when he himself becomes a social being for himself, just as society becomes a being for him in this object."[31] Black radicalism, the invagination and rematerialization of what Cedric Robinson calls "the ontological totality," might be performed in and as the arrival at becoming-social in the vexed and vexing exchange of roles; in and as the differentialized and ensemblic recalibration of the senses. For Marx, "[t]he domination of the objective essence within me, the sensuous outburst of my essential activity, is passion, which here becomes the *activity* of my being."[32] Aunt Hester's objective passion anticipates this Marxian formulation that is later reconfigured by Piper's seemingly passionless objection. In the *Untitled Performance for Max's Kansas City*, Piper silently transmits Aunt Hester's shriek, opening herself to its disruptive force even as she closes herself off to the sensory experience of the "artworld." To think Aunt Hester and Piper, individually and together, is to think not only what it means to recognize and deny, protect and risk, the complex interiority of the object, but also what it means to re-objectify the work of art, to revisualize it by way of an old recording, to rematerialize its opticality by way of the sound and song of what Marx couldn't even imagine, the commodity who shrieked, by way of what Fried couldn't even visualize, the object whose infusion with the resistant aurality of a tradition of politico-economic aspiration and whose concomitant and necessarily theatrical personhood bound to whatever lies before her own troubled self-making, made her art making art.

Notes

Resistance of the Object: Aunt Hester's Scream

1. Blackness, in all of its constructed imposition, can tend and has tended toward the experimental achievement and tradition of an advanced, transgressive publicity. Blackness is, therefore, a special site and resources for a task of articulation where immanence is structured by an irreducibly improvisatory exteriority that can occasion something very much like sadness and something very much like devilish enjoyment. To record this improvisational immanence—where untraceable, anoriginal rootedness and unenclosed, disclosing outness converge, where that convergence is articulation by and through an infinitesimal and unbridgeable break—is a daunting task. This is because blackness is always a disruptive surprise moving in the rich nonfullness of every term it modifies. Such mediation suspends neither the question of identity nor the question of essence. Rather, blackness, in its irreducible relation to the structuring force of radicalism and the graphic, montagic configurings of tradition, and, perhaps most importantly, in its very manifestation as the inscriptional events of a set of performances, requires another thinking of identity and essence. This thinking converges with the re-emergent question of the human that self-critical articulation demands. Such articulation implies and enacts an unorthodox essentialism wherein essence and performance are not mutually exclusive. How does this field of convergence, this ensemble, work? By way of the affirmative force of ruthless negation, the out and rooted critical lyricism of screams, prayers, curses, gestures, steps (to and away)—the long, frenzied tumult of a nonexclusionary essay. Racism and oppression are necessary but not

sufficient conditions of such advance. This is to say that if alienation and distance represent the critical possibility of freedom, they do so where the question of the human is most clearly rendered as the question of a kind of competence that is performed as an infinite set of variations of blackness. Hartman's work seems to me to have brilliantly recalibrated the investigation of this set though the question concerning the proper objecthood of this object remains.

Asha Varadharajan addresses this problem. She writes: "Clearly, then, there is a need for a theory that is sensitive both to the complicity between knowledge and power and to the possibility of resistance on the part of the objects of the power-knowledge nexus." Varadharajan is interested not only in how the production of knowledge enables domination but in how it "can also serve the cause of emancipatory critique and of resistance." For Varadharajan, "Theodor W. Adorno's *Negative Dialectics* . . . seems to offer this double opportunity. His notion of the dialectical relation that obtains between subject and object simultaneously insists on the carapace of identity that encloses the subject and on the resistance of the object to the subject's identifications." Therefore, the goal of her project is "to shift the focus from the decentered subject to the resistant object and to disentangle the practice of epistemology from the violence of appropriation." While we differ, to a certain extent, on the place of Adorno (and poststructuralism) in the development of such a project, and while it seems to me that disentanglement might not be the proper way to think the relation between violence and the emergence of liberatory critique, I want openly to avow Varadharajan's projects and to acknowledge my echo of her phrasing. My intellectual debt to Hartman is even more fundamental and is manifest always and everywhere in this book. See Saidiya V. Hartman, *Scenes of Subjection: Terror, Slavery, and Self-Making in Nineteenth-Century America* (Oxford: Oxford University Press, 1997), 4, and Asha Varadharajan, *Exotic Parodies: Subjectivity in Adorno, Said, and Spivak* (Minneapolis: University of Minnesota Press, 1995), xii.

I'd like to acknowledge a few more influences. One of the most formative—especially in its investigation of black literature's disruptive reconfiguration of totality—is Houston Baker, *Blues, Ideology, and Afro-American Literature: A Vernacular Theory* (Chicago: University of Chicago Press, 1984). Any exploration of "resistant orality" (in its complex relation to an often submerged or subversive literacy) in slave narrative, of its gendered foundations and implications, is now impossible without the work of Harryette Mullen. I am indebted to her *Gender and the Subjugated Body: Readings of Race, Subjectivity, and Difference in the Construction of Slave Narratives* (Ph.D. diss., University of California, Santa Cruz, 1990). See also her "Runaway Tongue: Resistant Orality in *Uncle Tom's Cabin, Our Nig, Incidents in the Life of a Slave Girl,* and *Beloved,*" in *The Culture of Sentiment: Race, Gender, and Sentimentality in Nineteenth-Century America,* ed. Shirley Samuels (Oxford: Oxford University Press, 1992), 244–64. "Optic White: Blackness and the Production of Whiteness," *Diacritics* 24, no. 2–3 (summer–fall 1994): 71–89; and "Africa Signs and Spirit Writing," *Callaloo* 19, no. 3 (1996): 670–89. For a liberating disruption of Frederick Douglass's self-proclaimed, oft-echoed, and openly gendered representative priority, I have returned often to Deborah E. McDowell, "In the First Place: Making Frederick Douglass and the Afro-American Narrative Tradition," in *African American Autobiography: A Collection of Critical Essays,* ed. William L. Andrews (Engelwood Cliffs, N.J.: Prentice Hall, 1993), 35–58. The analysis of the impact of black vocal performance on ocularcentric Western notions of value in Lindon Barrett, *Blackness and Value: Seeing Double* (Cambridge: Cambridge University Press, 1999) has been especially helpful. In studying the ongoing development of the culture of the resistance to slavery I have relied on Sterling Stuckey, *Slave Culture: Nationalist Theory and the Foundations of Black America* (Oxford: Oxford University Press, 1987) and Lawrence W. Levine, *Black Culture and Black Consciousness: Afro-American Folk Thought from Slavery to Freedom* (Oxford: Oxford University Press, 1977). Kimberly W. Benston, *Performing Blackness: Enactments of African-American Modernism* (London: Routledge, 2000) and Aldon Lynn Nielsen, *Black Chant: Languages of African-American Postmodernism* (Cambridge: Cambridge University Press, 1997) are invaluable treatments of the experimental drive in black music, writing and performance. I have benefited from the address of the migratory shifts, submerged ground, and reproductive soundings of Afro-diasporic thought and performance found in Paul Gilroy, *The Black Atlantic: Modernity and Double Consciousness* (Cambridge, Mass.: Harvard University Press, 1993), and Joseph Roach, *Cities of the Dead: Circum-Atlantic Performance* (New York: Columbia University Press, 1996). Finally, for making me believe in the radical and sensual performativity of haints in literary, photographic, and phonographic narrative, I gratefully acknowledge Avery F. Gordon, *Ghostly Matters: Haunting and the Sociological Imagination* (Minneapolis: University of Minnesota Press, 1997).

2. See Judith Butler, *The Psychic Life of Power: Theories in Subjection* (Stanford: Stanford University Press, 1997). In this book I attempt to analyze

the limits and potentialities of black performance's re-en-gendering force and, in so doing, move along a trajectory illuminated by the whole of Butler's work.

3. Hartman, *Scenes of Subjection*, 4

4. Here begins a major element of this book: a respectful challenge to Peggy Phelan's ontology of performance that is predicated on the notion of performance's operating wholly outside economies of reproduction. See "The Ontology of Performance: Representation without Reproduction," *Unmarked: The Politics of Performance* (London: Routledge, 1993).

5. Derrida speaks of invagination within the context of a discourse on genre and its relation to the concept of set or totality: "It is precisely a principle of contamination, a law of impurity, a parasitical economy. In the code of set theories, if I may use it at least figuratively, I would speak of a sort of participation without belonging—a taking part in without being part of, without having membership in a set. With the inevitable dividing of the trait that marks membership, the boundary of the set comes to form by invagination an internal pocket larger than the whole; and the outcome of this division and of this abounding remains as singular as it is limitless." See Jacques Derrida, "The Law of Genre," trans. Avital Ronell, in *On Narrative*, ed. W. J. T. Mitchell (Chicago: University of Chicago Press, 1981), 55.

6. Nathaniel Mackey, *Bedouin Hornbook*, Callaloo Fiction Series, vol. 2 (Lexington: University Press of Kentucky, 1986), 34.

7. Here are the relevant passages in full. I'll return to them quasi-obsessively throughout this text. The first two passages are from *Bedouin Hornbook*, 30, 34–35.

"Some would say it's not my place to make comments on what I've written, but let me suggest that what's most notably at issue in the Accompaniments' he/she confrontation is a binary round of works and deeds whereby the dead accost a ground of uncapturable 'stations.' The point is that any insistence on locale must have long since given way to locus, that the rainbow bridge which makes for unrest ongoingly echoes what creaking the rickety bed of conception makes. I admit this is business we've been over before, but bear with it long enough to hear the cricketlike chirp one gets from the guitar in most reggae bands as the echoic spectre of a sexual 'cut' (sexed/unsexed, seeded/unsown, etc.)—'ineffable glints or vaguely audible grunts of unavoidable alarm.'"

"You got me all wrong on what I meant by 'a sexual "cut"' in my last letter. I'm not, as you insinuate, advancing severance as a value, much less pushing, as you put it, 'a thinly veiled romance of distantiation.' I put the word 'cut,' remember, in quotes. What I was trying to get at was simply the feeling I've gotten from the characteristic, almost clucking beat one hears in reggae, where the syncopation comes down like a blade, a 'broken' claim to connection. Here I put the word 'broken' in quotes to get across the point that the pathos one can't help hearing in that claim mingles with a retreating sense of peril, as though danger itself were beaten back by the boldness, however 'broken,' of its call to connection. The image I get is one of a rickety bridge (sometimes a rickety boat) arching finer than a hair to touch down on the sands at, say, Abidjan. Listening to Burning Spear the other night, for example, I drifted off to where it seemed I was being towed into an abandoned harbor. I wasn't exactly a boat but I felt my anchorlessness as a lack, as an inured, eventually visible pit up from which I floated, looking down on what debris looking into it left. By that time, though, I turned out to be a snake hissing, 'You did it, you did it,' rattling and weeping waterless tears. Some such flight (an insistent *previousness* evading each and every natal occasion) comes close to what I mean by 'cut.' I don't know about you, but my sense is that waterless tears don't have a thing to do with romance, that in fact if anything actually breaks it's the blade. 'Sexual' comes into it only because the word 'he' and the word 'she' rummage about in the crypt each defines for the other, reconvening as whispers at the chromosome level as though the crypt had been a crib, a lulling mask, all along. In short, it's apocalypse I'm talking, not courtship.

"Forgive me, though, if this sounds at all edgy, maybe garbled at points. My ears literally burn with what the words don't manage to say."

The third passage is from "Sound and Sentiment, Sound and Symbol," in *Discrepant Engagement: Dissonance, Cross-Culturality, and Experimental Writing*, Cambridge Studies in American Literature and Culture 71 (Cambridge: Cambridge University Press, 1993), 232.

"Gisalo songs are sung at funerals and during spirit-medium seances and have the melodic contour of the cry of a kind of fruitdove, the *muni* bird. This reflects and is founded on the myth regarding the origin of music, the myth of the boy who became a *muni* bird. The myth tells of a boy who goes to catch crayfish with his older sister. He catches none and repeatedly begs for those caught by his sister, who again and again refuses his request. Finally he catches a shrimp and puts it over his nose, causing it to turn a bright purple red, the color of the muni bird's beak. His hands turn into wings and when he opens his mouth to speak the falsetto cry of a muni bird comes out. As he flies away, his sister begs him to come back and have some of the crayfish but his cries continue and become a song, semi-wept, semi-sung: 'Your crayfish you didn't give me. I have no sister. I'm hungry. . . .' For the Kaluli, then, the quintessential source of music is the orphan's ordeal—an orphan being anyone denied kinship, social sustenance, anyone who suffers, to use Orlando Patterson's phrase, 'social death,' the prototype for which is the boy who becomes a muni bird. Song is both a complaint and a consolation dialectically tied to that ordeal, where in back of 'orphan' one hears echoes of 'orphic,' a music that turns on abandonment, absence, loss. Think of the black spiritual 'Motherless Child.' Music is wounded kinship's last resort."

8. Edouard Glissant, *Caribbean Discourse: Selected Essays*, trans. J. Michael Dash (Charlottesville: Caraf Books/University Press of Virginia, 1989), 123–24.

9. Karl Marx, *Capital: A Critique of Political Economy*, vol. 1, trans. Ben Fowkes (London: Penguin Books, 1990), 176–77.

10. Marx, "Communism and Private Property," in *Early Writings*, trans. Rodney Livingstone and Gregor Benton (New York: Vintage, 1975), 356.

11. Ibid., 352.

12. Ferdinand de Saussure, *Course in General Linguistics*, trans. Roy Harris (La Salle, Ill.: Open Court, 1986), 116–17. Derrida cites fragments of an earlier English version of this passage in *Of Grammatology*, trans. Gayatri Chakravorty Spivak (Baltimore: The Johns Hopkins University Press, 1976), 53. However, he mutes, by way of ellipses, the Marxian echo, thereby postponing or, more precisely, drastically slowing the tempo of his own critical engagement with Marx even as he moves within the revolutionary wake of Marx's dematerializing drive. This book is partly conceived as a kind of tarrying in the break or broken time of that encounter. For a brilliant reassertion, to or through Saussure, of the body and its materiality, see (especially the footnotes of) John L. Jackson Jr., "Ethnophysicality, or An Ethnography of Some Body," in *Soul: Black Power, Politics, and Pleasure* (New York: New York University Press, 1998), 172–90.

13. I borrow the term "passionate utterance" from Stanley Cavell, "Wagers of Writing: Has Pragmatism Inherited Emerson?" unpublished paper delivered at the University of Iowa, 22 June 1995.

14. Hortense J. Spillers, "Mama's Baby, Papa's Maybe: An American Grammar Book," *Diacritics* (summer 1987): 80.

15. Leopoldina Fortunati, *The Arcane of Reproduction: Housework, Prostitution, Labor and Capital*, trans. Hilary Creek (New York: Autonomedia, 1995), 10.

16. Ibid., 7–8.

17. See Cedric Robinson, *Black Marxism: The Making of the Black Radical Tradition* (Chapel Hill: University of North Carolina Press, 2000), 171.

18. Frederick Douglass, *Narrative of the Life of Frederick Douglass, An American Slave*, ed. Henry Louis Gates Jr. In *The Classic Slave Naratives* (New York: Mentor Books, 1987), 259.

19. Ibid., 262–63.

20. For a more elaborate reading of Brown's relation to Douglass, see my "Bridge and One," in *Performing Hybridity*, ed. May Joseph and Jennifer Fink (Minneapolis: University of Minnesota Press, 1999).

21. These are notes taken during a presentation by Abbey Lincoln at the Ford Foundation Jazz Study Group, Columbia University, November 1999.

1. The Sentimental Avant-Garde

1. Sigmund Freud, *An Outline of Psycho-Analysis*, trans. James Strachey (New York: W. W. Norton, 1949), 18.

2. There is archival footage of an interview with Ellington in which he says, "Oh but I have such a strong influence by the music of the people—*the people*! that's the better word, *the* people rather than *my* people, because *the* people *are* my people." See *A Duke Named Ellington*, dir. Terry Carter, perf. Duke Ellington, Clark Terry, Russell Procope, Ben Webster, Council for Positive Images and American Masters/WNET, 1988. See also the cogent and informative analysis of Ellington's use of the phrase "my people" and of his 1963 review/musical *My People* in Graham Lock, *Blutopia: Visions of the Future and Revisions of the Past in the Work of Sun Ra, Duke Ellington, and Anthony Braxton* (Durham, N.C.: Duke University Press, 1999), 114–18.

3. Freud, *An Outline*, 18.

4. Ibid., 18–19.

5. Ibid., 19.

6. See Andrew Benjamin, *Translation and the Nature of Philosophy: A New Theory of Words* (New York: Routledge, 1989).

7. See Freud, *An Outline*, 19.

8. Ibid., 20–21.

9. Ibid., 19.

10. Ibid., 21.

11. Quoted in David Leeming, *Amazing Grace: A Life of Beauford Delaney* (New York: Oxford University Press, 1998), 112.

12. Antonin Artaud, "Artaud the Mômo," in *Watchfiends & Rack Screams: Works from the Final Period*, ed. and trans. Clayton Eshleman with Bernard Budor (Boston: Exact Change, 1995), 161.

13. Billy Strayhorn, "Lush Life." Tempo Music, 1936.

14. I make this assertion by way of Randy Martin's brilliant work in *Critical Moves* (Durham, N.C.: Duke University Press, 1998). On pp. 205–6 he writes: "By extending a productionist model to domains not generally associated with an economy oriented toward exchange, I want to take seriously Marx's understanding of capitalism. He treats it as forcibly constituting, by the very organizing boundaries it erects and then transgresses, in pursuit of increasing magnitudes of surplus, the global collectivity, the 'combination, due to association,' that he understood as the socialization of labor. The extension of Marx's concept of socialization to a widening range of practices deepens rather than detracts from the power and aims of his analysis. To take the production of surplus seriously in these other domains should not reduce practices to mere instruments of the ends of domination where race, gender, or sexuality are in turn nothing more than products in a profit-taking market. Rather, the emphasis on surplus identifies what is productive in race, gender, and sexuality such that the proprietary claims of the dominant position in each system are exposed as emerging only through what dominance subordinates through appropriation. The unacknowledged dependence recurs along different dimensions of dominance on what it subordinates through appropriation. This dependency of the dominant is one reason that whiteness is both the hatred of and the desire for blackness, that misogyny aspires to the rape and the reverence of the feminine, and that homophobia is the rejection of sameness and the need for it. In short, the appropriation not only produces the divide between dominance and subalternity but also the demand for further appropriation as a very condition of social reproduction. That race, class, gender, and sexuality, as the very materiality of social identity, are also produced in the process indicates the practical generativity—the ongoing social capacity to render life as history—necessary for any cultural product. Therefore, it is not that a productionist approach assigns race, class, gender, and sexuality the same history, political effects, or practical means. Instead, this approach is intended to imagine the context for

critical analysis that would grant these four articulating structures historicity, politics, and practice in relation to one another, that is, in a manner that is mutually recognizable.

"To speak of practices rather than objects of knowledge as what disciplines serve privileges the capacity for production over the already given product-object as a founding epistemological premise. The focus on practices also allows production to be named historically so as to situate it with respect to existing political mobilizations. If the older set of disciplinary formations constantly had to ask, "Knowledge for what?" it was because the autonomy of knowledge from other social relations was assumed. The practices of cultural studies imply commitments that are constitutional to knowledge as such and can therefore be used to ask how one set of practices could be articulated with another."

I would briefly add a couple of small formulations:

- The epistemological shift that Marx allows, wherein practices are thought as if for the first time, as if in eclipse of objects, can itself be thought as an irruption of or into the sciences of value. The black avant-garde is an anticipatory manifestation of that shift/irruption.
- The black avant-garde works the second "as if" above in a specific way. The eclipse of objects by practices is a head, a necessary opening that vanishes here in the work of those who are not but nothing other than objects themselves. (Black) performance is the resistance of the object and the object is in that it resists, is in that it is always the practice of resistance. And if we understand race, class, gender, and sexuality as the materiality of social identity, as the surplus effect (and cause) of production, then we can also understand the ongoing, resistive force of such materiality as it plays itself out in/as the work of art. This is to say that these four articulating structures must be granted not only historicity, politics, and practice, but aesthesis as well. This is also to say that the concept of the object of performance studies is (in) practice precisely at the convergence of the surplus (in all the richness with which Martin formulates it—as, in short, the ongoing possibility or hope of a minoritarian insurgence that would be keyed to Deleuze and Guattari, on the one hand, and, say, Adrian Piper, on the other) and the aesthetic.

15. This paraphrases remarks of his given at a meeting of the Ford Foundation Jazz Study Group at Columbia University in 1999.

16. In an essay called "The Five Avant-Gardes Or . . . Or None," in *The*

Twentieth-Century Performance Reader, ed. Michael Huxley and Noel Witts (New York: Routledge, 1996), 308–25.

17. Leeming and, in Strayhorn's case, David Hajdu. See Hajdu's *Lush Life: A Biography of Billy Strayhorn* (New York: North Point Press, 1996).

18. Leeming, *Amazing Grace*, 169.

19. Ibid., 151

20. Ibid., 12–13.

21. Ibid., 157.

22. Ibid., 143.

23. Check his own version of the song—he accompanies his voice on piano, but there is already an interior accompaniment of the voice—recorded live at Basin Street East, New York City, and released as Billy Strayhorn, "Lush Life," rec. 14 January 1964, *Lush Life*, Red Baron, 1992.

24. Artaud, "Ci-git/Here Lies," *Watchfiends & Rack Screams*, 211.

25. Strayhorn, "Lush Life."

26. I mean to place in some sort of resonant relation to one another the following texts: Neil Smith, Besty Duncan, and Laura Reid, "From Disinvestment to Reinvestment: Mapping the Urban 'Frontier' in the Lower East Side," in *From Urban Village to East Village: The Battle for New York's Lower East Side*, ed. Janet L. Abu-Lughod et al. (Oxford: Blackwell Publishers Ltd., 1994), 149–67; Susan Howe, "Incloser," in *The Birth-Mark: Unsettling the Wilderness in American Literary History* (Hanover, N.H.: University Press of New England, 1993), 43–86; and Marcia B. Siegel, *At the Vanishing Point: A Critic Looks at Dance* (New York: Saturday Review Press, 1972).

27. If this were ever sounded, I wouldn't want the appearance of the cut to be marked by another voice. Just another voicing: which would not be reducible to a difference of voices; which would be marked only by the palpability of the cut—no glance, no sound outside, just a pause and don't stop the tape recorder. The question remains: whether and how to mark (visually, spatially, in the absence of sound, the sound in my head) digression, citation, extension, improvisation in the kind of writing that has no name other than "literary criticism."

28. Cecil Taylor, *Chinampas*, rec. 16 November 1987, Leo, 1991. I'm going to write (about) the piece's first section.

29. In the absence of reading, either or both of *these terms* might be just as reducible or virtual as *word* or *sentence*. Part of what I'd like to relate is the

way Taylor's *(work art ritual performance music poetry)*, the way that which is of Taylor, renders all of *these terms* unavailable. Nevertheless, I must retain them, at least for a minute, otherwise I Can't Get Started.

30. "Editors Note," *Moment's Notice: Jazz in Poetry and Prose*, ed. Art Lange and Nathaniel Mackey (Minneapolis: Coffee House Press, 1993), x.

31. Or, more precisely, the double absence: the disappearance of the performance that is not recorded; the loss of what the recording reduces or occludes by embodying an illusory determinacy and representativeness.

32. Implied here is that glow, aura, *sfumato*, hazy luminescence that smears the edge, the containment, of the image or the letter. Halogen, neon, Las Vegas—though I'm pretty sure Taylor's never played my home town—are in my head along with another, more recent, recording of Taylor's, *In Florescence*, rec. 8 June and 9 September, 1989, A & M, 1990.

33. Or, more precisely, a double phrasing: words' syntagmic ordering and the arrangement and enactment of their internal sonic resources.

34. Wilson Harris, "History, Fable, and Myth in the Caribbean and Guianas," in *Selected Essays of Wilson Harris: The Unfinished Genesis of the Imagination*, ed. A. J. M. Bundy (London: Routledge, 1999), 157.

35. Gracefully designed by Mike Bennion.

36. Spencer Richards, liner notes, Cecil Taylor, *Live in Vienna*, Leo, 1988. These notes consist largely of an interview with Taylor. The recording is of a performance by the Cecil Taylor Unit given on 7 November 1987, just nine days before the recording of *Chinampas*. Richards dates his notes May 1988.

37. "Idiom" demands a break. It demands some extended quotation, first from *The Compact Edition of the Oxford English Dictionary* (1971), then from Derrida, "Onto-theology of National Humanism (Prolegomena to a Hypothesis)," *Oxford Literary Review* 14 (1992): 3–23. Idiom, according to the *OED*: "peculiarity, property, peculiar phraseology"; "the form of speech peculiar or proper to a people or country"; "the variety of a language which is peculiar to a limited district or class of people"; *"the specific character, property, or genius of any language"*; *"a peculiarity of phraseology approved by the usage of a language and having a signification other than its grammatical or logical one"* (my emphasis). Idiom, according to Derrida: "I shall say simply of this word 'idiom,' that I have just very rapidly thrust forward, that for the moment I am not restricting it to its linguistic, discursive circumscription, although, as you know, usage generally folds it back towards that limit—idiom as linguistic idiom. *For the moment, while*

keeping my eye fixed especially on this linguistic determination which is not all there is to idiom, but which is not just one determination of it among others, I shall be taking 'idiom' in a much more indeterminate sense, that of prop(ri)e(r)ty, singular feature, in principle inimitable and inexpropriable. The idiom is the proper" (my emphasis). Let me add a couple of propositions to which I'll return: race ("a peculiar or characteristic style or manner—liveliness, sprightliness or piquancy," according to the *OED*) and idiom, in their determination by a conceptual apparatus made up of uninterrogated differences, classes, and sets, are interchangeable; t(race) and phrase constitute an improvisation of race and idiom, one activated within a certain understanding of totality or ensemble in which idiom is defined as the t(race) of a general idiom that is nothing other than the generativity (i.e., what is produced by and is the possibility of the production) of idiom.

38. Richards, liner notes, *Live in Vienna*.

39. Ibid.

40. Ibid.

41. Or, more precisely, doubly illegible words: the sonic/visual blurring of the words; the fundamental absence of the written text. And note the echo of Baraka's oft-repeated claim that poetry is "speech *musicked*." The particular manifestation of the phrase to which I refer is quoted in D. H. Melhem, "Amiri Baraka: Revolutionary Traditions: Interview," *Heroism in the New Black Poetry* (Lexington: University Press of Kentucky), 221.

42. Richards, liner notes, *Live in Vienna*.

43. Derrida, "Onto-theology of National Humanism," 3.

44. Cecil Taylor, "Sound Structure of Subculture Becoming Major Breath/Naked Fire Gesture," liner notes, *Unit Structures*, LP 84237. Blue Note, 1966.

45. David Parkin, "Ritual as Spatial Direction and Bodily Division," in *Understanding Rituals*, ed. Daniel de Coppet (London: Routledge, 1992), 18.

46. Claude Lévi-Strauss, *Structural Anthropology*, vol. 2, trans. Monique Layton (Chicago: University of Chicago Press, 1977), 66; and quoted in Parkin, "Ritual as Spatial Direction," 11.

47. Parkin, "Ritual as Spatial Direction," 16.

48. Elizabeth Hill Boone, "Introduction: Writing and Recording Knowledge," in *Writing without Words: Alternative Literacies in Mesoamerica and the Andes*, ed. Elizabeth Hill Boone and Walter D. Mignolo (Durham, N.C.: Duke University Press, 1994), 15.

49. On metavoice, see Mackey, "Cante Moro," *Sound States: Innovative Poetics and Acoustical Technologies*, ed. Adalaide Morris (Chapel Hill: University of North Carolina Press, 1997), 194–212.

50. See Joanne Rappaport, "Object and Alphabet: Andean Indians and Documents in the Colonial Period," in *Writing without Words*, 284.

51. Derrida, "Structure, Sign, and Play in the Discourse of the Human Sciences," in *Writing and Difference*, trans. Alan Bass (Chicago: University of Chicago Press, 1978), 278–80.

52. See Taylor's comments on Bill Evans in Nat Hentoff, liner notes, Cecil Taylor, *Nefertiti, the Beautiful One Has Come*, FLP 40106 LP, Arista/Freedom, 1975. First published in *Down Beat*, 25 February 1965, 16–18.

53. Quoted in Derrida, "Structure, Sign, and Play," 287.

54. Ibid.

55. Parkin, "Ritual as Spatial Direction," 16.

56. See James A. Winn, "Music and Poetry," in *New Princeton Encyclopedia of Poetry and Poetics*, 3d ed., ed. Alex Preminger, T. V. F. Bogan, et al. (Princeton, N.J.: Princeton University Press, 1993), 803. Please take note that this entry in this definitive encyclopedia says very close to nothing about the life and shape of the synthesis of music and poetry in the "New World" or in non-Western societies. Taylor's concern with precisely these registers is certainly a constitutive feature of his improvisation through the determinations of the dominant understanding of that synthesis. In his work the trace of *mousike*, the ghostly affect and effect of a certain *free* mode of organization, gives us to imagine a thought not grounded in the architectonics and dynamics of difference that harmony both marks and conceals. It's as if the real/phantasmatic duality of the encounter with the other opens that which demands an improvisation through the condition of its possibility.

57. See back cover of Taylor, *Chinampas*.

58. Check the sentence (in Lange and Mackey, "Editors Note," *Moment's Notice*, x) that follows Charles Lloyd's expression of doubt concerning the capability of words to arrive at music: "Writers influenced by jazz have been variously rising to the challenge of proving him wrong."

59. Ralph Ellison, *Invisible Man* (New York: Vintage, 1990), 6–7.

60. Ibid., 8–9.

61. Ibid., 9–11.

62. Ibid., 12.

63. Derrida, "Onto-theology of National Humanism" 3–23.

64. Eve Kosofsky Sedgwick, *Tendencies* (Durham, N.C.: Duke University Press, 1993), 8–11.

65. And the break or cut was always thus. Armstrong disseminates the break—that's what we hear in "Black and Blue" and, even more iconically, in "West End Blues." The break animates the entirety of the solo rather than simply functioning as the "home" of something that approaches the solo, some local and locatable habitation (of the name). This is what jazz comes to, this dissemination of the break. Such *jouissance*, which we'll come to see as the animation—the essence and historicity—of an invaginative tradition of joy and pain, is just that nonlocalizable dis/continuity. The new thing in jazz was in Armstrong already—this is the old-new thing.

66. Or, as in Amiri Baraka's "The Burton Greene Affair," where the irreducibly antinatal occasion of the homoerotics of hybridity is embodied in the punctual and unfruitful playing of Green (and the specter of Cecil Taylor-as-influence). Or, as in the sad embrace of Ray and Jimmy at the end of Baraka's *The Toilet*. Is it new? The danger of national emasculation is embedded in the homoerotics of the aphorism. Again, the sexual cut is an evasion of the natal. We'll return to these last two examples.

67. And part of what's at stake here, in this re-en-gendering sexual cut, this lackness (sorry: blackness) of blackness into which we've fallen, is, again, a performative queerness where originary maternity and the hypermasculine are given as convergent figures of a kind of degradation that has liberation at its heart. This thing at the center is unreachable for Ellison precisely because the language that would give us access to it is broken or unavailable. But, as Sedgwick writes, "That's one of the things that 'queer' can refer to: the open mesh of possibilities, gaps, overlaps, dissonances and resonances, lapses and excess of meaning when the constituent elements of anyone's gender, of anyone's sexuality aren't made (or *can't be* made) to signify monolithically. The experimental linguistic, epistemological, representational, political adventures attaching to the very many of us who may at times be moved to describe ourselves as (among many other possibilities) pushy femmes, radical faeries, fantasists, drags. Clones, leatherfolk, ladies in tuxedoes, feminist women or feminist men, masturbators, bulldaggers, divas, Snap! Queens, butch bottoms, storytellers, transsexuals, aunties, wannabees, lesbian-identified men or lesbians who sleep with men, or . . . people able to relish, learn from, or identify with such." Sedgwick

goes on to acknowledge "intellectuals and artists of color ... [who] are using the leverage of 'queer' to do a new kind of justice to the fractal intricacies of language, skin, migration, state. Thereby, the gravity (I mean the *gravitas*, the meaning, but also the *center* of gravity) of the term 'queer' itself deepens and shifts." I want to move in the trajectory of this shifting sound in order to range as much as possible across the entirety of the experimental field of blackness that it opens. This is after a sounding and resounding of the sound of the black avant-garde and its political, theoretical, aesthetic erotics that is given only in the sexual cut. See Sedgwick, *Tendencies*, 8–9.

68. Baraka, "BLACK DADA NIHILISMUS," in *The Dead Lecturer* (New York: Grove Press, 1964), 61–64.

69. Ellison, *Invisible Man*, 564.

70. Mackey, *Bedouin Hornbook*, 34.

71. Ibid. 34.

72. Ibid.

73. Taylor, "Sound Structure."

74. Baraka, "New Black Music: A Concert in Benefit of the Black Arts Repertory Theatre/School Live," in *Black Music* (New York: William Morrow, 1967), 176.

75. Derrida, *The Post Card*, trans. Alan Bass (Chicago: University of Chicago Press, 1987), 500–502. This quotation is from a section of *The Post Card* called "Du Tout." That section is introduced in the following manner: "First published in *Confrontation* I (1978), preceded by this editorial note: 'On 21 November 1977, a session of "Confrontation" with Jacques Derrida was organized around [Derridean] texts in thematic relation to the theory, movement, and institution of psychoanalysis. ... In response to René Major's initial questions, Jacques Derrida advanced several introductory propositions. We are reproducing them here in the literality of their recording. Only the title is an exception to this rule.'" Note the small phrase that accompanies Derrida is: *Ce-n'est-pas-du-tout-une-tranche*. Bass offers the following translator's note: "This sentence plays on lexical and syntactic undecidability. *Une tranche* is the usual French word for a slice, as in a slice of cake, from the verb *trancher*, to slice. In French psychoanalysis slang, *une tranche* is also the period of time one spends with a given analyst. There is no equivalent English expression. Further, the expression *du tout* can mean either 'of the whole' or 'at all.' Thus, the sentence can mean 'This is not a "slice" [a piece, in the analytic sense or not] of the

whole,' or 'This is not at all a "slice" [in any sense].' The verb *trancher* can also mean to decide on a question or to resolve in a clear-*cut* way; the English 'trenchant' has a similar sense. Throughout this interview, the sense of *tranche* and 'trench' beckon toward each other, finally coming together in the concluding discussion of schisms and seisms (earthquakes, cracking ground)." I can't discuss, here, the interview in its entirety; but the thematics of the slice or cut, of shifting or cracked ground, of their relation to and constitution of the whole, is at the heart of this project, all of which is scored by these motives.

76. Derrida, "'This Strange Institution Called Literature': An Interview with Jacques Derrida," in *Acts of Literature*, ed. Derek Attridge (New York: Routledge, 1992), 35.

77. Derrida, "An Interview with Derrida," trans. David Allison et al., in *Derrida and Différance*, eds. David Wood and Robert Bernasconi (Evanston, Ill.: Northwestern University Press, 1988), 73–74.

78. Derrida, "The Original Discussion of *Différance*," trans. David Wood, Sarah Richmond, and Malcolm Bernard, in *Derrida and Différance*, eds. Wood and Bernasconi, 87.

79. Is it a "Derridean hope," an echo or reformulation or deconstruction of the Heideggerian hope to which Derrida alludes in *Différance*? Or is it otherwise? Is it of the cultures, of Algeria and elsewhere, marked by more than what would always have been the origin? See Derrida, *Margins of Philosophy*, trans. Alan Bass (Chicago: University of Chicago Press, 1982), 27.

80. Derrida, *Memoires: For Paul de Man*, rev. ed., trans. Cecile Lindsay, Jonathan Culler, Eduardo Cadava, and Peggy Kamuf, Wellek Library Lectures at the University of California, Irvine (Stanford, Calif.: Stanford University Press), 221. This is part of Derrida's first public response to the discovery of de Man's wartime journalism.

81. There is another Derridean cut that has been operative here all along, or at least since the invocation of (Artaud's) voices/forces. In 1965, toward the end of "La Parole Soufflée," Derrida asks: "Liberated from diction, withdrawn from the dictatorship of the text, will not theatrical atheism be given over to improvisational anarchy and to the actors' capricious inspirations? Is not another form of subjugation in preparation?" The final question sounds differently, bears an alternative stress, after and of the whole. There is another form of subjugation *in* preparation and so we come, with foresight, unprepared but adorned with a phrase, a sound. Perhaps another way of thinking magic and black magic,

a magic disidentification in which the scene of hasty and deliberate—improvi-sational—objection irrupts into doubled theatricality as an artist or actor who embodies the process of making art or making acts in order to recalibrate this constellation: madness and its other; the work and its absence; subjugation and its improvisation. We'll return to these questions by way of Adrian Piper who is concerned, as in Artaud according to Derrida, with the discovery of "a universal grammar of cruelty." See Derrida, "La Parole Soufflée," *Writing and Difference*, 169–195. The quotations above are from 190 and 191.

82. Nat Hentoff, liner notes, *Charles Mingus Presents Charles Mingus*, LP 9005, Candid, 1960.

83. Ingrid Monson, *Saying Something: Jazz Improvisation and Interaction* (Chicago: University of Chicago Press, 1996), 84–85.

84. Jaki Byard, interview with Ingrid Monson, *Saying Something*, 179.

85. Nathaniel Mackey, *Atet A.D.* (San Francisco: City Lights Books, 2001), 118–19.

86. Eric Dolphy, remarks at the conclusion of "Miss Ann," rec. 2 June 1964, *Last Date*, Fontana, 1991.

87. Douglass, *Narrative*, 263.

2. In the Break

1. The question of the name is unavoidable. It is bound to the question of where radicalism goes, or how radicalism develops, in Baraka's work after the seizure/opening of 1962–1966 upon which my study of him has been concen-trated. Why refer to the author in question now as Baraka even though his texts of the period here examined appear under the name LeRoi Jones? In part to honor the nominative marker of his own conception of his radicalism, to indi-cate that what was radical in the moment examined did not disappear but was transformed and continues to transform into new Barakan figurations that have both attenuated and amplified the tradition they inhabit. But it is also to indicate, along with Lula—the embodiment of predatory white femininity in Baraka's play *Dutchman*—that talking to and with and about somebody's name ain't the same as talking to/with/about them. Taking Lula as a model is, of course, problematic, but how she works here and in the scene *Dutchman* is and delineates could never be absolutely separated from how Bessie Smith, say, (or Lady Day) or Bird, could or will work here and in that scene whose trace demands excavation. If the radical scene of that moment were underground and

moving, like a train, traversed and scarred by racial, sexual, and class difference and desire, where is the location of that scene now? How do we reenact that submergence in the interest of a more authentic upheaval? How do we avoid the perennial call of a performed oppositional purity? And these questions, implying as they do that the long seizure that I investigate is the scene of Baraka's radicalism at its opening and at a level of intensity that would never be surpassed, are not reducible to the assertion that bohemianism or interracialism or homoeroticism are that radicalism's very constitution. Rather, it is in the ensemble that they rupture and exceed that the radicalism, *which is also to say the blackness*, of Baraka in/and the tradition, is anarchically grounded.

2. Baraka, "Apple Cores #6," in *Black Music* (New York: William Morrow, 1967), 142.

3. See Martin Heidegger, "'Only a God Can Save Us': The Spiegel Interview (1966)," trans. William J. Richardson, S.J., in *Heidegger: The Man and the Thinker*, ed. Thomas Sheehan (Chicago: Precedent Publishing, 1981).

4. Ludwig Wittgenstein, *Tractatus Logico-Philosophicus*, trans. C. K. Odgen (London: Routledge and Kegan Paul, 1986), 65.

5. Wittgenstein, *Remarks on the Philosophy of Psychology II/ Bemerkungen über die Philosophie der Psychologie II*, ed. C. G. Luckhardt and M. A. E. Aue (Chicago: University of Chicago Press, 1980), 2e, 89e.

6. Wittgenstein, *Remarks on the Philosophy of Psychology I/ Bemerkungen über die Philosophie der Psychologie I*, ed. G. E. M. Anscombe and G. H. von Wright, trans. G. E. M. Anscombe (Chicago: University of Chicago Press, 1980), 6e.

7. Wittgenstein, *Philosophical Investigations*, 2d ed., trans. G. E. M. Anscombe (Oxford: Blackwell Publishers, 1997), 193e. Quoted in Stephen Mulhall, *On Being in the World: Wittgenstein and Heidegger on Seeing Aspects* (New York: Routledge, 1990), 6.

8. Wittgenstein, *Last Writings on the Philosophy of Psychology I: Preliminary Studies for Part II of Philosophical Investigations/Letzte Schriften über die Philosophie der Psychologie I: Vorstudien zum zweiten Teil der Philosophiche Unterschungen*, ed. G. H. von Wright and Heikki Nyman, trans. C. G. Luckhardt and M. A. E. Aue (Chicago, University of Chicago Press, 1992), 100e.

9. Derrida, "'This Strange Institution Called Literature': An Interview with Jacques Derrida," 65.

10. See Charles Sanders Peirce, "The Icon, Index, and Symbol," In *Collected Papers, vol. 2: Elements of Logic,* ed. Charles Hartshorne and Paul Weiss (Cambridge: Harvard University Press, 1931).

11. Stephen Mulhall, *On Being in the World: Wittgenstein and Heidegger on Seeing Aspects* (New York: Routledge), 11.

12. Peirce, "One, Two, Three: Fundamental Categories of Thought and Nature," in *Peirce on Signs,* ed. James Hoopes (Chapel Hill: University of North Carolina Press), 181.

13. The tragic life produces, is produced by, the one for whom we always mourn, the one who is most acutely recognizable in mourning. One mourns for itself: singularity and totality, effects of a determining nascence, are never present, never moved from or arrived at through whatever possible nostalgic direction. Miles is their effect; his tone is tragic, mournful; we mourn for him, and in so doing, long to reproduce that tone, which exists, as his voices, as the trace of a singularity and a totality that never were. In mourning Miles we mourn the mournful trace of what never was. More later.

14. Baraka, "BLACK DADA NIHILISMUS," 63.

15. Ibid., 61.

16. Cool, here, is the fullness with which Baraka enacts Charles Olson's famous dicta from "Projective Verse": "Form is never more than an extension of content"; "The HEAD, by way of the EAR, to the SYLLABLE/the HEART, by way of the BREATH, to the LINE." See Olson, "Projective Verse," in *Selected Writings* (New York: New Directions, 1966), 19.

17. Wittgenstein, *Last Writings on the Philosophy of Psychology I,* 65e, quoted in Mulhall, *On Being in the World,* 11.

18. See Baraka, "BLACK DADA NIHILISMUS," 73, and note the final lines of the poem: "may a lost god damballah, rest or save us/against the murders we intend/against his lost white children/black dada nihilismus." Note, too, the anticipation of Heidegger, "Only a God."

19. Mackey on Baraka: "The way in which Baraka's poems of this period [the period referred to is the early sixties when Baraka wrote "BLACK DADA NIHILISMUS" as well as "History as Process," the poem that occasions Mackey's comments: FM] move intimates fugitive spirit, as does much of the music that he was into. I recall him writing of a solo by saxophonist John Tchicai on an Archie Shepp album: 'it slides away from the proposed.'" See Mackey, "Cante Moro" 200.

20. What I'm after here is the *properly* metaphysical faith in the constitutive absence at metaphysics' very heart: the ensemble metaphysics spurns and craves as totality is obscured by singularity, its name(s), its trace(s), and *vice versa*.

21. Ekkehard Jost, *Free Jazz* (New York: Da Capo Press, 1981), 21.

22. See Ray Monk, *Ludwig Wittgenstein: The Duty of Genius* (New York: Penguin Books, 1990).

23. It has also been called, by William J. Harris, his transitional period, the period in which he moves from bohemianism to Black Nationalism [social-structural dynamics paralleled by the movement from bebop to free jazz discussed above], from one kind of political despair to another. See William Harris's editorial arrangement of *The Jones/Baraka Reader* (New York: Thunder's Mouth Press, 1999).

24. John R. Searle, *Intentionality* (Cambridge: Cambridge University Press, 1983), 143.

25. See Mackey, "Cante Moro."

26. Baraka, "When Miles Split," *The Village Voice*, 15 October 1991, 87.

27. Leon Forrest, "A Solo Long-Song: For Lady Day," *Relocations of the Spirit* (Wakefield, R.I.: Asphodel Press/Moyer Bell, 1994), 344–95. See especially 344–55.

28. Billie Holiday with William Dufty, *Lady Sings the Blues* (New York: Penguin Books, 1992), 104–5.

29. The performance was recorded on 10 November 1956, issued later as *The Essential Billie Holiday*, Verve V6-8410.

30. Forrest, "A Solo Long-Song," 344.

31. Forrest quoting Finis Henderson in "A Solo Long-Song," 356.

32. Forrest, "A Solo Long-Song," 345.

33. Holiday with Dufty, *Lady Sings the Blues*, 5.

34. Undated letter to William and Maely Dufty, quoted in Donald Clarke, *Wishing on the Moon: The Life and Times of Billie Holiday* (New York: Penguin Books, 1994), 399.

35. Holiday with Dufty, *Lady Sings the Blues*, 192.

36. Joel Fineman, *Shakespeare's Perjured Eye* (Berkeley: University of California Press, 1986), 5.

37. Ibid., 16–17. We'll see how Baraka insists upon something Monk names and performs with sublime, oxymoronic precision. Check him at the

piano, machine gun over his shoulder, on the cover of an album entitled *Underground* that includes his composition "Ugly Beauty." Or, back to the subject at hand, and along lines that we'll see Baraka begin to work out, listen to Lady singing "You've Changed": more later.

38. Fineman, *Shakespeare's Perjured Eye*, 15.

39. See William Shakespeare, *Shakespeare's Sonnets*, ed. with analytical commentary by Stephen Booth (New Haven, Conn.: Yale University Press, 1977), 387–92.

40. Derrida, "This Strange Institution," 67.

41. Derrida speaks elsewhere (see Derrida, "Politics and Friendship: An Interview with Jacques Derrida," in *The Althusserian Legacy*, ed. E. Ann Kaplan and Michael Sprinker [London: Verso, 1993], 226) of deconstruction as just such an everything, the "open and nonself-identical totality of the world." This fragment of the Derridean discourse on totality shows something of another— both descriptive and prescriptive—awareness of the whole as wholly restructured by and in that ongoing event at the intersection of invagination and improvisation that is, who is, nothing other than the Dark Lady. This is so in spite of, and sometimes quite clearly at the precise moment of his statements of, his reticence toward improvisation, which is why formulations of Derrida such as the one above are more fully experienced when broken and expanded by whatever version you happen to have of "Billie's Blues" (sometimes she sings, "I'll quit my man"; sometimes she sings, "I'll cut my man").

42. See Laurel Brinton, "The Iconic Role of Aspect in Shakespeare's Sonnet 129" (*Poetics Today* 6, no. 3 [1985]: 447–59), for a more detailed exposition of certain aspects of these matters.

43. Booth reminds us that for the Elizabethans "sonnet" could refer to any short lyric, even the six iambic couplets that make up number 126. Booth also points out that the last of those couplets refers to and enacts a "quietus," cessation or cut that the thematics of the entire poem puts forward as the unavoidable shadow of a temporality, embodied in the young man, which seems to resist the End. The oneness of growth and decay never achieves the equilibrium of a pause; such a pause would only be precisely that end that it desires to avoid. "Having" would be precisely this stasis that is not one, but it and its representation are impossible. Left hanging, out of time in a cut that really isn't there, we move to another accounting or encountering, the arhythmics

and thematics of blackness that takes the sequence out. Here are sonnets 126 and 127 (*Shakespeare's Sonnets*, 108–11):

O thou, my lovely boy, who in thy pow'r
Dost hold time's fickle glass, his sickle-hour,
Who hast by waning grown, and therein show'st
Thy lovers withering, as thy sweet self grow'st–
If nature, sovereign mistress over wrack,
As thou goest onwards still will pluck thee back,
She keeps thee to this purpose, that her skill
May time disgrace, and wretched minute kill.
Yet fear her, O thou minion of her pleasure;
She may detain but not still keep her treasure.
Her audit, though delayed, answered must be,
And her quietus is to render thee.

In the old age black was not counted fair,
Or if it were it bore not beauty's name.
But now is black beauty's successive heir,
And beauty slandered with a bastard shame;
For since each hand hath put in nature's pow'r,
Fairing the foul with art's false borrowed face,
Sweet beauty hath no name, no holy bow'r
But is profaned, if not lives in disgrace
Therefore my mistress' eyes are raven black,
Her eyes so suited, and they mourners seem
At such who, not born fair, no beauty lack,
Sland'ring creation with a false esteem.
    Yet so they mourn becoming of their woe,
    That every tongue says beauty should look so.

44. These are fairly faithful variations on entries found under "race" in *The Compact Edition of the Oxford English Dictionary*, vol. 1, 1971 edition.

45. Baraka, "The Dark Lady of the Sonnets," in *Black Music*, 25.

46. D. H. Melhem, "Amiri Baraka: Revolutionary Traditions: Interview," in *Heroism in the New Black Poetry* (Lexington: University Press of Kentucky, 1990), 257.

47. Annette Michelson, "The Wings of Hypothesis: Montage and the Theory of the Interval," in *Montage and Modern Life, 1919–1942*, ed. Matthew Teitelbaum (Cambridge: MIT Press), 67–68.

48. Trinh T. Minh-ha, *Framer Framed* (New York: Routledge, 1992), 120.

49. See Sergei Eisenstein, "The Filmic Fourth Dimension," in *Film Form*, ed. and trans. Jay Leyda (New York: Harcourt Brace, 1949), 64–71.

50. Baraka, "Apple Cores #5—The Burton Greene Affair," in *Black Music*, 136.

51. I'm saying that Baraka is part of a long line of what he disparagingly calls "Negro deconstructors"—Du Bois is that tradition's capstone, a precursor and anticipatory critic of Gates and Baker, ones who are, paradoxically, anathema to Baraka in that they might be said to arrest rather than extend that tradition.

52. See Baraka, "Hunting Is Not Those Heads on the Wall," in *Home*, 173–78.

53. See Mackey, "Cante Moro," for more on such stammers and divisions.

54. Heidegger, "Only a God," 56–57.

55. Baraka, "New Black Music," 175.

56. Heidegger, "Only a God," 57.

57. Jost, *Free Jazz*, 94.

58. Ibid., 95.

59. Derrida, *Cinders*, trans. Ned Lukacher (Lincoln: University of Nebraska Press, 1991), 22.

60. Derrida, "*Geschlecht*: Sexual Difference, Ontological Difference," trans. Ruben Berezdivin, *Research in Phenomenology* 13: 65–83.

61. Martin Heidegger, *Being and Time*, trans. John Macquarrie and Edward Robinson (New York: Harper & Row, 1962).

62. Heidegger, *Being and Time*, quoted in Derrida, "*Geschlecht*," 69.

63. Derrida, "*Geschlecht*," 71–72.

64. Samuel Beckett, *The Unnamable*, in *Three Novels by Samuel Beckett* (New York: Grove Press, 1965), 22.

65. Derrida, *Cinders*, 25.

66. Ibid., 21.

67. Baraka, "Home," in *Home*, 10.

68. See Theodore Hudson, *From LeRoi Jones to Amiri Baraka* (Durham, N.C.: Duke University Press, 1973).

69. Johannes Koenig is the signature affixed to "Names and Bodies," a

brief text that opens the possibility of a brief and partial tracing of Baraka's turns and declensions—from white bohemianism and aestheticism to black cultural nationalism; from subjectivist to socialist; from the aesthetico-philosophical to the historico-political—and that forces us to ask if these parallel certain turns of Heidegger: for instance, from the attempt to define Being in terms of man and within a historico-structural hermeneutic to an attempt to define Being in terms of a linguistic event and a topology (thus a turn away from subjectivism). How is Baraka's awareness of this turn to be read—as an "anti-humanism," a reading through anthropocentrism that parallels the effort to determine "the highest form of Being" in Heidegger's *Introduction to Metaphysics*? The question, finally, is of the status of Baraka's reading of Heidegger—of, for instance, Heideggerian *Dasein*:

>   If
> *Life* an abstract noun, living (Life-ing) is not (i.e., it is living.)
> Be (I think Olson sd its root from the sanscrit Seen or Being seen)
>   And it is Verb. The Act.
>   Doing. Seeing. Being.
>   Seinde. (Heidegger's Being. & its Projection
> or what he called Dasein   Da-Sein,   Sein is To Be. Da is
> literally There. To Be There. Or the positing of an existence that is
> not literally where we are now. The colloquial mean-ing) Where
> you are.   Now.(Also colloquial) Where you at?   Or.   where are
> you at?   An existence(tial) question. What is the disposition of
> your Life (forces), &c?

See Diane di Prima and Amiri Baraka, *The Floating Bear: A Newsletter* (La Jolla, Calif.: Laurence McGilvery, 1973), 271.

    70. This group of words, which I reluctantly call a sentence only because I can then, by way of a certain principle of expansion, think of it anacrustically, as an opening of an improvisation of rhythm, is also the opening of both a convergence and divergence with Kristeva. Indeed, it is her notion of expansion, employed in "Word, Dialogue, and Novel" that I appeal to above, just as it is her distinction between sentence and phrase—also given in "Word, Dialogue, and Novel" and elaborated in "The Novel as Polylogue" (Julia Kristeva, *Desire in Language: A Semiotic Approach to Literature and Art*, ed. Leon S. Roudiez, trans.

Thomas Gora, Alice Jardine, and Leon S. Roudiez [New York: Columbia University Press, 1980], 64–91, 159–209)—which I both invoke and seek to critique and transform. I do not intend to fulfill the imperatives of a Kristevan rigor, one that would, for instance, require a certain "nonexclusive opposition" between sentence and phrase, reason and instinctual drive; to do so would require a submission to the rigors of the sentence that I would here neither move through nor forget but improvise in the name of what lies before it. Nevertheless, Kristeva's work is crucial to what I am attempting here, not only because of her original movement within a conceptual field I must now negotiate, one characterized by a certain understanding of music that remains to be worked, but also because of her understanding of the relations between that conceptual field and sexual difference.

71. See Wittgenstein, *Philosophical Grammar*, trans. Anthony Kenny (Berkeley: University of California Press, 1974), 97.

72. Merrill B. Hintikka and Jaakko Hintikka, *Investigating Wittgenstein* (Oxford: Basil Blackwell, 1986), 155. See also Wittgenstein, *Philosophical Remarks*, ed. Rush Rhees, trans. Raymond Hargreaves and Roger White (Chicago: University of Chicago Press, 1975), 119.

73. Nor is the question of what it means for the performance of blackness to be done through spirit, breath, and against rhythm lost. We'll return to this.

74. Heidegger, "Kant's Thesis about Being," trans. Ted E. Klein and William E. Pohl, *Southwestern Journal of Philosophy* 4, 10–11.

75. Edmund Husserl, *Ideas: General Introduction to Pure Phenomenology*, trans. W. R. Boyce Gibson (New York: Collier Books, 1962), 6.

76. Derrida, "*Différance*," 27.

77. Michel Foucault, "Maurice Blanchot: The Thought from the Outside," in *Foucault/Blanchot*, trans. Brian Massumi and Jeffrey Mehlman (New York: Zone Books, 1987), 54.

78. Baraka, "The Burton Greene Affair," 138–39.

79. Derrida, *Of Spirit*, trans. Geoffrey Bennington and Rachel Bowlby (Chicago: University of Chicago Press, 1989), 28.

80. According to Baraka, Burton Greene's style is pointed toward Taylor. On the other hand, if we extrapolate to Brown from Jones's description of Sanders, the saxophonists want "to feel the East, as … oriental m[e]n." See Baraka, "The Burton Greene Affair," 137.

81. See Andrew Ross, "Hip and the Long Front of Color" in *No Respect:*

Intellectuals in Popular Culture (New York: Routledge, 1989), 65–101, and Sally Banes, *Greenwich Village, 1963: Avant-Garde Performance and the Effervescent Body* (Durham, N.C.: Duke University Press, 1993).

82. Frank O'Hara, "The Day Lady Died," *The Collected Poems of Frank O'Hara*, ed. Donald Allen (Berkeley: University of California Press, 1995), 325.

83. Andrew Ross, "Hip and the Long Front," 66.

84. Baraka, "American Sexual Reference: Black Male," *Home: Social Essays* (New York: William Morrow, 1966), 216–33.

85. Ross, "Hip and the Long Front," 66–67.

86. Ibid., 241, n. 4.

87. See Brad Gooch, *City Poet: The Life and Times of Frank O'Hara* (New York: Harper Perennial, 1994), 334, and take note of the intensity with which Baraka was the object of consumptive hipster desire. See also Hettie Jones, *How I Became Hettie Jones* (New York: Penguin, 1990).

88. Samuel R. Delany, *The Motion of Light in Water: Sex and Science Fiction Writing in the East Village, 1957–1965* (New York: Plume, 1988), 110.

89. Ibid., 113.

90. Ibid.

91. Ibid., 115.

92. Ibid., 173.

93. Ibid., 174.

94. Ibid.

95. Joan W. Scott, "Experience," in *Feminists Theorize the Political*, ed. Judith Butler and Joan W. Scott (New York: Routledge, 1992), 22–40.

96. Gayatri Chakravorty Spivak, "Supplementing Marxism," in *Whither Marxism? Global Crises in International Perspective*, ed. Bernd Magnus and Stephen Cullenberg (New York: Routledge, 1995), 117.

97. Catherine Clément, *Syncope: The Philosophy of Rapture*, trans. Sally O'Driscoll and Deirdre M. Mahoney (Minneapolis: University of Minnesota Press, 1994), 1.

98. Ibid., 1–2.

99. Baraka, *The Toilet*, in *From the Other Side of the Century II: A New American Drama, 1960–1995*, ed. Douglass Messerli and Mac Wellman (Los Angeles: Sun and Moon Press, 1998), 126.

100. Ibid., 128.

101. Ibid.

102. That question of development that the changing name (LeRoi Jones, Amiri Baraka; Foots, Ray) or same indexes and that must be recalibrated by thinking it through the figure and fissure of montage recurs throughout Baraka's work. *The Toilet* is no exception. What does montage do to development? How does montage reconfigure advent? These questions are themselves tied not only to an investigation of the relation between all of the well-known plays Baraka produced in 1964—*The Toilet*, *The Slave*, and *Dutchman*—but also to what we might call the development of his own critical attitude toward *The Toilet* in its relation to the other plays of this "trilogy" and to his work as a whole. There is, suffice it to say, an interesting temporal dynamic in his discourse regarding *The Toilet*. In discussions of the play at or around the time of its initial production, Baraka speaks of it as emerging from the memory-driven frenzy of a single all-night's writing, a kind of jet-propelled radiophonic zoom clash given in one sitting. Later, the play's ending is figured as a tacked-on sentimentalism that does not much more than mark Baraka's temporary occupation of a transitional phase (read the specific combination of immaturity and degradation that becomes, *for him*, his particular bohemianism and bohemianism in general), a moment remarkable mainly in that it signifies both development and a certain arrest of development. I'm concerned with valorizing and investigating the political erotics of such arrest, cessation, break, syncope, as it animates Baraka's work and tradition. This is not to denigrate or undermine the value of development but to think its montagic interinanimation with such moments of disruptive, interruptive intensity. I want to linger, with and against Baraka, in this music.

Another, necessarily condensed and therefore inadequate way to put it is this: one condition of possibility of black arts is bohemianism, is the rejection of bohemianism; the limits of black arts are set by the rejection of a certain revolutionary embrace that is embedded in bohemianism, and the possibility of their transgression is given in the rejection of a certain retrogressive privilege that bohemianism retains and that is manifest in and at its hip and unhip poles. There are questions here concerning decadence or deviance. The black arts are, in part, the cultural vehicle of return to a certain moral fundamentalism, one based on (the desire for) African tradition rather than white/bourgeois normativity. This is to say that they would enact a return to the former after having enacted the bohemian rejection of the latter. The embrace of the homoerotic is, here, an opening and not an aim. And while the embrace of the homoerotic and the embrace—rather than repression—of the maternal lesson/lesion/mark do not operate in some simple and direct relation, they brush one another in such a way as to make possible the disruption of all manner of retrograde national symbolisms of markable and marketable maternal soil. That earth erupts its own refusal—dark, incontinent, air, fold.

For more on this issue see Nielsen, *Black Chant*, and Lorenzo Thomas, *Extraordinary Measure: Afrocentric Modernism and Twentieth-Century American Poetry* (Tuscaloosa: University of Alabama Press, 2000), 118–61. I have only glanced off the issue of Baraka's career trajectory, preferring to focus on one extended moment. Obviously there is much more to be said, and I hope to say some of it. The investigation of this issue has been initiated in the following texts: Hudson, *From Jones to Baraka*; Kimberly W. Benston, *Baraka: The Renegade and the Mask* (New Haven, Conn.: Yale University Press, 1976); Werner Sollors, *Amiri Baraka/LeRoi Jones: The Quest for a "Populist Modernism"* (New York: Columbia University Press, 1978); William J. Harris, *The Poetry and Poetics of Amiri Baraka: The Jazz Aesthetic* (Columbia: University of Missouri Press, 1985). Two recent texts advance this investigation by reversing the priority the preceding critics give to aesthetics over politics: Komozi Woodard, *A Nation within a Nation: Amiri Baraka (LeRoi Jones) and Black Power Politics* (Chapel Hill: University of North Carolina Press, 1999), and Jerry Gafio Watts, *Amiri Baraka: The Politics and Art of a Black Intellectual* (New York: New York University Press, 2001).

103. Banes, *Greenwich Village, 1963*, 154.

3. Visible Music

1. David Leeming, *James Baldwin: A Biography* (New York: Henry Holt, 1994), 34.

2. Lee Edelman, "The Part for the (W)hole," *Homographesis* (New York: Routledge, 1994), 68–69.

3. Edelman struggles against the constraints of the hole/whole binary that, in certain circles, constitutes the range of figuration for identity: "Can identity itself be renegotiated in the force field where 'race' and sexuality are each inflected by the other's gravitational field? Can it open itself to self-difference without being figured either as 'hole' or 'whole'?" Leaving aside the question of what is implied by the inverted commas that bracket "race" and the absence of such a mark for "sexuality" (Does the mark indicate constructedness as opposed

to the natural, the fantasmatic as opposed to the real? Can we remain comfortable with such oppositional formulation?), one is left to consider the possibility that for a critical discourse on Baldwin in particular and black performances in general, hole and whole both remain operative even in their sublation. That possibility has already been investigated by Houston Baker, in part by way of a consideration of Baldwin's extended critical engagement with Richard Wright: "Transliterated in letters of Afro-America, the *black hole* assumes the subsurface force of the black underground. It graphs, that is to say, the subterranean *hole* where the trickster is ludic. Deconstructivebeing. Further, in the script of Afro-America, the hole is the domain of *Wholeness*, an achieved relationality of black community in which desire recollects experience and sends it forth as blues. To be *Black* and *(W)hole* is to escape incarcerating restraints of a white world (i.e., a *black hole*) and to engage the concentrated, underground singularity of experience that results in a blues desire's expressive fullness." I've already attempted to show, by way of Baraka and Delany, that the black underground is a sexual underground, a space re-en-gendering aesthetic and political experiment. Edelman's work helps to emphasize even while it strains to hear the music that Baraka speaks. I'll return to this question of music shortly but wanted to pause here to acknowledge Baker's formative presence as a thinker of "the ontological totality" at this point in the proceedings. See Edelman, "The Part for the (W)hole," 59; and Baker, "A Dream of American Form: Fictive Discourse, Black (W)holes, and a Blues Book Most Excellent," in *Blues, Ideology, and Afro-American Literature*, 151–52.

4. Derrida, "The Law of Genre," 55.

5. Félix Guattari, *Chaosmosis: An Ethico-Aesthetic Paradigm*, trans. Paul Baines and Julian Pefanis (Bloomington: Indiana University Press, 1995), 4–5.

6. Amiri Baraka, *Eulogies* (New York: Marsilio Publishers, 1996), 98.

7. Here is a relevant quote from the title essay of Edelman's *Homographesis*, 9–10: "Following ... from Derrida's post-Saussurean characterization of writing as a system of '*différance*' that operates without positive terms and endlessly defers the achievement of identity as self-presence, the 'graphesis,' the entry into writing, that 'homographesis' would hope to specify is not only one in which 'homosexual identity' is differentially conceptualized by a heterosexual culture as something legibly written on the body, but also one in which the meaning of 'homosexual identity' itself is determined through its assimilation to the position of writing within the tradition Western metaphysics. The

'writing,' in other words, as which homosexuality historically is construed, names, I will argue, the reduction of 'différance' to a question of determinant difference; from the vantage point of dominant culture it names homosexuality as a secondary, sterile, and parasitic form of social representation that stands in the same relation to heterosexual identity that writing, in the phonocentric metaphysics that Derrida traces throughout Western philosophy from Plato to Freud (and beyond), occupies in relation to speech or voice. Yet as the very principle of differential articulation, 'writing,' especially when taken as a gerund that approximates the meaning of 'graphesis,' functions to articulate identity only in relation to signs that are structured, as Derrida puts it, by their 'non-self-identity.' Writing, therefore, though it marks or describes those differences upon which the specification of identity depends, works simultaneously . . . to 'de-scribe,' efface, or undo identity by framing difference as the misrecognition of a 'différance' whose negativity, whose purely relational articulation, calls into question the possibility of any positive presence or discreet identity. Like writing, then, homographesis would name a double operation: one serving the ideological purposes of a conservative social order intent on codifying identities in its labor of disciplinary inscription and the other resistant to that categorization, intent on *de*-scribing the identities that order has so oppresively *in*-scribed."

8. Guattari, *Chaosmosis*, 7. There he writes: "Grafts of transference operate in this way, not issuing from ready-made dimensions of subjectivity crystallized into structural complexes, but from a creation which itself indicates a kind of aesthetic paradigm. One creates new modalities of subjectivity in the same way that an artist creates new forms from the palette. In such a context, the most heterogeneous components may work towards a patient's positive evolution: relations with architectural space; economic relations; the co-management by patient and carer of the different vectors of treatment; taking advantage of all occasions opening onto the outside world; a processual exploitation of event-centered singularities—everything which can contribute to the creation of an authentic relation with the other."

9. Jacques Lacan, "The Direction of the Treatment and the Principles of Its Power," *Écrits: A Selection*, trans. Alan Sheridan (New York: W. W. Norton, 1977), 232.

10. Lacan, "Alienation," *The Four Fundamental Concepts of Psycho-Analysis*, ed. Jacques-Alain Miller, trans. Alan Sheridan (New York: W. W. Norton, 1978), 212.

11. Guattari, *Chaosmosis*, 5.

12. Lacan, "The Mirror Stage as Formative of the Function of the I," *Écrits*, 4.

13. Ibid.

14. See Harris, "History, Fable, and Myth," for more on phantom limbs.

15. Baraka, *Wise, Why's, Y's: Djeli Ya (The Griot's Song) (1–40)* (Chicago: Third World Press, 1995), 7.

16. Adorno, "On Jazz," trans. Jaime Owen Daniel, *Discourse* 12, no. 1 (fall–winter 1989–90), 53.

17. Henry Dumas, "Will the Circle Be Unbroken," in *Goodbye, Sweetwater: New and Selected Stories*, ed. Eugene B. Redmond (New York: Thunder's Mouth Press, 1988), 85–91.

18. See John Brenkman, "The Other and the One: Psychoanalysis, Reading, the *Symposium*," in *Literature and Psychoanalysis: The Question of Reading: Otherwise*, ed. Shoshona Felman (Baltimore: The Johns Hopkins University Press, 1982), 393–456. Brenkman deals with this in his staging of an encounter between Plato and Lacan, philosophy and psychoanalysis. He writes: "This relation between the denial of castration and philosophical discourse acquires a specifically social dimension when viewed from the standpoint of the subject's history. It allows us to glimpse how an unconscious formation can, with the help of the educational process that intervenes during latency, be fitted to the exigencies of an existing and ideological order" (444).

19. Edelman, "Homographesis," 9.

20. Brenkman, "The Other and the One," 444.

21. Lacan, "The Mirror Stage," 1.

22. *James Baldwin: The Price of the Ticket*, dir. Karen Thorsen, perf. James Baldwin, Maya Angelou, Bobby Short, David Baldwin, Nobody Knows Productions, Maysels Films, Inc., 1991.

23. Thorsen, *James Baldwin: The Price of the Ticket*.

24. Lacan, "What Is a Picture?" in *The Four Fundamental Concepts*, 117–18.

25. Ibid., 118–19.

26. Such anticipation is lacking even though the sound of Lacan's voice irrupting into these texts called seminars, seminars called texts, aural in their provenance and therefore full of the scandal/chance of the voice's extension through meaning, song and speech, voice itself to metavoice: this, too, is the

baraka, as it is played in Robert Pete Williams or Rev. Gary Davis, the singing preachers of whom Baldwin is one and not just one among others. His text is a long sermon on the *baraka*.

27. Presumably here he is speaking of the horn as an object devoid of instrumentality and wholly uninflected by its aural function, something moving out toward a certain realm of voice and spirit, a certain interruptive noisiness that is problematic precisely to the extent that it disturbs the spatial/visual ground for this strange occlusionary intersection of woman in sexual difference and sound in the holoesthetic field. What I mean here is that this negation of the aural function of the horn, of the aural possibility of the horn, is bound up with the visual/spatial hegemony that is the condition and condition of possibility of the understanding of the sign and the sign's relation to sexual difference (and racial difference—though this is not Lacan's concern) that Lacan works within. He would like to speak of those innumerable other things whose appearance is clear, whose appearance is not augmented by sound or sound's potential, a potential that disturbs the protocols of meaning that the sign, in its relation to visualizable difference, imposes and follows.

28. Adorno speaks of the rhythm of the iron system, a hypnotic agent that puts folks to sleep for the purposes of a fucked-up deception. He thereby forces the question concerning jazz and enlightenment by asserting a necessary relation between jazz and enlightenment-as-mass-deception. He moves theoretically to foreclose any possible relation between the music and another enlightenment to be determined neither by rampant instrumental rationality nor an irrationalism that emerges from the instrumentalism it would oppose.

In *Dialectic of Enlightenment* (trans. John Cumming [New York: Continuum, 1994]), Adorno and Max Horkheimer suggest that the enlightenment always carried the seed of its own reversal. This seed would then have to be suppressed, not allowed to disseminate. Enlightened thought in jazz as jazz—the notion contains the seeds of its own destruction as much as any particular historical manifestation. How, then, to protect against the seeds and their dissemination? By way of a prophylactic gaze, perhaps, or a beneficent sound, protecting reason on its journey from itself. Here jazz is aligned—as a kind of essence or, as Lacan might put it, "cunning" of reason (an invagination or sexual cut that goes all the way back to Hester('s scream) and before and enacts that *mater*ialization of the phallus to which Baldwin is especially attuned (again, one thinks of Abbey Lincoln's "Tryptich")—both with the seed of reason's destruction and, perhaps, the prophylaxis that guards against that destruction. It is a danger and a saving power that works to threaten and protect reason, to save enlightenment from itself by being more of what it already is. Reason is reason's seed, its destruction and regeneration. Reason's seed: reason's jazz. The prophylactic sound is what had earlier been thought of as destruction. The seed that destroys turns out to have been that which protects. That seed or sound becomes a blessing, maybe Ornette's. But you have to listen. Strange that the true prophylactic allows all that insemination and dissemination, opens everything to all that is thought in terms of hybridity and impurity, popularity and deception, all that is signified by and in a certain rhythm, a certain (as Queen Latifah might say) gift of body, as jazz, as the new and necessarily un/successful, ir/rational rhythm method. It wasn't always just the rhythm of the iron system; it was also rhythm *in* spirit—whatever all of spirit means—*against* the spirit of system.

Adorno's reaction is no simple sound-induced seizure; it is tied to a particularly embodied sound, a sound bound up both with what exceeds sound and with what seems to be excessive in terms of the body, with a certain regression, a tympanic logic of enrapture. This brings us to the question of intoxication and improvisation and to the relation of intoxication and insemination and how that might get us to the place of jazz: how sexual desire and musical rapture both contain that which might either endanger or revive reason; how, at the locus of the lunatic, the lover, and the poet, another kind of thinking, another enlightenment might operate. Baldwin is hip to this breaking connection: the sexuality of the music, the fact that the music is infused with sexuality and that that sexuality marks the spot of a double rapture, sexual and musical, a rapture of intoxication by way of love and sound and an overpowering invasion of body: all of this is there from beginning to end, from *Go Tell It on the Mountain* to *Just above My Head*, from illuminative fire to heard and not seen evidence.

29. Leeming, *James Baldwin*, 76.

30. Derrida, *Of Grammatology*, 53.

31. Houston A. Baker Jr., "Caliban's Triple Play," in *"Race," Writing, and Difference*, ed. Henry Louis Gates Jr. (Chicago: University of Chicago Press, 1986), 394. Quoted in Edelman, "The Part for the (W)hole," 73.

32. Derrida, *Of Grammatology*, 57.

33. James Baldwin, *Just above My Head* (New York: Dell Publishing, 1978), 209.

34. Edelman, "The Part for the (W)hole," 70–71.

35. Derrida, *Of Grammatology*, 63.

36. Guattari puts it this way: "How do certain semiotic segments achieve their autonomy, start to work for themselves and to secrete new fields of reference? It is from such a rupture that an existential singularization correlative to the genesis of new coefficients of freedom will become possible. This detachment of an ethico-aesthetic "partial object" from the field of dominant significations corresponds both to the promotion of a mutant desire and to the achievement of a certain disinterestedness" (*Chaosmosis*, 13).

37. On Baldwin's awareness of the gap between lyric and song, see José Esteban Muñoz, *Disidentifications: Queers of Color and the Performance of Politics* (Minneapolis: University of Minnesota Press, 1999), 21.

38. In Thelma Golden, ed., *Black Male: Representations of Masculinity in Contemporary American Art* (New York: Whitney Museum of American Art, 1994), 102. For a more comprehensive account of Till's murder, the events leading up to it, and its aftermath, see Stephen J. Whitfield, *A Death in the Delta: The Story of Emmett Till* (Baltimore: The Johns Hopkins University Press, 1988).

39. Mackey, *Bedouin Hornbook*, 51–52.

40. Ibid., 201–2.

41. Roland Barthes says that "[p]hotography has something to do with resurrection." Later, I'll try to extend this assertion by way of, against, and through some of Barthes's formulations of photography. See his *Camera Lucida: Reflections on Photography*, trans. Richard Howard (New York: Hill and Wang, 1980), 82.

42. Whitfield informs us that "Bobo was self-assured despite a speech defect—a stutter—that was the consequence of nonparalytic polio that he had suffered at the age of three." See Whitfield, *A Death in the Delta*, 15 and note, also, Whitfield's documentation of Ms. Bradley's argument that the attribution to Till of an attempted transgressive, transracial seduction on the part of his murderers was in part the function of their inability to decipher Till's broken speech. See also Mackey's "Cante Moro" for more on the enabling disabilities of "crippled speech," its relation to referents unavailable to moaning's or humming's cutting augmentation of the verbal.

43. Whitfield, *A Death in the Delta*, 15.

44. Julia Kristeva works fruitfully in the field determined by the opposition of mimesis and analytic-interpretive knowledge. I want to acknowledge

that work here as well as the necessity for a full account of that work. That necessity is particularly pronounced in work that is, on the one hand, attuned to the encountering of maternity and phonic materiality in a way that is very much influenced by Kristeva and, on the other hand, driven by an engagement with Barthes at a moment in his career when the influence of Kristeva is especially evident in his work. I intend to provide such an account very soon. Meanwhile, Kristeva speaks very lucidly on the relation between mimesis and knowledge in "A Conversation with Julia Kristeva," in *Julia Kristeva: Interviews*, ed. Ross Mitchell Guberman (New York: Columbia University Press, 1996), 31.

45. I want to acknowledge, here, the work of Karen Sackman on the relation between overtone and political mobilization. The chance to discuss these matters with her was crucial to the development of my ideas in this essay. I should say, too, that our discussion was prompted in large part by Randy Martin's extraordinary book *Critical Moves*.

46. Amiri Baraka, "When Miles Split!" in *Eulogies* (New York: Marsilio Publishers, 1996), 145–46.

47. There is more to be said elsewhere regarding the photographic apparatus, the production of a sound that allows the production of image. Thanks to my colleague Barbara Browning for opening this up.

48. Mackey speaks, with regard to Baraka and his reading and rewriting of Lorca in the late 1950s and early 1960s, of "a well-known, resonant history of African-American fugitivity and its well-known, resonant, relationship to enslavement and persecution." He adds, "The way in which fugitivity asserts itself on an aesthetic level . . . is important as well. The way in which Baraka's poems of this period move intimates fugitive spirit, as does much of the music that he was into. He writes of a solo by saxophonist John Tchicai on an Archie Shepp album, 'It slides away from the proposed.' . . . That sliding away wants out." Again, see Mackey, "Cante Moro."

49. Barthes associates the state, shall we say, of having made no observations with kindness: "In this little girl's image I saw the kindness which had formed her being immediately and forever, without her having inherited it from anyone; how could this kindness have proceeded from the imperfect parents who had loved her so badly—in short: from a family? Her kindness was specifically *out-of-play*, it belonged to no system, or at least it was located at the limits of a morality (evangelical, for instance); I could not define it better than by this feature (among others): that during the whole of our life together, she never

made a single "observation." This extreme and particular circumstance, so abstract in relation to an image, was nonetheless present in the face revealed in the photograph." It remains for us to think the consequences, beyond all of what might be seen as admirable or loveable, of the placement, by and in relation to Barthes (himself figured earlier in his own text as a definite sentimental and theoretical observer), of this idealized preobservationality. See Barthes, *Camera Lucida*, 69.

50. This is all to say that ultimately what remains constant in Barthes's thinking on photography is the use of the black example. And one must think hard about what that allows him to do; it's neither liberal acknowledgment nor petty racist invocation/dismissal, though that's the trajectory his use takes, and we could talk about that as well. Ask the North African workers of the Goutte d'Or district of Paris? Ask the parents of Emmett Till? OK.

51. Ibid., 76–77.

52. Ibid., 26.

53. Ibid., 40.

54. Ibid., 25–28.

55. Ibid., 71 (Barthes's emphasis).

56. Barthes, "The Great Family of Man," in *Mythologies*, trans. Annette Lavers (New York: Hill and Wang, 1972), 101.

57. Ibid.

58. Ibid., 102.

59. In *The Threshhold of the Visible World* (and here I thank David Eng for bringing this to my attention), Kaja Silverman looks at Barthes's distinction between the wounding effect of the *punctum* and the normative "'voice' of 'knowledge' and 'culture'" with which he associates the *studium*. Silverman cogently critiques Barthes's valorization of and failure to displace the ego, noting "the limited nature of the gains to be realized when [Barthes's] revisionary act of looking does not involve at the same time a realignment of self and other." She adds, "One is left with the disquieting sense that whereas Barthes consistently apprehends the photographs about which he writes from a viewing position which is radically divergent from that indicated by the metaphoric geometral point (associating an African American woman, for instance, with his aunt), his own sovereignty vis-à-vis the object remains unquestioned." Ultimately, as Silverman claims, "The figures depicted in the photograph serve only to activate [Barthes's] own memories, and so are stripped of all historical

specificity. Barthes's recollections might thus be said to 'devour' the images of the other." The simultaneously lost and operative singularity that Barthes grieves for is his own. And the problem, here, is not the loss of the object that was there but the never having been there of Barthes's own absolutely singular objectlessness. Again, Silverman's formulations here seem absolutely correct. I would only augment them in the following ways. One, the refusal or inability to displace the sovereign ego is not only a failure to realign self and other but a failure to realign the individual and the collective, so that the repression of difference is also the repression of a certain ensemblic publicity that is activated in and as sound, where sound is irreducible to voice and, thus, to the meanings that comprise dominant culture and knowledge. Two, the devouring of the images of the other in which Barthes engages is, in some ways, a predictable effect of the specific theory of history that animates Barthes's ahistoricism. The discourse of slave narrative, for instance, is massively infused with examples of the submission of black bodies to a scopic regime that has, as one of its effects, the renewal, if not instantiation, of white interiority. This process is no less pronounced for the development of that white interiority that is identified as radically divergent (from the metaphoric geometral point or from the political and/or aesthetic norms that are associated with that geometral point) or avant-garde. This is not to say that it is not surprising that Barthes associates an African American woman with his aunt; it is to say that it is *also* not surprising that Barthes makes such an association.

I will try to say more about how such interiority as that of Barthes is possible only in contradistinction to that incapability of science or theory, that inability to make—or lack of concern with making—observations, that interminably looked-at failure to look, that specifically black phonic materiality that marks, if you will, the return of the repressed *studium* in the *punctum*, in short that presubjective position outside of history that has been associated with the African with equal vigor in valorizations of tradition, on the one hand, and discontinuity, on the other. As I imply here and elaborate below, a fuller attempt to move past such a structure would require an attunement not only to the ways in which the aesthetics of black spectatorship and audition as black performance is tied to a general phonography of the photograph, but to how that complex is, in turn, tied to an improvisation through the opposition of interiority and ensemblic publicity. Of course, Silverman's work—including especially *The Acoustic Mirror*, her wary critique of the phallocratic deployment of what she understands to be a degrading reduction of feminine voice to feminine scream in classic cinema—is very useful to such a project. See *The Threshold of the Visible World* (New York: Routledge, 1996), 180–85.

60. Barthes, *Camera Lucida*, 64.

61. Louis Althusser, "The International of Decent Feelings," in *The Spectre of Hegel*, trans. G. M. Goshgarian (New York: Verso, 1997), 21–35.

62. If I have taken Barthes to task for his overlooking of Ms. Bradley's role in the ongoing production and display of the famous, terrible, beautiful photograph of her murdered son, it has been, in part, a result of a comparison of Ms. Bradley's willingness, and Barthes's refusal, to show the image of the loved one who is dead. In basing my analysis at least in part on such a comparison, I failed to take into account two things: first, Ms. Bradley's more recent and more enduring reticence at reproducing the photograph of her son (which is partly why I do not reproduce it here); second, the experiential knowledge of how terrible, if terribly beautiful, it is to look at and show the image of the lost. Nevertheless, I cannot disavow the arguments I have made here; the problem is not that they are wrong but that I didn't know how right they were, and so failed to fully account for the intensity of the knowledge of loss in Barthes and in Ms. Bradley. Now, after a spell of looking at pictures I can't look at, of being unable to show you a photograph of my mother in a book that is about nothing but her, I know more about what I thought I knew.

63. Now's the time briefly to consider the place of aural performance in the lecture, a form J. L. Austin says he hates. How, for instance, is one to take the relation between aurality and repetition? Specifically, what is the status of the repetitions that begin each chapter, which is to say each lecture in the set of transcribed lectures that make up Austin's *How to Do Things with Words*, second edition, ed. J. O. Urmson and Marina Sbisa (Cambridge: Harvard University Press, 1962, 1975)? Are Austin's recapitulations—designed to help him and us remember our place by abbreviating previously enacted elaborations—marks of an iterability he can't control, signs of an immaturity of speech that writing will have overcome, an ancillary quality of speech that Saussure decries that is exacerbated by the para-verbal, gestural baggage of speech that is particularly disturbing to Austin? What have these repetitions, what has this messy iterability, to do with the constellation of pitch, tone, sound, voice? Does the concern with voice in philosophy of Austin's student, Stanley Cavell, parallel Derrida's concern with idiom? Nation is an immediate background against which idiom

emerges for Derrida; it's no less powerful in Cavell. Voice and sound in philosophy are both personal and national for him—not to hear Thoreau's or Austin's voice/sound is not to notice their distinctiveness and their nationality. Or, not to hear Emerson's sound in Nietzsche is not to hear a specific Americanness in Nietzsche. For Cavell, to have an ordinary language is to have a national language, an idiom. Here voice is tied to speech, to the nationalized performance of an ordinary language. And for Derrida, idiom is always tied to sound and, for that matter, to autobiography: the achievement of the old-new language will have been, for him, a coming into voice, as bell hooks might say, that is or will have been a coming into or upon, a recording, of "the sound of Algeria." If we back up and think this idiomatic mark in speech as a kind of habitation within an ordinary language, and if we think a given ordinary language along the lines of the distinction between competence and performance, as Chomsky outlines it, then we see another essential point of commerce between ordinary language and performance: this is to say that ordinary language exists only in performance. This will be, then, another source of Austin's profound ambivalence with regard to the constellation of performance, drama, theatricality. *The search for a universal language is to be carried out only by way of a lecture whose phonetic and gestural performativity is irreducible.* And this is, of course, tied to the sense Austin begins with of performatives as masqueraders, utterances that look like but are not statements. One way we could put the problematic Austin hips us to is this: how can a performance or performer be essential to and as the ordinary?

Or, put another way: Austin begins with a desire to isolate and valorize ordinary language over against the language of metaphysics and the phantasmic language of positivism. He specifically wants to argue, against the logical positivists, that there are utterances that are, on the one hand, not verifiable statements and, on the other hand, not nonsense. More precisely he wants to "play Old Harry" with two "fetishes," which is to say two binary oppositions, two of what Cavell calls false alternatives (and note the interesting way the idea of the fetish, the notions of value it carries by way of Marxian and Freudian registers comes into play here as tied to or clearly manifest in the "false alternative"): the value/fact fetish and the true/false fetish, two fetishes, or dogmas, one might say, of positivism. The originary distinction between performative and constative and its complex elaboration and/or degradation into the field delineated by locution, illocution, and perlocution is the way Austin wants to get to this game of Old Harry and here is where all the problems and the interest lie. In order to obliterate false alternatives Austin must first indulge in a performance (pretend, masquerade, be, in some sense, nonserious or poetic or theatrical), and he must broach a kind of generality that his mode of analysis, his exclusionary choices, decries. Austin's aspiration demands a totalizing performance. One question this raises: is there anything other than totalizing performance? I think there is not. Part of what I'd like to think about is how it is that what I take to be the undeniable fact of iterability is the condition of possibility of a totalizing performance.

Meanwhile, Austin needs to perform in order to bring off his serious intentions. Derrida says that the serious utterance is always shadowed by an internal other that is its condition of possibility. What is spoken or taken seriously can always be, must always potentially be, spoken or taken otherwise. This is to say that Austin's performance anxiety is part of a general phenomenon. Nevertheless, and this is Cavell's central and decisive contribution—a reminder given him by Wittgenstein and Austin, prophets of the ordinary—in spite of the risk iterability bears, something is often said by way of an utterance; something—*content*—is carried, smuggled, carried across or over or off, conveyed. And the point is that the danger inherent in iterability (the specter of the theater, of pretense, of nonseriousness) is the saving power of such conveyance. Performatives, those utterances that masquerade as statements but are neither verifiable nor nonsensical, are tied to a kind of nonseriousness manifest in and as some dissociative "backstage artiste" who would duplicate or reiterate the play. On page 10, Austin attempts to distinguish, in a beautiful little footnote, between types of performers—those who would enable as opposed to those who would duplicate the play; I don't think the distinction holds. Performatives are always performers, dark ladies, wearing the mask that grins and lies, bearers of uncategorizable infelicity in the make-up of well-formedness.

Derrida and others after him show that the problem of iterability is tied to the problem of theatricality, of the necessary, multiple, anarchic, and tragicomic performances of performatives. These problems are tied to that of totality as well. This is to say that avoidance of the univocal need not be tied to or instantiated in an avoidance or refusal of the general. This requires recasting the parasitic, duplicative backstage artiste as well as the fastidious and enablingly codependent backstage techie out of their fetishistic opposition to one another. It demands a breakdown of the opposition between original (authentic, sincere, paradoxically serious) performance and duplicative performer by way of an assertion of the multiplicative, invaginative, cutting, augmentative, ensemblic force of a performance. (This will have recognized the antipathy toward duplication or reproduction as an antipathy toward a performance or theatricality, one manifest most clearly in the need for any given performance's disappearance in lieu of metaphysical formulations of Performance or Performativity.) That force is essential and essentializing. And this, in turn, is all bound up with the distinction—shall we say a true alternative—between meaning and force that Austin gives us as replacement for a certain false alternative between force and truth. This is to say you have to think about the conveyance and the truth value of the "merely" phonetic act and think, more generally, about what's at stake when imagining another idea of truth—as unconcealment and not adequation—the relation between truth and saying something is animated as well.

Cavell argues, against a certain symptomatic Derridean reading, that Austin is actually enabled, rather than stymied, by the breakdown between the performative and the constative and, more generally, by the way his classes (of the classes of acts, speech acts, locutions, illocutions, infelicities) blur such that "all aspects are present in all classes." The erotic response (an) ordinary language gives to analytic violence is felicitous for Austin; the breakdown of the orginal distinction between performative and constative works in relation to a totalizing intuition or drive in the ordinary, the ensemblic force of iteration instantiated by and in the "merely" phonetic act, the conveyance, the feeling, of a structure. Black performance is, in part, the amplified, previously given soundtrack of this masquerade, this pageant of "aspect dawning." There will have been no performance without it. It requires thinking more rigorously how the "merely" phonetic act has illocutionary force or produces perlocutionary effects. Again this is a question of aspect, where the ethico-temporal problematic blurs and blurs into the problematic of class, set, ensemble. One has to think about what's at the core and envelops and blurs the set of the sets, of locution (saying something with meaning [sense + reference]), illocution (doing something in saying something), and perlocution (doing something by saying something).

At the same time, according to Cavell, voice does not exist in the purely phonetic act. Here's where the distinction between sound and voice that breaks down in his usage of them re-emerges. The sound of philosophy that Cavell wants to recover is always tied to meaning. I would here join with Derrida where Cavell charges him with indulging in a certain animism. I'd even link such indulgence to a kind of animalism that Austin is always pointing out, where the mere making of noises is the purview of monkeys. There are limits to Derrida's animism or animalism, his sense of soul you might say, that I'd wanna go past. I have to linger in the music in the interest of a more elemental or anim(al)istic sound of/in philosophy, one that disrupts meaning and the sign, and the hegemony of the signifier over the psyche. I would follow Austin and Cavell, then, in acknowledging the importance of the circumstances of the speech act, but I would also point to the need for a more detailed and expansive engagement with that which we could think about, using Austin's designation, as the accompaniments of the utterance: not only winks, pointings, gestures, frowns, and other such visible markers but tones of horror and, beyond and before that, certain cut augmentations of voice (meaning, a certain look or style or make-up tied to a performance that visualizes, thereby mut(at)ing, sound; interesting, though, to think the effects of sound looking like a black woman) by way of multiple self-accompaniment. The point, here, is that iterability instantiates (the) ensemble, and it does so not as a pure effect of writing but as the effect of soundwriting, of a phonographic interruption of voice/speech/tone/look by the generalizing writing of the phonetic act. The phonetic act cuts and abounds the phono-logo-phallo-centric field presided over by meaning and the sign in their impossible phonetic reduction. The phonetic act marks the interinanimation of birth and inheritance; it's the old-new thing, cutting mastery and the master's passionate utterance by way of an out response, its circumstances, accompaniments, and anim(al)ism. This is the new science and old inheritance of value. It moves through the fetish and materiality's disruption of the fetish. It moves through, or by way of, the ordinariness of performances.

Finally, how can we begin to ask more rigorously what performance studies will be in the renewed light of performances and their ordinariness. Paying close attention to Austin's attention to performatives is a crucial element to that more rigorous asking. This is to say that we must follow that trajectory, that conveyance or telepathy, feel that structure, between performatives and performances across the unbridgeably vast and immeasurable small "distance" between them. That path moves through these three lectures. That path moves through these lectures as they mark certain ordinary events. It moves also through the intersection of the two sets of three lectures I'm interested in here. A passage in Derrida's lecture which remains partially unheard in Cavell's reading of Derrida's partial hearing of Austin marks the last step of this

choreography: *Différance*, the irreducible absence of intention or assistance
from the performative statement, from the most 'event-like' statement possible,
is what authorizes me, taking into account the predicates mentioned just now,
to posit the general graphematic structure of every 'communication.' Above all,
I will not conclude from this that there is no relative specificity of the effects of
consciousness, of the effects of speech (in opposition to writing in the traditional sense), that there is no effect of the performative, no effect of ordinary
language, no effect of presence and of speech acts. It is simply that these effects
do not exclude what is generally opposed to them term by term, but on the
contrary presuppose it in dyssemtrical *[sic?]* fashion, as the general space of
their possibility." Derrida goes on in the section called "Signatures" to say that
that general space of possibility of the list of effects (of speech, of the performative, of ordinary language, of presence, of speech acts) is writing in the non-
traditional sense, writing as "spacing, as the disruption of presence in the mark."
My concern has been to examine these effects in the light of this at once other
and more fundamental writing and to think them in their relative specificity or
within the relative specificity of a particular and differentiated "context" or
"history." More specifically, I'm trying to examine, in the light of writing, the
effects of the black ordinary, of black speech, of black presence. My suspicion is
that such examination is fruitful precisely to the extent that it puts the Derridean asymmetry in play such that presence and absence are each the other's
condition of possibility; so that writing and the ordinary are interlocking total-
ities, each invaginative of the other, each disruptive and augmentative of the
other as mutual conditions of possibility. These specificities and generalities
are known by way of the materialities of various workings of various surfaces,
by way of what Butler calls the residue of the social.

Another formulation of this project, mentioned above in my acknowledg-
ments, is then given in Cavell, at the end of *A Pitch of Philosophy*, by way of its
own schedule (Nietzsche, Bloch), fully intelligible for me only after the fact of
Derrida (since speech is only given to us now after we've been given writing—
there is no phoné but for phonography, the cut augmentation and condition of
possibility of phonetic writing): "Am I ready to vow, as when Bloch asked us
whether we heard through to Bloch, that I have the ear, that I know my mother's
mother tongue of music to be also mine?" One of the aims of the encounter of
lectures and lecturers that this note attempts to prepare is technical. Perhaps
Austin, Cavell, and Derrida only partially hear each other because the speakers

(Marvin Gaye, Kenneth Cockrel, Angela Davis)—in all of their phonographic disruptiveness and distortiveness—weren't properly, or elsewhere were too properly, hooked up.

See Cavell, *A Pitch of Philosophy: Autobiographical Exercises* (Cambridge: Harvard University Press, 1994), and Derrida, "Signature Event Context," in *Margins of Philosophy*, trans. and with additional notes by Alan Bass (Chicago: University of Chicago Press, 1982), 309–30.

64. *Finally Got the News*. Prod. Stewart Bird, Peter Gessner, René Lichtman, and John Louis Jr., in association with the League of Revolutionary Black Workers. Perf. Kenneth Cockrel, John Watson, Chuck Wooten. Black Star Productions, 1970.

65. Gayatri Chakravorty Spivak, *A Critique of Postcolonial Reason* (Cambridge: Harvard University Press, 1999), 68–69.

66. Ibid., 68–69, n. 86.

67. Ibid., 75.

68. Ibid., 75, n. 97.

69. Ibid.

70. Dan Georgakas and Marvin Surkin, *Detroit: I Do Mind Dying*, updated ed. (Boston: South End Press, 1998).

71. Fredric Jameson, "Cognitive Mapping," in *Marxism and the Interpretation of Culture*, ed. Cary Nelson and Lawrence Grossberg (Urbana: University of Illinois Press, 1988), 347.

72. Ibid.

73. See Silverman, *The Acoustic Mirror*, 72–78.

74. Michel Chion, *The Voice in Cinema*, ed. and trans. Claudia Gorbman (New York: Columbia University Press, 1999), 24.

75. Marvin Gaye, *What's Going On*, Motown, 1971.

76. Marvin Gaye, "Since I Had You," *I Want You*, Motown, 1976.

77. Dipesh Chakrabarty, *Rethinking Working Class History: Bengal 1890–1940* (Princeton, N.J. Princeton University Press, 1989), 68.

78. See Angela Y. Davis, "Afro Images: Politics, Fashion, and Nostalgia," in *The Angela Y. Davis Reader*, ed. Joy James (Oxford: Black Publishers, 1998).

79. Spivak, *A Critique of Postcolonial Reason*, 68, n. 86.

80. See Davis, *Blues Legacies and Black Feminisms: Gertrude "Ma" Rainey, Bessie Smith, and Billie Holiday* (New York: Pantheon, 1998).

81. Davis, "Afro Images," 278.

Resistance of the Object: Adrian Piper's Theatricality

1. See Robert Storrs, "Foreword," in Adrian Piper, *Out of Order, Out of Sight* (Cambridge: MIT Press, 1996), 1: xviii–xix. Piper discusses Krauss's formulation without naming Krauss, placing it within the framework of a larger critique of the convergence of ontological fallacy and socioeconomic presumption in the (construction of the) art world, in "Critical Hegemony and Aesthetic Acculturation," *Noûs* 19, no. 1 (1985): 29–40. Piper revises and expands this critique in "Power Relations within Existing Art Institutions," in *Out of Order*, 2: 63–89. Here are the relevant passages from "Critical Hegemony," 30–31.

"A commitment to a career as an art practitioner requires that one is financially independent, or that one's family is, or that one possesses other economically remunerative skills, or that a permanently Spartan lifestyle can be regarded as a novelty or a virtue, rather than as proof of social failure.

"This precondition to professional commitment functions as a mechanism of selection among creatively inclined individuals for whom economic hardship has been, up to that point, a central reality. Art institutions in their present incarnations will tend to attract individuals for whom economic and social instability are not sources of anxiety, for they have correspondingly less reason to sacrifice the vicissitudes and satisfactions of self-expression to the necessities of social and economic pressure.

"One immediate effect of this social and economic preselection is to create a shared presumption in favor of certain artistic values, i.e., a concern with beauty, form, abstraction, innovations in media, and politically neutral subject matter. Let us roughly characterize these as *formalist* values. Since economically advantaged individuals often import such values from an economically advantaged, European background environment, and since existing art institutions favor the selection of such individuals, it follows that these institutions will be popularized by individuals who share these values.

"... [T]hose creative products dominated by a concern with political and social injustice, or economic deprivation, or that use traditional, or 'ethnic,' or 'folk' media of expression, are often not only not 'good' art; they are not art at all. They are, rather, 'craft,' 'folk art,' or 'popular culture'; and individuals for whom these concerns are dominant are correspondingly excluded from the art context.

"The consequent invisibility of much non-formalist, ethnically diverse art of high quality may explain the remark, made in good faith by a well-established critic, that if such work didn't generate sufficient energy to 'bring itself to one's attention,' then it probably did not exist. It would be wrong to attribute this claim to arrogance or disingenuousness. It is not easy to recognize one's complicity in preserving a state of critical hegemony, for that one's aesthetic interests should be guided by conscious and deliberate reflection, rather than by one's socioculturally determined biases, is a great deal to ask. But by refusing to test consciously those biases against work that challenges rather than reinforces them, a critic insures that the only art that is *ontologically* accessible to her is art that narrows her vision even further. And then it is not difficult to understand the impulse to ascribe to such work the magical power to 'generate its own energy,' introduce itself to one, garner its own audience and market value, and so on. For nearly all objects of consideration can be experienced as animatedly and aggressively intrusive if one's intellectual range is sufficiently solipsistic."

I intend briefly to address this solipsism as it manifests itself in the criticism of Michael Fried. This address is, however, only in the interest of framing an engagement with Piper's art and thought. I hope to show why the frame is necessary and essential even as it is broken. Part of what's at stake is the recognition that Piper's critique of critical hegemony and critical solipsism is structured by an asserted disbelief in, or critical debunking of, the fetish character of the art object. Notions of the artwork's essential energy or aggressivity— whether demonized, as we shall see, in Fried or valorized in Krauss—are unacknowledged ideological effects of an acculturation that emphasizes formalist values, according to Piper. However, part of what I'll begin to argue here is that Piper's work—which is, in a quite specific way, to say Piper—constitutes a massive and rigorous rematerialization of the art object whose most prominent feature is the ongoing and resistant assertion of self-generated energy, impulse, drive. I intended to show that to experience Piper or the Piperian artwork is to enter a zone of ontic aesthetic productivity and a history of performance that undermines Piper's own Kantian formulation that "artworks without words are dumb" ("Critical Hegemony," 33). This is to say that I intend to argue—by way of Aunt Hester and her line, which includes Piper (who knows much about the complex and open relationship between slavery, art, and the freedom of the object)—against Piper's notion (later extended and elaborated by Phelan) that performance, in its nonreproductivity, constitutes a bulwark against (or a solution to the problem of) the fetishization of the art object. Performance is, rather, the occasion to think the fetish character of the art object and its secret, its mystery, anew. To assert this is to move with and against Piper's richly internally differentiated—if not contradictory—discourse on the object. See her "Performance and the Fetishism of the Art Object," in *Out of Order*, 1: 51–61; "Talking to Myself: The Ongoing Autobiography of an Art Object," in *Out of Order*, 1: 29–53; and "Pontus Hulten's Slave to Art," in *Out of Order*, 1: 187–92. See also Peggy Phelan, "Broken Symmetries: Memory, Sight, Love," in *Unmarked*.

2. See Piper, *Out of Order*, 2: 127–48.

3. Michael Fried, "Art and Objecthood," in *Minimal Art: A Critical Anthology*, ed. Gregory Battcock (Berkeley: University of California Press, 1999), 116–47.

4. See Clement Greenberg, "Modernist Painting," in *The Collected Essays and Criticism* (Chicago: University of Chicago Press, 1993), 4: 85–93.

5. See Zora Neale Hurston, "Characteristics of Negro Expression," in *The Sanctified Church* (Berkeley: Turtle Island, 1981), 49.

6. Piper, *Out of Order*, 2: 177.

7. Fried, "Theories of Art after Minimalism and Pop," in *Discussions in Contemporary Culture*, ed. Hal Foster (New York: New Press, 1987), 55–56.

8. Fried, *Courbet's Realism* (Chicago: University of Chicago Press, 1990), 6. An earlier version of this formulation is quoted and analyzed by Stephen Melville in his *Philosophy beside Itself: On Deconstruction and Modernism* (Minneapolis: University of Minnesota Press, 1986), 13.

9. Fried, "Art and Objecthood," 144–47.

10. Derrida, *Of Grammatology*, 53.

11. Fried, "Art and Objecthood," 145.

12. Amiri Baraka, "John Coltrane (1926–1967): I Love Music," in *Eulogies* (New York: Marsilio Publishers, 1996), 2.

13. Piper, *Out of Order*, 1: 27.

14. See Derrida, *Resistances of Psychoanalysis*, trans. Peggy Kamuf, Pascale-Anne Brault, and Michael Naas (Stanford, Calif.: Stanford University Press, 1997); and Gilles Deleuze and Félix Guattari, *Anti-Oedipus: Capitalism and Schizophrenia*, trans. Robert Hurley, Mark Seem, and Helen R. Law (Minneapolis: University of Minnesota Press, 1983).

15. Piper, *Out of Order*, 1: xxxix.

16. Ibid., xxxix–xl. For an excellent analysis of the cultural import of racial and sexual minorities' restricted rights of privacy, see Phillip Brian Harper,

Private Affairs: Critical Ventures in the Culture of Social Relations (New York: New York University Press, 1999).

17. Greenberg, "Modernist Painting," 85.

18. The thing (*Ding*) is passive, according to Kant. It's that to which nothing can be imputed, and is opposed to "a person [who] is a subject whose actions can be imputed to him." The thing is without freedom and spontaneity. A human being acting in response to inclinations, acting as means to another's ends, is a thing. At the same time, the thing or thing as such is metaphysical substance, that undetermined thingness in general that is a condition for the possibility of experience in general and is, likewise, a condition for the possibility of objects of experience. A *Gegenstand* is an object that conforms to the limits of intuition and understanding. When an object of experience is made into an objects of knowledge, it becomes an *Objeckt*. Part of what's at stake here, which I can only begin to explore, is the paradoxical character of intuition (space and time, the transcendental aesthetic) as condition of and conditioned by objects of experience or sense, as both the immediate relation to objects and that which occurs only insofar as the object is given to us. This temporal gap of the object is like the temporal gap of the subject—that it must be called into existence, that the fact that it is called indicates it already exists—that Butler isolates and reads with a rhythmically rigorous insistence in *The Psychic Life of Power*. Just as the subject, according to Althusser, is made possible by the call that its prior existence makes possible, so is the object made possible by the intuition that its prior existence makes possible. This immediacy of intuitive apprehension is presentness, in Fried's language.

I should here acknowledge the usefulness of Howard Caygill's *A Kant Dictionary* (Oxford: Blackwell, 1995). The quotation above from Kant is in *A Kant Dictionary*, 304.

19. Derrida, *The Truth in Painting*, trans. Geoff Bennington and Ian McLeod (Chicago: University of Chicago Press, 1987), 45.

20. Ibid., 54–55.

21. Ibid., 64.

22. Ibid., 59.

23. See Spivak, *A Critique*, 1–111; also Robert Bernasconi, "Who Invented the Concept of Race? Kant's Role in the Enlightenment Construction of Race," in *Race* (Oxford: Blackwell, 2001), 11–36.

24. For me, that link is constituted by Artaud and Derrida's reading of

him. In "La Parole Soufflée" Derrida addresses Artaud's critique of the way speech and writing have worked in the theater. Artaud desires writing, according to Derrida, that is not a transcription of speech but a transcription of the body, a writing on the body, gesture, movement, something, according to Derrida, no longer controlled by the institution of the voice. Artaud is after "the overlapping of images and movements [that] will culminate, through the collusion of objects, silences, shouts, and rhythms, or in a genuine physical language with signs, not words, as its root." As Derrida says, "the only way to be done with freedom of inspiration and with the spiriting away of speech [la parole soufflée] is to create an absolute mastery over breath [le soufflée] within a system of nonphonetic writing." Deleuze and Guattari, again by way of Artaud, speak of this nonphonetic writing as "primitive inscription," and their language marks the spot of a metaphysics that is always primitively anthropological, primitive in its need and desire for the anthropological object, the anthropological order, the one Spivak now calls, but in a different way, the native informant.

Piper enacts this object of desire under the veiled rubric of the primitive that is structured where and when the sciences of in/human/e administration and the new sciences of value meet (anthropology, psychoanalysis, the critique of political economy, the genealogy of morals, general linguistics, evolutionary biology). But in Piper, the primitive is critically unveiled as that which is not what it is. Improvised, this collusive writing of "*objects*, silences, shouts, rhythms" is her performative language. "A universal grammar of cruelty."

In the end, Derrida, picking up on his critique of Foucault's *Madness and Civilization*, also in *Writing and Difference*, wants to challenge the notion that madness is purely the absence of the work. He wants to say that madness is the work as well and, more importantly, that madness is just as much a part of the history of metaphysics as its other. This is to say that the appeal to madness or to the absence of the work is still operating within the metaphysical, logocentric reserve. Artaud and Foucault still operate within or "belong to the epoch of metaphysics that determines Being as the life of a proper subjectivity." This is to say that madness is still operative in its relation to proper subjectivity. This is the metaphysics "which Artaud destroys and which he is still furiously determined to construct or to preserve within the same movement of destruction ... At this point, different things ceaselessly and rapidly pass into each other and the *critical* experience of *difference resembles* the naïve and *metaphysical* implications *within difference*, such that to an inexpert scrutiny, we could appear to be criticizing Artaud's metaphysics from the standpoint of metaphysics itself, when we are actually delimiting a fatal complicity. Through this complicity is articulated a necessary dependency of all destructive discourses: they must inhabit the structures they demolish, and within them they must shelter an indestructible desire for full presence, for nondifference.... The transgression of metaphysics through the 'thought' which, Artaud tells us, has not yet begun, always risks returning to metaphysics. Such is the question in which we are *posed*. [Remember—as one poses a net, surrounding the limit of a discursive net.] A question which is still and always enveloped each time that speech, protected by the limits of a field, lets itself be provoked from afar by the enigma of flesh which wanted properly to be named Antonin Artaud" (194–95). You inhabit the discourse you're trying to destroy as a function of the urge to destroy it and of a formal tie, a tie of necessity to what you would destroy, a tie that is not fixed but is determinate. The thing is, at the end of *La Parole Soufflée*, which I just quoted, something else is going on, first in the body of the text and then in the little appendage or attachment that cuts and augments it like a fold, a messy, unfoldable fold or gap in the envelope, a disruption of the pose. To speak of the envelope, to thereby push it, so to speak, is to invoke the trace of a future discourse in Derrida, a discourse of invagination that will emerge in relation to a certain understanding of the ear—the body and its folds will have literally come to disrupt the artificial or artifactual totality of the pose. In "The Law of Genre" Derrida speaks of invagination as that which cuts and augments the whole, that which ruptures the limit in the interest of a larger reestablishment. Not a dismantling of the house but a stringent and rigorous remodeling and expansion that is predicated on a critique of the idea of ownership and authorship, of a certain exclusionarily determined architectural propriety. Meanwhile, the (delimiting and illimitable folds of the) body becomes the figure for what the flesh will have always done to speech. This is the enigma of the flesh (as distinguished from the body by Spillers) that provokes speech from outside of speech's protective limits. Such provocation is the very structuring possibility of Derrida's work that his work is designed to mute as if it moves only in disbelief of the ghost that is its constant companion, as if caught up in the desire for a listening out of earshot, as if folded into an old avoidance of material accent. Derrida's work is bound up not only with the repression of accent's irreducible differences, but with the unfortunate way that the French language conflates voice and speech. To articulate the difference between body, voice, and speech is what remains (to articulate flesh as a kind of *Geschlecht*, a gathering of differences, the ante-logos, the afterparty), what Artaud attempts to do by way of the body's mastery over breath, spirit. Derrida's attachment of the appendix to the essay betrays an awareness of an overheard difference, the differential wedge that articulates it. The hole, the force, the new whole, is a re-en-gendering, as Spillers points out. It is an unmanning, as Schreber describes and Artaud enacts (their link being articulated in the work of Deleuze and Guattari). They carry the knowledge of the mother's touch and tongue, but repressively project it away from themselves in and as the image of the primitive. As we've seen, Spillers describes this operation with regard to blackness, *as* blackness—the cut of cutting, burning flesh, the fleshly remainder in the absence—the cut augmentation and dispossessive spiriting (away)—of the maternal body. The ongoing stealing away of and from maternal body, maternal shore, maternal language. Steal away (from) home. Born not in bondage but in fugitivity, in stolen breath and stolen life.

25. See Gilles Deleuze, *Kant's Critical Philosophy: The Doctrine of the Faculties*, trans. Hugh Tomlinson and Barbara Habberjam (Minneapolis: University of Minnesota Press, 1984).

26. See Marx, *Capital*, 1: 126.

27. See Louis Althusser and Étienne Balibar, *Reading Capital*, trans. Ben Brewster (London: NLB, 1970), 145–57.

28. Marx, "Communism and Private Property," in *Early Writings*, trans. Rodney Livingstone and Gregor Benton (New York: Vintage, 1975), 352.

29. Ibid., 358.

30. Ibid., 348.

31. Ibid., 352.

32. Ibid., 356.

Index

Fred Moten is associate professor of African-American studies at the University of California, Irvine.